Village Women and Grameen Bank in Bangladesh

VILLAGE WOMEN AND GRAMEEN BANK IN BANGLADESH

Asma Begum

GYAN PUBLISHING HOUSE

NEW DELHI - 110002

Village Women and Grameen Bank in Bangladesh

ISBN : 81-212-0926-9
Rs. 590

Published in 2007 in India by
Gyan Publishing House,
5, Ansari Road, Daryaganj, New Delhi-110002
Phones : 23282060, 23261060
Fax : (011) 23285914
E-mail : books@gyanbooks.com
Website : www.gyanbooks.com

Laser Type-setting by : Shagun Graphics, Delhi
Printed at : Salasar Imaging System, Delhi

Dedication

Late Professor Muhammad Abdul Hai
---Father-in-law

Justice Abdul Wahab
---Father

Contents

	List of Tables	*7*
	Preface	*13*
1.	Introduction	15
2.	The Status of Woman in Bangladesh	59
3.	The Grameen Bank	90
4.	Methods Followed in the Study	108
5.	Findings I	138
6.	Findings II	164
	Appendix A Interview Schedule	294
	Bibliography	302
	Index	319

List of Tables

2.1 Literacy Rate for Persons of All Ages by Sex in Census Years, 1961-1991, in Bengladesh. 68

2.2 Literacy Rate for Persons of All Ages by Sex and Residence in Census Years, 1961-1991, in Bangladesh. 68

2.3 Involvement of Women in Non-farm Production in Bangladesh. 75

2.4 Employed Persons Aged 10 years and above by Status in Employment and Sex, 1990, in Bangladesh. 76

2.5 Economic Activity Rate (by Sex) in Bangladesh.77

2.6 Distribution of Women Employed in Establishments Employing 10 Persons or more by Professional Category, in Bangladesh. 78

5.1 Population by Thana and Locality, 1991, in Narsingdi District. 140

5.2 Dwelling Households by Locality (1961-1991), in Narsindi District. 141

5.3 Household size of Dwelling Unit by Locality, in narsingdi District. 142

5.4 Household Distribution by Main Sources of Income, in Narsingdi District. 143

5.5 Literacy by Sex and Locality 1961-91, in Narsingdi District. 144

5.6 Economic Participation Rates by Sex and Locality, in Narsingdi District. 145

5.7 Ranking of Thana in Respect of Basic Characteristics, 1991, in Narsingdi District. 147

5.8 Population 10 years and Over by Sex, working Status and Main Activity, in Narsingdi District (with detailed information of rural area). 148

5.9 Population (10 years and Over) by Source of Household Income and Main Activity, in Narsindi District (With detailed information of rural area). 149

5.10 Area, Total Household, Dwelling Househlods by Material of Roof of Main House and Population and Literacy by Sex, at Panchdona Union. 151

5.11 Population (10 years and over) by Main activity at Panchdoan Union. 152

5.12 Loanee and Non-loanee Women, by Age. 156

5.13 Loanee and Non-loanee Women, by Education. 157

5.14 Loanee and Non-loanee Women, by the Types of their Families. 158

5.15 Loanee and Non-loanee Women, by Per-capita Monthly Income of their Families. 158

5.16 Loanee and Non-loanee Women, by Their Family Size. 158

5.17 Loanee and Non-loanee Women, by Duration of their Marriage. 159

5.18 Loanee and Non-loanee Women's Husbands, by Education. 159

5.19 Loanee and Non-loanee Women's Husbands, by Occupation. 160

5.20 Loanee Women, by the period of their Membership of The Grameen Bank. 161

5.21 Loanee Women, by Their Monthly Income. 161

5.22 Loanee Women, by Their Occupation. 162

6.1 Loanee and Non-loanee Women, by their Participation in the Decision Making Process in relation to Family Budget, Education, Medical Treatment and Marriage of Family Members. 166

6.2 Loanee and Non-loanee Women, by Their Decision-Making on the Number of Children. 210

6.3 Loanee and Non-loanee Women, by Their Control over Family Income / Expenditure / Savings. 214

6.4 Loanee Women, by Their Control Over Their Own Income. 221

6.5 Loanee Women, by Their Control Over Expenditure of Their Own Income. 222

6.6 Loanee and Non-loanee Women, by Their Freedom, to Sell Their Property. 224

6.7 Loanee and Non-loanee Women, by Their Freedom to Talk to Male Outsiders. 226

6.8 Loanee and Non-loanee Women, by Their Husbands' and other Family Members' Approval of Their Direct Conversation with Male Outsiders. 231

6.9 Loanee and Non-loanee Women, by Compulsion to Abide by the Disapproval of Their Family Members of Their Conversation with Male Outsiders. 233

6.10 Loanee and Non-loanee Women, by Their Freedom of Movement. 235

6.11 Loanee and Non-loanee Women, by the

Nature of Decision on the Casting of Vote. 237

6.12 Loanee and Non-loanee Women, by the Levels of Their Participation in the Decision-Making Process. 240

6.13 Loanee and Non-loanee Women, by Their Age and The Level of Their Participation in the Decision-Making Process. 242

6.14 Loanee and Non-loanee Women, by Their Education and the Level of Their Participation in the Decision-Making Process. 246

6.15 Loanee and Non-loanee Women, by the Types of Their Families and the Levels of Their Participation in the Decision-Making Process. 250

6.16 Loanee Women and Non-loanee Women, by Duration of Their Marriage and The Levels of Their Participation in the Decision-Making Process. 254

6.17 Loanee Women, by the Period of Their Membership of the Grameen Bank and the Level of Their Participation in Decision-Making Process. 255

6.18 Occupations of Husbands of Loanee Women and Non-loanee Women and the levels of Their (the Respondents') Participation in the decision-making Process 258

6.19 Education of Husbands of Loanee Women and Non-loanee Women and the levels of Their (The Rdspondents') Participation in the decision-Making Process 261

6.20 Loanee and Non-loanee Women, by the Time devoted by Them per Day to Household Chores and Economic activities. 262

6.21 Loanee and Non-loanee Women in Terms of Help Received by Women in Day-to-Day Activities. 265

6.22 Loanee Women, by Their Perception of the Quantity of Their work-load. 266

6.23 Loanee Women, by Their Opinion of the Nature of Their Work-Load. 267

6.24 Loanee and Non-loanee Women, by Their Opinion. Regarding the Role of Husbands and Wives in Running the Household. 270

6.25 Loanee and Non-loanee Women, by Their Opinion Regarding the Disirability of Taking Decisions conjointly by Husbands and Wives. 273

6.26 Loanee and Non-loanee Women, by Their Perception of Happiness. 277

6.27 Non-Loanee Women, by Their Primary Reason for not Taking loan from the Grameen Bank 284

Preface

The present study is concerned with an important aspect of the interrelation between the Grameen Bank of Bangladesh and poor rural women of the country. This aspect relates to the status of poor women in the countryside, after they had started getting a modicum of income from economic activities aided by the credit from the Grameen Bank. Discussions centre round on the status of women emanating from the existing reality of the inequality between men and women, their access to various resources and the association between the economic activity independently carrried out with the credit received from the Grameen Bank by the women and the resulting difference.

I express my deep sense of gratitude to Dr Krishna Chakraborty and Professor Swapan Bhattacharyya, Department of Sociology, University of Calcutta, without whose guidance and help I could not have completed this work. I am grateful to Professor Bela Dattagupta and Dr Gayatri Bhattacharyya for their kind help and to Professor Partha Majumdar of Indian Statistical Institute for his valuable suggestions and help in the quantitative analysis of the data.

I graefully acknowledge the award of Government of India Scholarship under the auspices of the Indian Council for Cultural Relations which enabled me to undertake this study. I received all cooperations from the national Library, Ramkrishna Mission Institute of Culture and British Council Library, all in Kolkata.

In my own country, I have the most profound debt to the village women who, as subjects of this study, have provided me with detailed information of their experience which constitute the basis material of the study. They have given me their precious time even at the cost of depriving their husband and children of the same. The moments I passed in their company are unforgettable. I record my sense of appreciation the cordiality of the authorities of the Grameen Bank, particulary, Nizamul Haque, I recall with respect the support I received from my mother-in-law, late Begum Anisa Hai, my parents Justice Muhammad Abdul Wahab and Late Saria Banu, Dr. Sila Basak, Dr. Sudeshna Basak, Mr. Parag Rakshit, Mrs. Sudipta Rakshit, Dr. Manzoor Hasan and Professor Akramuzzaman in course of my academic pursuits.

I must name Ihtisham and Inzamam–my two sons, but for whose pleasant company, I could not have completed this book with satisfaction. I am also grateful to my husband Mr. Ishtiaque Hasan for his constant support and help.

January 1, 2007 **Asma Begum**
Dhaka, Bangladesh

1
Introduction

The present micro-study is concerned with an important aspect of the relation between the Grameen Bank of Bangladesh and the poor rural women of the country. This aspect refers to the status of poor women in the countryside of Bangladesh, after they started getting a modicum of income from economic activities aided by the credit from the Grameen Bank. Discussion on the status of women emanates from the existing reality of the inequality between men and women which manifests itself in differential access of men and women to various resources.

More specifically, this study presents the data regarding the association between the economic activity independently carried out with the credit received from the Grameen Bank by the women and the differences, if any, in the status of the loanee and the non-loanee-women in two villages, viz., Bhatpara and Pachdona, in Narsingdi district of Bangladesh.

To clarify the objective and importance of this research, the study seeks to explain the background with brief references to sociological theories of different schools regarding the status of women. It will, for this purpose, also present information on the status of women in different countries of the world; facts about social, political, economic, educational and legal conditions of the women in Bangladesh, the Grameen Bank, its *modus operandi* and the various programmes launched by it for the uplift of the underprivileged women in the villages.

Comprising almost half of the world's population, women form a variable human resource base. But to harness the human resource potential of women for the well-being of the mankind, the human society will have to recognise the important role of women and their ability to contribute, as much as, if not more than men, to the family and to the wider community.

In reality, however, inequality in the status between men and women has stood in the way of society's granting recognition to women and resulted in the denial of opportunities for them and the utilization of their potentialities for the community's welfare. Women have been subordinated to men almost always and everywhere, though they seem to have recognized and protested that situation in some from or other (Chafetz and Dworkin, 1986, cited in Ritzer, 1988, p. 403). Even today, in many societies like that of Bangladesh, women's control over their own lives and belongings remains significantly limited, despite their contribution to the economy through household chores and in case of certain strata, through income from work outside the household.

Women are still found generally to lag behind men in educational attainment, earning and other aspects (Kalbagh, 1992, pp. 21 - 22). They are forced into a disadvantageous position in getting the information and opportunities that they need in order to work more productively for themselves and for the society. Women's low profile in public life is associated with their dependence on men in the family for physical, economic and other social support (Mahadevan, 1989, p. 345).

It is interesting to note that feminist concerns according

to which the situation or situations and experiences of women in society should be a major "object" for investigation have been addressed to by male and female theorists who were marginal to professional sociology, when they wrote (for example, Marx and Engels). According to Engels, the material bases for women's transformation from the status of equal members of society to that of the subordinate spouses, lag in the development of valuable productive resources as private property——a process which was initially evidenced in the domestication of large animals. This transformation started the process of the subordination of women in all subsequent modes of production in which quite different forms of private property became significant. The ultimate restoration of female sex to its rightful position could only come into existence with the total abolition of private property, i.e., with socialism. Engels urges that "the premise for the emancipation of women is the re-introduction of the entire female sex into public industry". Despite the element of truth in it, Engels' thesis provides only one strand in the large corpus of the theories seeking to explain women's subordinate position. Some of these theories, e.g., the gender stratification theory proposed by Blumberg (1991, p. 99), stress economic factors, but they are, as their propounders assert, not monocausal.

Again, several theories in the field highlight a number of important aspects of women's subordinate position as well as the plausible factors responsible for them, which have not been adequately stressed by Marx and Engels.

The theories of scholars showing feminist concern, centre around two basic questions :

1. And what about the women ? In other words, where are the women in any situation being investigated ?

2. Why is women's situation as it is ? There is, of course, a third question haunting many social scientists with

feminist concern. How can we change and improve the world ? If they are not found, why ? In case they are present, how do they experience the situation and what do they contribute to it ?

Obviously, any answer to the third question depends on an understanding of the first two questions. Following Ritzer, (p. 19), one would discern three categories of answers to the first question which provide the bases for three major varieties of theory trying to describe women's social situation : (1) it is different for men's (2) it is unequal to men's and (3) it is that of an oppressed group and the oppressors are men or the male-constructed patriarchal social system. Each of these broad categories of theories ... relating to difference, inequality and oppression, respectively... evinces further variations on the question of why women's situation is as it is. Theorists stressing the difference between men's and women's situation explain the differences in terms of (*i*) bio-social conditioning, (*ii*) institutional socialization and (*iii*) socio-psychological interfacing. Theorists providing explanations in terms of inequality account for women's positions in terms of (liberal feminism's view of) unequal opportunity structures and (Marxian accounts of) women's position as segment of a complex class-system of exploitation. Theorists who perceive, mainly, oppression as women in women's situation seek to explain that oppression (*a*) with the help of psychoanalytic theories regarding men's innate need to subjugate women or (*b*) taking the aid of radical feminist discovery of the root of patriarchal oppression in male's greater ability and readiness to use brute force to subjugate others or through the socialist feminist analysis with attempts to synthesize various forms and theories of oppression and highlight the different systems of oppression like class, age, ethnicity, sexual preference, global position as well as gender. These feminist theories have contributed to the development of sociological literature analysing the socio-economic situation of women particularly in relation to men in different parts of the world (Wallace, 1989).

The differences between feminist theory and sociology for women or what is euphemistically called sociology of gender is that the former seeks to present a woman-centred patterning of experience whereas the latter is more concerned with the study of socially constructed male and female roles, relations and identities——a somewhat different field from feminism's concentrated attention to women. The fact, however, remains that some sociologist who begin from a sociology of gender standpoint have come out with works of importance for feminist theory. Rac Lessor Blumberg's attempt provides a good example of the above. He points out that all the varieties of non-feminist theories concerning development share a common trait : "............. near 'gender blindness' that pays only peripheral attention to half the human race" i.e., women (1989, p. 161). The same view is shared by Muhammad Yunus, originally a Professor of Economics in the Chittagong University but later on the initiator of the Grameen Bank Project. "Whenever we make plans, observes Yunus, "for providing employment to our vast population, we unconsciously plan for men only. It is assumed that women economically at least are an unnecessary part of society, and if they happen to be poor, then they simply do not enter into any economic picture at all" (Yunus, 1991. p. xv). Yunus further states, "Our society simply refuses to accept the fact that these women are 'persons' by their own right, having independent identities and potentials of their own. The sense of values of these women have gradually become so deeply influenced by male domination that they have come to accept the fact that it is only right for them to be repressed and persecuted (ibid, p.xvi).

While the theoretical stance of Blumberg resembles that of the theorists highlighting the unequal situation of women prompted by the relatively poor control by women of economic resources, Yunus' theoretical baggage seems to be a mixed one emphasizing both inequality and oppression. The latter is, however, more interested and actively involved in changing and improving the world for women through organization of the Grameen Bank which caters to the needs of poor men as well as women in villages of Bangladesh.

Blumberg's "general theory of gender stratification" attempts a convergence of the feminist theory of development (Wallace, 1989, p. 16) with sociological viewpoint regarding gender stratified societies, i.e., societies marked by a categorically greater access enjoyed by males in comparison with females to the scarce values of their society (Chafetz, 1989, p. 137).

Blumberg claims to have conducted field work in more than a dozen countries around the world. He finds it difficult to reconcile the rich diversity of gender role ideologies, cultural practices, patterns of socialization, normative and legal systems among third world countries having more or less similar economic levels with the plausibility of explaining gender stratification by economic variable alone. Nonetheless, his theory proposal specifically that the key variable influencing overall gender equality is relative male/female control of economic resources... income, property, and other means of production. In other words, neither mere work in economic activities nor even ownership of economic resources is enough if the person doesnot control them.

(a) Furthermore, the degree of control over surplus allocation is more important for relative male/female economic power than is the degree of control over resources needed for bare subsistence (i.e., withholding food from hungry children is rarely an option at the micro level).

(*b*) Relative male/female economic power varies........and not always in the same direction........at a variety of "nested "levels ranging through the micro-macro continuum. These levels extend from the male/female dyad, to the household, the community, the class, the ethnic group, the state, and even our world capitalist economy.

(*c*) The macro levels influence the micro levels more than vice versa once they emerge historically. (For example, Khomeini's decrees in Iran drastically restricted women's position within the family as well as the larger society).

(*d*) The more macro levels of the 'pyramid of political economy' in stratified societies are highly male—dominated, although the degree varies.

(*e*) Therefore, the extent to which the more macro levels are male-dominated and repressive of females affects how much actual leverage a women can wield for any given amount of economic resources she controls at the micro level :

1. In other words, the macro levels act as a kind of "discount rate" on the exercise of women's relative economic power at the micro levels.
2. Such discount rates are most often negative : Greater relative male control of the macro levels means that economic, political, legal, religious, and ideological factors (including their internalization in gender socialization patterns) act to nibble away at the amount of economic power a women actually can realize from any given amount of micro-level economic resources.

(*f*) The greater the women's relative economic power, the greater their control over their own lives.

1. The greater a women's relative economic power, the greater the likelihood that her fertility pattern will reflect her own perceived utilities and preferences (rather than those of her mate, family, state, and so forth).
2. The greater her relative economic power, the greater her control over a variety of other "life options," including marriage, divorce, sexuality, overall household authority, and various types of household decisions.

(g) Women's relative economic power rises and falls in different trajectories with different consequences. In general, it falls more rapidly than it rises.

1. On the up side, when a women's relative economic leverage increases (net of the various macro- and micro- level "discount factors" mentioned above), her self-confidence and sense of self also increase (Kusterer, Estrada de Batres, and Cuxil, 1981; Crandon with Shepard, 1985; Blumberg, 1985, 1989b). Her input into household decision making (domestic, economic, and fertility issues) also tends to grow, albeit slowly and not always smoothly or uniformly. In such times of transition, violence may result if men use their greater power of force to keep women from consolidating a rising economic position (Roldan, 1982, 1988).
2. On the down side, however, a decline in her base of independently controlled resources often portends a quite rapid decrease in her relative power position in household decisions (Blumberg, 1985; 1989a, 1989b).

In short, there is a whole chain of consequences that emerges from a change in the micro-level gender balance of economic power between male and female. One of the most important consequences affects family well-being. As indicated in the following section, a number of studies show that women tend to spend income that flows through their hands differently than men, holding back less for personal use and devoting more to children's nutrition and family welfare (Blumberg, 1991, pp 100 - 101).

Thus, any discussion related to women's problems cannot remain confined within women's affairs merely; it must necessarily be viewed in the perspective of the entire family and society. Especially women's problems are no less social problems. While listing the problems of women, we are in fact required to ascertain the position, the status, the role and the contribution of women to society vis-à-vis those of men. Society usually attaches different values to the contribution of men and women. These variations in valuation of women relative to that of men, however, vary widely in different societies and in different social and cultural contexts. The status of women in a society, therefore, have to be viewed in the context of the historical conditions from which it emerged as well as the economic, political and cultural forces determining the status of women (United Nations, Department of Economic and Social Affairs, 1975).

One of the biggest disadvantages that working women have to face is the double burden of work. During to economic reasons as well as cultural practices even a full time job does not excuse Bangladeshi women from their regular domestic chores. The old habit of people involves elaborate cooking which is customarily done by women. Women are also responsible for washing, cleaning and child rearing. All these take away a large part of their productive energy. Domestic labour saving devices and implements are not within the reach of these poor families and except for a handful of fortunate women, it is economically not feasible to engage domestic helps. Income earning women are found to be working from 10 to 16 hours a day which is normally more than an income earning male (Khanam, 1990, p. 50). The burden of jobs and family and the social view that a women's first responsibility is to her home work act as detrimental to achieving equal opportunity in the labour market (Khan, 1988, p. 77).

Work for women outside the home has implications for the financial well-being of the family alone. Since work participation involves skills, women can bring in interpersonal skills by which they may gain a stronger say in matters relating to the utilization of family resources. How far this participation is translated into women's decision-making power is obviously a timely topic for sociological research. Thus far, the theoretical and empirical implications of this question have been neglected by Bangladeshi researchers (Mizan, 1992, p. 89).

Currently, Bangladesh, like several other countries, is showing special interest in enhancing women's status and ensuring women's participation in family welfare and national development efforts, in both rural and urban areas (Duza, 1989, p.142). So, the number of employed women has increased in recent years. For example, in 1981 only 1.2 million women participated in the civilian labour force, while in 1986 this figure increased to 3.2 million (Government of Bangladesh 1990). Civilian labour force in Bangladesh refers to the population of age 10 years and above who earns income from their work. This excludes housewives, students, the disabled and the beggars. Even though women's participation relative to men's remains considerably lower, their earnings and income contribution to the family have been substantial. This gain in women's employment was primarily confined to the urban areas of the society.

However, against the background of this changing socio-economic context, the study has sought to ascertain the status of women in contemporary rural Bangladesh in relation to development schemes initiated by the Grameen Bank.

Recently, the introduction of the Grameen Bank has widened cash-earning opportunities for rural women who participate in the programme as loanees/borrowers. While this kind of gainful economic participation at the grass-roots level was virtually non- existent for women a decade ago, today the Grameen Bank's programme provides many thousands of its female members all over the rural areas of Bangladesh with the capacity of playing economic contributor's role.

Does this shift in rural women's economic role has any measurable alteration on their decision-making status in the family, specially in economic contribution ? How does this alteration-role of a woman as cash income earners influence spousal decision-making among the poor in the rural sector of the society? In addition, does this income earning role enable women to have control over their family decision-making?

These are some of the questions that I seek answer in this study. This study reviews the status of women in their families vis-à-vis their extent of economic contribution towards the management of their homes.

The main focus of this research is to investigate the concern of women's economic contributions and earnings and their participation in the process decision-making.

The context is important because the association between women's economic status and contribution, the area of decision-making and their related indicators which obtain in developed countries may have much relevance for the rural cultures of the developing countries.

Some of the common items suggested by the family sociologist in the area of decision-making are decisions concerning the husband's job, buying a car, choosing a family doctor, taking vacations etc. These indicators of western decision-making are irrelevant in rural Bangladesh. Also, the rural bazaars, where everyday household consumption items are bought and sold, are generally restricted to women. Generally, men buy and sell in a rural bazaar. Thus, daily purchase of goods in the rural families of Bangladesh remains under men's control. What items to be purchased, however, may be decided by the women (Mizan, 1992, p.7).

In rural Bangladesh, women do not have access to the formal employment market nor do they have the necessary funds to engage in income generating activities. So, the Grameen Bank and its extension of credit to rural women in several regions of the country have provided them with unique opportunities to earn an income. This credit generated work for women in the informal Sector. The Grameen Bank thus has created a situation which enables me to test the proposed association between women's economic contribution and their decision-making power. To put it in a more specific manner, the present study may formulate the following proposition :

Considering these inquiries into the nature of the relationship between woman's status in the family, and their contribution to the family's subsistence, it may be assumed that when a woman supports her family, economically, she would be included to a greater extent in the family's decision-making process than one who is merely a housewife. At the same time she will also enjoy some freedom which her non-supporting counterparts are deprived of.

This proposition may be further broken into several more specific hypotheses :

(a) There is an association between the economic contribution of women to their families and their participation in the household decision-making process.

(b) There is an association between the economic contribution of women to their families and the extent of their participation in the decision-making process regarding the number of children.

(c) There is an association between the economic contribution of women to their families and the extent of their control over their family income.

(d) There is an association between women's economic contribution to their families and the extent of their control over the sale of the property owned by them.

(e) There is an association between the economic contribution of women to their families and their freedom of movement.

(f) There is an association between the economic contribution of women to their families and their freedom of speech and expression.

(g) There is an association between the economic contribution of women to their families and their independence in exercising their voting right.

(h) There is an association between the economic contribution of women to their families and their opinion regarding the role of husbands and wives in running the household.

(i) There is an association of Literacy

The focus of the present study is on the status of the rural women who are gainfully employed vis-à-vis those who are not engaged in any economic activity.

A number of studies on the association between the participation by women in economic activity and improvement of status of the women have taken place and are taking place throughout the world. These studies, however, have not come and are not coming to the same conclusion.

If these studies could be broadly categorised, several patterns of thought would emerge from them. First, some studies on women's work have linked their involvement in income-generating activity to an improvement in their status within the household. Bhatty (1980, p. 41) in her study of women workers in the *beedi* (country made cigarette) industry of Allahabad, a city in India, finds a positive relationship between women's status and their participation in employment. She concludes : "A greater economic role for women definitely improves their status within the family. A majority of them have more money to spend, and even more importantly, have a greater say in the decisions to spend money. Most women claim to be better treated as a result of their contribution to household income. Their attitudes show a clear perception of the significance of their work to family welfare and their own status within the family."

Chatterjee (1981) also shares Bhatty's viewpoint on the basis of her research on women sweepers in Benaras, another city of India. She has shown that lower class women had control over the household finances. Their improved status was highlighted by the fact that the husbands of these sweepers usually handed over the salary to the wives. She finds that, "Sweeper women go out to work as municipal sweepers and not only do they do the same work as their menfolk but they also earn as much, if not more. In the majority of cases they control the household finances as well, the husband handing over all his earning to his wife, and keeping only a specific sum for pocket money (p.1)."

These studies infer that work outside home confers on the working women prestige and status as compared to the housewives. Because, no matter, how meagre is the pay packet, it never fails to bring its own recognition to these women in the eyes of others in the household. Similar views are also provided by Gulhati (1975, p. 37); Nayak and Kala, (1992, p. 204).

Even when a woman is engaged in the unorganised sectors she enjoys a better treatment in the family than a woman who is simply a housewife. It has been noted in Banerjee's survey (1985) that an increase in the contribution of a woman to the family income is followed by an increase of her power in the management of the family funds independently, or along with others. That they have separate savings and/ or earnings is also an indicator of the fact that these women enjoy financial independence (p. 100)

Ahmad (1980) has stated that the economic activity sets, the stage for improved female status. She also mentions, "Of course, the stark reality of economic pressure as the cause affecting male support towards working female is the ultimate reason for the upward surge in women's economic activity (p. 35).

Similarly, Ahmed's study, (1985) show women's perception of improvement of their socio-economic status. The increased self-confidence of women accompanies an improvement in the attitude of men also.

An independent source of income assures a female member that she is no longer financially dependent on her husband, and this contributes to her self-confidence and sense of individuality. As a violent husband becomes aware of his wife's growing autonomy, he realises that continued abuse on his part might very well drive her away and deprive him of the extra income. A woman who contributes to the family income is no longer viewed as lazy and as an economic burden, but as an economic asset (Shehabuddin, 1992, pp. 102 -103; Rahman, 1986, pp. 77 - 79).

Moreover, economic activities give women a feeling of being united in a group. They also generate confidence and self-esteem in women and empower them to establish themselves as independent entities (Rahman, 1986, pp. 77 - 79).

Noponen's findings suggest that the independent source of income of the women plays a critical role in the family. A comparison of the women's earnings with those of other household members reveal that being self-employed in many cases is more remunerative than being a wage-worker in the informal sector. The self-employed women's income is not a mere supplement; rather it is the backbone of the family income (Noponen,1987, p.236).

However, Ahmad (1991), observes that cash earning improves female status in the family, far more than does wage earned in kind, such as food or other non-food items (p.62).

It is well documented in development programmes and research that a woman's status in the household and the community rises with an increase in her personal income and control of assets (Fuglesang & Chandler, 1993, p.26).

On the other hand, social scientists like Karlekar and Kazi have stressed that women are not free of their men inspite of their participation in economic activities. Their status remains unchanged. Kazi has put forward reasons as to why the status remains unchanged. The change in the status depends very much on the patriarchy. Patriarchy prevails in most of South Asia; the patriarchal system is described as a set of social relationships with a material base, which enables men to dominate over women. According to this system males have power over women through control of property and household income. Since female economic independence is thus limited in these societies, this automatically leads to their lower status relative to men (Kazi, 1986, pp. 45 - 46).

Mies highlights another important aspect of the phenomenon. She points out, "although the lace-makers and the agricultural labour women, *defacto* belong to the same class of pauperized peasants and agricultural labourers, they are separated because members of one category conceive of themselves as housewives, and the other as workers (Mies, 1988, p.16). The improvement in the status depends significantly on the perception of the women themselves.

The forgoing discussion on the status of women vis-à-vis their participation in economic activity has been limited to a general aspect. There are studies, which deal with a specific indicator of the status of women, viz., their participation in the decision-making process. But in this realm also, different studies on decision-making role have established different kinds of opinions.

Some Family Sociologists argue that women's economic participation is positively related with their status. They focus predominantly on the study of power relationships between husband and wife in the areas of decision-making. At the household level, some research findings show that an earning wife shares more power in decision-making with her husband than a non-earning wife (Mizan, 1992, p. 196; Ramu, 1988, p. 50; Blood and Wolfe, 1960, p. 45).

In developing countries survival of low income families may compel all members to engage in productive activities. However little the improvement in total household earnings, a woman's status is likely to be affected by an increase in bargaining power as a result of her crucial contributions to family subsistence. This implies that when the wife's contribution becomes a valued resource for the welfare of the family the wife will have more influence in decision-making within the family.

The women who contribute to their family income in a substantial way, understood in the sense suggested above, are found to have broken through the barriers of many social taboos which bound them to the old social behavioural norms. These two factors contribute towards increasing the independence of women. They have also substantially contributed towards their role in family decision-making. None of these women are mute observers and victims of decisions made by their husbands (Kalbagh, 1992, p. 235). This fact, partly, explains why women's participation in many developmental projects in Bangladesh was trageted to ensure the awareness, building among them about their status and oppertunities of making their own decisions especially in the reproductive behaviour and health care practices. Kabir and Amin have found in their study based on the data derived from the three (BRAC, BRDB and GB) village- based development agencies in Bangladesh that informal sector enterprise and opportunities to work outside homestead are likely to empower women. Their study suggests that work in the informal sector provides opportunities for women's mobility and decision-making power in the family and it also, probably, enables them to regulate the desired fertility. Women's involvement in economic activities beyond home surroundings and in cash generation is likely to have a more positive impact on the endeavour towards the achievement of decline in fertility (1995, p. 36).

Kabir and Amin further observe that women's sense of collective power is enhanced by opportunities for women to move around not only outside the their homes but also, beyond their village as well, attendance in outside meetings, to speak out in larger gatherings and to assume leadership. 'These findings lead us to believe that there may have been an increase in female status and autonomy" (Kabir and Amin, 1995, pp. 36-37)

Cultural constraints on women are changing in the lowest strata of society also, where women are being pushed into the labour market out of dire economic necessity. Evidence from South Asia indicates that the vast majority of women work in response to economic need. These women undertake a diverse range of economic activities to meet their subsistence needs (Kazi, 1989, p. 47).

The growing incidence of households headed by women in South Asia provides further evidence of changing socio-cultural norms. Economic pressures are overriding the basic tenets of the patriarchal system—that males should provide for their female relatives. In 1982, more than 15 per cent of the total households in Bangladesh were headed by women. (BBS. 1986).

Another factor leading to the emergence of women as *de facto* heads of households is the migration of males which is likely to have major implications on the decision-making role of the women. Migration to the Middle-East has been a development of great importance to the economy of most South Asian countries. Research, on the impact of the absence of men from rural areas in Pakistan, India and Bangladesh indicates conflicting effects of male migration on the families left behind. Though not all, but some of the studies highlighted that male migration leads to a greater say for the females in decision-making process (Kazi, 1989, p. 48).

As a woman's contribution to the family income increases, the probability of her managing the family funds independently or along with members increases. Nevertheless, even among women earning 50 percent or more of the family income, one third were not consulted on important matters. A related indicator of their financial independence was their ability to think in terms of having separate personal savings. Though at these levels of income, it would not be easy for most individuals to save any significant amount, but the fact that they could envisage the idea of being financially independent, indicated their level of maturity and the lack of family pressures to stop them from doing so (Banerjee, 1985, pp. 100 - 101).

The consequence of women having a source of income, which is an unmistakable sign of their greater importance in household decision-making process, is the increased say they have on how money is spent (Bhatty, 1987, p. 46).

Most of the participants in the International Seminar on Role of Rural Women in Development held at the Nassau Inn, Princeton, New Jersey on December 2-4, 1974, concurred that greater economic independence is desired by most women in most countries and is crucial to their status, options and ability to participate in other programmes. "Women's economic independence can", they further observed, "be fully assured only if their income is theirs to control and if they know, how best to utilize it. Many women currently play a significant role in the family's economic decisions and should be better trained to do so" (Weisblat, 1975, p.3). In another similar international seminar, supported by the ADC, Geliat. T. Castillo who works in the Philipines reported that in the Filipino household which is more egalitarian but rather patriarchal, the Filipino wife is the keeper of family joint with household finances and participates in the management not only of matters concerning household and family, but also of farming and livelihood. The issue [regarding economic independence and participation in decision-making], therefore, in the Phlilipine case, is not the degree of authority and influence which a woman exercises in the farm and family-related matters, but rather the quality of her input into the decision-making process and what might be done to enhance the content of what she contributes"

(Castillo, 1977, p. 6)

That women are at all deciding independently to take up paid work, is an achievement in the context of the village society in countries like Bangladesh. Supported by the fact that men endorse their action provides ample emphasis to the acceptance of women's decision-making, and the new view on women as active participants (Ahmed, 1980, p. 35).

Mabud has shown that once they are given the exposure to vocational training and work opportunities in the production workshops, the rural women are capable of increasing their income, and during the programme they become a source of family income. The data also shows that their opinion in the family is weighted more, and their status in the family decision-making process is increased (Mabud 1985, p. 150).

Various other studies, on the other hand, have elucidated that despite economic independence, women played a very insignificant role in the decision-making process of the family.

These studies showed a lesser degree of freedom is enjoyed by women than men in household decision-making in rural India and Bangladesh even today. Women's role in the family decision-making process is marginal although they engage themselves in both productive and reproductive work (Nayak and Kala, 1992, p. 201).

Westergard (1983) found in his study, based on the data derived from Comilla District of Bangladesh, that half of these women reported that their husbands asked for some or all the money. For all the women the proceeds were so meagre that even in cases where the women did not have to work hard over the money, the income gave them little autonomy in decision-making (p. 119).

Reddy (1985), on the basis of his analysis of several empirical studies, points out that in the Indian context male control over female labour, their activities and participation, continues to be preponderant not only in rural areas but also among urban families (p. 47). The women who perform agricultural work have least participation in decision-making regarding farm-management. However, it is assumed by some concluding anthropologists that women who work for wages and even those women who work as family labourers would have greater say in household matters than women who perform household work. This assumption was, Reddy immediately adds, rejected by Ursula Sharma (1980). According to Sharma, the female labourer "usually earns wages which are too small and sporadic to lend her any special leverage in household politics and the work of female family labourers does not give women any particular control over the products of their labour" (Sharma, 1980, p.196).

Ursula Sharma was considering the situation of the Himachali and Punjabi women, of India, or more particularly, of the north-west part of India. She noted important differences between these two categories of women. The contrast between the restrained public demeanor of the Punjabi women and their spontaneity in the private company of other women seems striking to her. The Himachali women appeared to her to be more reserved though less obliged to refer their behaviour and movement to men. But the similarities in the underlying structure of the female situations in both the cases turned out to be very great. "The chances for economic independence and the control over their economic activities which this might bring are as limited for Himachali women as for Punjabi women" (ibid, pp.195-196). As in agricultural decision-making so "in other areass of social life, women's capacity to influence decisions and exert control was just as likely to depend on factors unrelated to the kind of productive work"(ibid). Sharma, claims to have examined the particular sphere of matchmaking in some detail. In this aspect "the power which women wielded and their importance in determining household policy depended on factors quite other than their capacity to work or generate income" (idem). According to her, the ideology of dependence of women on men, which is perceived in the male-dominated communities like the ones she found in Himachal and Punjab is required by the material structure of production. "A little well-meaning intervention from the rural development experts, a few schemes to stimulate local crafts among village women—these are not going to change the structure of production, although they will, undoubtedly be worthwhile for the women who benefit from them directly" (ibid. p. 208).

In her field survey among the agricultural labourers in Punjab, Raj Mohini Sethi found that the male wage rate is always higher than the female rate for similar number of hours of work. What is more relevant for the purpose of the present study, is that household work and child care continued to be the responsibility of women only, even though they were also doing wage work. These women did not enjoy any decision-making powers within the household and the worst trend of it all is that the practice of dowry raised its ugly head even in the poor, agricultural labour households (Sethi, 1981, cited in Desai and Krishnaraj, 1990, p. 81).

In a later work carried out by her among the women family-labourers in Himachal Pradesh of North India, Sethi has observed that in the prevailing agricultural structure in Himachal Pradesh "women's contribution to agricultural work is more than of men in Himachal Pradesh" (1989, p. 223). What is interesting is that "women's dominant participation in economic activities...does not give them a dominant role in decision-making" (ibid, p. 228). Her data shows that in taking decisions on education and admission of children in schools, in selecting an occupation or a mate for children, expenditure on children's marriages, and the observance of rituals and social ceremonies, women at best, patricipate along with other men in the household; "only seven to ten percent women take such decisions independently of men" (ibid, p. 228). Her analysis reveals that all the major decisions in the family are taken by men either individually or jointly with women, "in all the economic and prestige groups. Thus men wield considerable domestic power by exercising control over decisions affecting the household economy. Women who are the productive and reproductive agents, exercise exclusive control over peripheral areas of domestic life" (idem). Sethi notes that the prevailing political ideological and cultural factors cause increasing marginalisation of women despite their high rate of work participation on family farms. On the other hand, men "perform only productive agricultural work and non-agricultural work and when unemployed prefer to remain idle, than share housework. Housework continues to be the responsibility of women only, even if they increasingly perform the agricultural work. On the other hand, increasing participation of women in family farms is accompanied by an increasing withdrawal of men from these farms leading to the 'feminisation' of the agricultural labour force.

Sethi perceives in her field a situation akin to what Maria Mies would call "housewification" under certain circumstances the subsistence—based agricultural work represents an extension of housework for women. It is this process of housewification as elaborated by Mies (1987) that helps in the reduction of labour costs on the one hand and the exclusion of women from any involvement in the decision-making process at different levels by maintaing their seclusion from public life on the other.

This spells another kind of danger. Sethi rightly points out, "Women's seclusion keeps them out of the decision-making process related to various rural development activities such as the utilisation of loans and subsidies under the various IRDP (Integrated Rural Development Programme Schemes" (Sethi, 1089, p.232).

Desai and Krishnaraj in their analysis of the conditions of middle class employed women in post independence India have found that the control over the income earned by these women is not necessarily in the women's hands. "Nor does it always improve the women's position with respect to authority and decision-making, within the family" (Desai and Krishnaraj, 1990, p. 95).

In a study conducted by Qadir (1988) among a number of employed women in the urban and rural areas indicates that in the rural areas, even though women are allowed to keep a part of their income. they are not completely free to spend their income in the way they like to (cited in Ahmad, 1991, p. 67). "This may be due to their lack of education which in turn impairs their self confidence and ability to earn respect" (Ahmad, 1991, p. 67).

Though income earning women felt satisfied that they could maintain themselves or could help their guardians financially, they were as subordinate to their guardians as to non-income earning women. Though women's incomes, were a measure of economic relief to their families, this was not openly appreciated by their husbands or their guardians. This may be due to the fact that maintaining the household is considered the responsibility of men and when they are unable to do so, they feel inadequate. As such, recognising women's role in this regard may mean recognition of what guardians may regard as their own shortcomings. This also reflects how, like their labour, women's contributions are often underestimated. Money earning alone, while it may improve their conditions of life, cannot change the attitude of men towards women (Desai, 1990, p. 95).

One finds in the above paragraphs, repeated references to "the status of women" or "women's status". Status is understood here mainly in the sense of capacity for participation in the decision making process in the family. This understanding seems in conformity with the sociological interpretation of the word, status.

Status is a complex, dynamic and relative concept, encompassing certain power derived either from one's own achievements and/or from ancestors. The power is manifested in prestige and privileges along with rights, roles and autonomy for independent action. Status generally grows periodically and also fluctuates. It normally exists among members of a society irrespective of age and sex, but varies on the basis of class, caste and several other positions and achievements.

One may take, as illustrations, the definitions offered by Max Weber and Ralph Linton. Max Weber pointed out that there are three major dimensions of social stratification: status, class or income and political power. Status is, according to him, "an effective claim to social esteem in terms of positive or negative privileges" (Weber, 1978).

In saying this Weber emphasised the relational base of status and that a status claimant must have an audience from which to receive or to demand deferent response. Later, Gerth and Mills (1953) stressed that a status situation is not fixed but inclines to be played out on the uncertain grounds of claimant and audience negotiation and compromise.

A different type of interpretation seems to emerge from the work of anthropologist, Ralph Linton (1936). According to him, status is primarily a position in a social structure, involving rights, duties and reciprocal expectations of behaviour, none of which depends on the personal characteristics of the status-occupant. Davis (1948) further developed this idea for sociology. And, Merton (1957) went on to postulate that individuals have an array of social positions, constituting a composite or status set.

In fine, then, two major conceptualisations of status have grown:

(1) status, as seen by Weber and his followers, is relational and intersubjective; (2) status, as outlined by Linton and others, is positional and highly structured "Much of today's work takes an uneasy path between the two" (Wolf, 1985, p. 826) And this tension is reflected in the considerations of status of women in countries like Bangladesh and their participation in the decision-making power in the family.

Prior to a discussion of the connection of status and participation in the decision-making power in the family, it may be mentioned that Linton, in his discussion of status refers to an associated concept, viz., role. He has referred to role as the dynamic aspect of status; a role is the totality of all the cultural patterns associated with a particular status. This view, according to many, comprehends roles as essentially prescribed and static expectations of behaviour, as prescriptions inherent in particular positions. These prescriptions flow from the society's culture. This understanding of roles as embodiment of cultural prescriptions seems to admit that roles are often defined in relation to other roles, but not that interaction produces or modifies roles. One may point out that this view of role does not hold good in modern societies which are frequently fragmented, marked by diverse elements, and where different groups (and, therefore, individulas) are characterised by a lot of indeterminacy of roles. In traditional societies, however, one finds that the cultural prescriptions deriving from age-old, relatively static tradition do not allow much freedom to the incumbents of particular statuses and roles. They have to obey what is traditionally envisioned for them. "Lintonian view of social structure, status and role seems to be overidingly present in such cases. This is particularly true of status and role of women in a male-dominated society" like the one in Bangladesh (Sen, 1991, p. 238). But, at the same time, it seems that women have started experiencing changes in their status and role because of differnt social forces.

Herein one may expect to find a dent in the relatively static picture of status-system and role-system and, concomitantly, a certain degree of indeterminacy in the roles of women, making way for changes in their status.

Whether and how far measures like opportunities of income-generating activities by women help the process is a moot point in this research.

The status of women in the real and complete sense is a recent and emerging concept, though women, in general, enjoyed certain privileges, positions, rights, duties, roles, power and authority in varying degrees in different societies. However, one nearly universal fact is that they did not enjoy equal and extensive status in society as did men. In analysing the status of women, the term status is used, first, as an access to resources such as education, gainful employment or employment in income-generating activity fetching income for women independently of their husbands, and health services, and, second, the position (power, prestige, authority) that a woman has in different situations. The term, 'role', refers to the different activities that a woman performs in relation to her status in a given situation (Oppong, 1970 and Dixon, 1978, as cited in Mahadevan, 1989, p. 349).

In this connection, it seems very relevant to mention the distinction made by Safilios-Rothschild between women's power and women's status and also the connection pointed, out by her, lying between the two. "Women's power can be distinguished from women's status, in that status refers to women's overall position in the society while power refers to women's ability to influence and control at the interpersonal level. Power can be defined as the 'ability to control or change the behaviour of others'.............. Thus, female power can be defined as women's ability to control or change other women's and men's behaviours and the ability to determine important events in their lives, even when men and older women are opposed to them" (Safilios-Rothschild, 1982, p.117). [Interestingly enough, the credit of authorship of the preceding view, rather, the preceding sentences, is given by Mahadevan, et. al., to Dixon (1978). See Mahadevan, et. al. 1989 p.349).] Saffilios-Rothschild suggests a number of indicators on women's status. And the selection of the indicators is based on the notion that (i) the higher women's ability to control important events in their lives e.g., age at marriage, remarriage, etc.), the higher is their status, and (ii) the more women that have the same life options as men in the same age-group and social class with respect to food, education and training, occupations, remuneration and occupational advancement, migration, use of time and leisure, land and property ownership, and life expectancy, the higher is the status. The indicators of women's status, most often used in macro-level studies, are not detailed enough to facilitate an accurate measurement of the degree to which women's status indicating their overall position in the society is translated into power at the individual level. There may be, at times, disjunctions between women's status at the macro=level and women's power at the micro-level. Hence, information at the micro-level is very important for understanding women's status. Safilios-Rothschild rightly observes, "while the indicators of women's status are important for macro level studies of different societies, the indicators of women's power in the household are important methodological tools for case studies of individual women (or networks of relatives)." (ibid, p.128). Considering this view of Safilios-Rothschild, Mahadevan remarks, "Safilios-Rothschild (1982) defines the status of women in terms of power they wield in the family and society" (Mahadavan (ed). 1989, p. 12; emphasis added), though in another article in the same book Mahadevan along with other writers observes, "Safilios-Rothschild (1982 : 117) differentiates between power and the status of women". (Mahadevan, et. al. 1989 in Mahadevan (ed.) 1989, p. 349).

Be that as it may, the indicators of women's power are, according to Safilios-Rothschild, as follows : —

"– Women's ability to control decisions about their productive and economic activities, including freedom of movement and control over the resulting wages of income.

– Women's ability to control the services of others (unpaid family members or paid help) who substitute for them in household and child-care tasks and responsibilities.

– Women's ability to control the type of household structure in terms of composition (extended or not and with which relatives female-headed or not; polygamous or not and with second wife, etc.), size of duration.

– Degree of discrepancy between men's and women's ratios of time spent in income-earning activities to leisure time.

– Degree to which the women's time budgets show

unreciprocated special services rendered to husbands.

- Percentage of own expenses and children's expenses paid by mother.
- Women's membership in economic and social collectives, and formal or informal groups (credit or loan association, co-operatives, etc.).
- Degree of discrepancy between men's and women's wages or income from productive activties in the household.
- Women's ability to have an important say (if not make the actual decision) in decisions which affect their lives, such as major purchases, building a house, family size (including having a child at a particular time of life and work), moving or not to another town, etc. Or, in other words, women's ability to play an important role in decisions which are not stereotyped as 'feminine'—such as what to eat, how to decorate the house, minor household purchases or the rearing of childern" (Safilio-Rothschild, 1982, pp. 128-129).

Safilios–Rothschild reminds the researchers of the fact that the above indicators are all behavioural, and the assessment of them can be best carried out through brief observation and intensive interviewing of the women being studied. During the intensive interviews, she remarks, it should be fairly easy to assess the prevailing attitudes towards male supremacy and dominance and towards women's economic, social and psychological independence.

Participation in decision-making power by women and its association with women's participation in gainful employment or income-generating activities have been considered an important indicator of women's status and role in society in several other studies which have gained recognition from the social scientists, e.g., Blood and Wolfe, 1960, in the USA, Mizan (1992) herself has done it in the context of Bangladesh, and she cites several other similar works done by others in differnt context, (e.g., Heer, 1963, Blood, 1963 ; Kenkel, 1961 and 1963; Wilkening and Bharad, 1967). The researchers have argued, according to Mizan, that the power-balance within marriage is determined by the comparative valued resources of spouses. "Thus a working wife bringing valued resources such as incomes into the family is expected to gain a significant increase in decision-making power relative to her husband and have more power than a non-working wife" (Mizan, 1992, p. 33).

It seems relevant to note the views of Blood and Wolfe in some detail. According to them, in a patriarchal system both the husband and the wife will, ordinarily, take for granted that the husband should take most of the decisions. But even in a tradition-bound society, there are variation between couples, not to speak of those societies which are relatively free from the shackles of tradition. The sources of variations in the power of the husband and the wife must be sought in the comparative resources which the husband and wife bring to the marriage, beside authority. Power according to them, accrues almost automatically to the partner who has the greater resources at his/her disposal. They mention a second factor closely related to resources. Any one who succeeds in making a contribution is, almost by definition, a competent person–i.e., someone with special skills. To possess a skill enables the individual to make a contribution; in addition, it implies special competence in decision-making as such. "Thus a wife may not only depend on her husband for 'brining home the bacon' but recognize that in this work he becomes familiar with some of the complexities of life outside the home. Therefore, she may defer to his superior knowledge in decisions about politics, taxes, and cars" (Blood and Wolfe, 1960, p. 13).

But, if authority patterns and personal resources both influence the balance of power, are they equally important? The answer is, according to Blood and Wolfe, not likely to be entirely one or the other—since change in one are bound to affect the other, sooner or later. "If husbands become infected with democratic ideas and start giving their wife more freedom, the wives will gain more competence. On the other hand, if wives gain increased resources, old patriarchal nations are not likely to remain unaffected for very long" (ibid, p. 14).

In order to measure the precise balance of power between husbands and wives, it is necessary to assess their influence in all the family decisions which had ever been made–or at least all those which had been made over a considerable length of time. But a complete record of decisions is difficult to obtain for various reasons. Therefore, any study which seeks to examine the balance of power between husband and wife must rely on a sample of decisions to represent the larger whole. Blood and Wolfe selected "eight decisions" or decisions in eight areas of family life. However, their list is not applicable to the situation prevailing among the poor strata in Bangladesh, which are being considered in the present study. But the relevance of the work by Blood and Wolfe for the present study lies in that they operationalise power through a number of indicators of decision-making in various areas of family life.

What the present researcher likes to highlight is that the status of women, like the general concept of status, is a multi-dimensional and dynamic concept which is considered (by researchers carrying out empirical studies like the present one) on a relative basis. It is comprised of several dimensions. As Mahadevan and others rightly point out, "these dimensions of status may have value over a particular period of time, with reference to a situation, and may be able to function on their own lines." And, 'Autonomy' and 'Decision' which include 'Participation in Decision-making' have been considered one of the Status Affecting Variables (SAVs) by Mahadevan and others who have drawn the list of SAVs in the light of extant knowledge regarding the status of women.

In this study, women's status has been defined as women's capacity for participation in the family decision-making process which where found to more relevant to family dynamics of rural Bangladesh from the pilot study may be detailed in the following manner:

1. Participation in decisions on family budget :–

A budget is a financial plan which a person, institution, or Government has and which shows in detail how much money is available and how it is to be spent. To budget something means to plan your expenditure carefully so that you know how much money you can spend on something.

A household or a family, if it is not a destitute one household usually makes budgets for meeting its different needs. Though there are differences in ways in which a rural family and an urban family will do it, there is in both the cases the process of making decisions as to what portions of the income of the family will be spent on what specific items or needs, e.g., food, clothing, entertainment of guests, etc.

The present study, makes an attempt to fathom to what extent the respondents participate in making decisions on family budget.

2. Participation in decision concerning the education of the offspring :—

The women, usually lack in the appreciation of the educational needs of their children. Since they are denied the freedom of movement outside and do not have their separate earning, they are hardly consulted in matters concerning the education of the offspring. If at all the family takes any decision in the matter, it is the husbands or other male members take the decision, since they earn the income necessary for the family. It is the husbands or male members who will pay the expenses for education. Hence it is the husbands or male members in the family who take decisions regarding children's education. It indicates the superior status of men to women in the family in this respect.

If the women take decisions solely on their own or participate along with their husbands in decision-making in relation to the education of their children, it indicates, for the purpose of this study, their status or power to influence what goes on in the family. This study examines whether the loanee-women who have their independent earning can make decisions or participate in making decisions concerning their children's education and whether there is any difference between them and the non-loanee-women in this respect.

3. Participation in the making of decisions regarding the marriage of the offspring :—

In patriarchal and patrilineal Muslim society in Bangladesh, it is the father or in his absence any one of his male relatives who is guardian of the children or even of the whole the mother takes a lot of responsibility for the nurturing and socialization of the children in the family. Indeed, in most of the cases she takes a much heavier responsibility than her husband for the upbringing of the children, though she may not financially contribute like him to the family. But in all important matters, including the matter concerning the marriage of the offspring, because of the prevalance of patriachy, it is the father (or some other male relative in his absence) who takes the decision. The power of a person to take decision in the matter indicates his/her status in the family. This study, therefore, seeks to examine and see, if and how far loanee-women who make financial contribution to their respective families independently of their husband, take part in making decision relating to the marriage of children in the family.

4. Participation in making decisions regarding the nature of medical treatment to be adopted in the event of sickness or illness in the family :

Health is an important aspect of life in the family. According to the World Health Organisation, health is a "state of complete physical mental and social wellbeing and not merely the absence of disease and infirmity". The Committee on the Status of Women in India has observed in its report that health is an important factor in the achievement of status as well as an indicator of social status, particularly for women, whose health is conditioned to a great extent by the prevailing social attitudes. (Government of India, 1974, p. 310). To drive home the point, the Committee cites the findings of a study by conducted Kumudini Dandekar in rural Maharashta in 1957. Dandekar observed in her study of six villages in Maharashtra in 1957, "Invariably, in all the centres except Dhanore money spent on male adults exceeded than that spent on female adults" (1959, p.124). She further observed that "on the whole, expenditure on male children was higher than that on female children in all the centres." (ibid, p. 125). In rural Bangladesh also a similar situation prevails. "Social and environmental patterns play a very important part in the lives of rural woman. So deep is the impact of social constraints on a woman that her movement within the area specified by parents, husband and in-laws has to be followed strictly, even at the cost of her health" (Mahtab and Ahmad, 1979, p. 35). A study conducted by the Ministry of Social Welfare and Women's Affairs of the Government of the Peoples Republic of Bangladesh points out that female population like the male counterpart is vulnerable to malnutrition and various diseases. But to this "must be added the diseases of mothers related to deprivation, unregulated fertility and fatigue···" (Ahmed, et al ed. 1985,

p. 87, quoted in Sen, 1991, p. 270). Women refrain form "utilizing available health facilities because of distance of health centre from home; cultural barrier and inadequate resource provision (op. cit. 88). Another constraint is that women, although they are very much conscious of health of other members of the family, "give less importance to their own health and nutrition a traditional practice/prejudice" (idem).

This is a reflection of the prevailing patriarchy and bias in favour of the male gender, rather, male domination in the family in the countryside of Bangladesh. Women's inferior status in the family is evident in the sphere of deciding questions regarding health in the family. It is the husbands or male members who earn money for the family would take decision when and how much money would be spent for treatment of illness or sickness of the members of the family. They would decide which system of medical treatment should be availed of. Women, who lack in the mobility to move outside their homes and the capactiy to contribute money earned from some income-generating activities to their family, hardly enjoy the power to take decisions in the matter. Their opinion is scarcely given importance. Do the loanee-women who financially contribute to the family find an alteration in the stituation and a change in their position or status in the family in the matter of making decisions or taking part in decision-making in this sphere, i.e., health ? And is there any difference between loanee and non-loanee-women in this respect ? This study seeks answers to these queries for a proper understanding the association of the status of women as reflected in their power of taking decisions relating to health and treatment and the fact of their earning an income.

5. Participation in decisions on the mode of expenditure of the family income :—

When one considers the social norms and institutions

in relation to the status of women in Bangladesh, one observes that whatever may be a woman's position at different stages of life, "one common feature··· is her inferiority to husband and domination of male members of the family in household finance. At no stage of life does she exercise control over the family resources or have access to the family funds. She depends on man for essential purchase - including purchase of food" (Islam, 1979, p. 243). True, the eldest female member of the family, usually the mother, is sometimes consulted at the time of seasonal buying and selling in rural household. "But man is the final arbiter in household finance. Every husband keeps strict vigilance over his wife stealthily giving money or grain to her relative on the paternal side. Any such action by wife, if detected, is severely handled" (idem). The power to decide how the income available for the family will be spent is a very important component of the status of a person in the family. This study, therefore, wants to examine whether the loanee-women who make an income of their own and financially contribute to the family have any power to take decisions regarding the way of disposal of the income of the family and compare their status in regard that of non-loanee-women. In order to understand whether and, if so, what kind of association exists between the fact of earning separate income by the loanee-women and the power of taking decisions by them or participation by them in decision-making with regard to the expenditure of income in the family.

6. Participation in decisions regarding the mode of expenditure of the income earned by one for one's own purpose or according to one's choice :—

In view of the male domination, in general, and control of men over finance in the family, in particular, it is important to learn whether and how far the women can control the income they earn from their own income-generating activities. A woman may be allowed, for one reason or another, to engage in income-generating activity. A loanee-woman-may earn a modicum of income on her own. But does she have any power to decide as to how it will be dealt with ? Does a loanee-woman who has an independent income have any control over it? Or is she denied any power to decide whether and how much of it should be spent or saved ? To have an understanding of the questions like the above and thereby of the status of loanee-women the study tries to find some answers.

7. Participation in decisions regarding the number of children a family should have :—

In a situation of poverty and scarcity in the traditional society of Bangladesh it is the women who suffer most. The sanctification of motherhood, self-sacrifice, and obedience to husband as head of the family leads women to forego their own education, and their freedom is affected adversely. Sattar wrote in 1979, "Over fifty per cent of Bangladeshi women suffer from anaemia; eating last they eat least and less of protein food, having served the best of what is available to their husbands and children, particularly male ones. Repeated pregnancies undermine their health and reduce their capacity to work" (Sattar, 1979, p. 13, emphasis added). Since the women have to bear the burden of child-bearing and also the most of the responsibility for child-rearing, they should, logically speaking, have the power to decide regarding the number of children they should have. But women are conditioned by the extent of the automony which they enjoy in the family. The inferior status of women in the family makes them dependent on the desires of their husbands or male members in this sphere also. As Noman points out in villages in Bangladesh women "cannot decide freely on the number and spacing of childrn to be born to her" (Noman, 1983, p. 6). Hence, this study seeks to examine whether the loanee-women who have an independent earning and make financial contribution to the family experience any alteration in the situation. In other words, whether they have any power to take decisions or take part in decision-making with regard to the number of children they should have. The power to take decision in the matter is considered to be relevant for the status of women. Also, the study compares the status of the loanee-women with that of non-loanee-women, in this respect.

8. Particpation in decisions regarding the freedom of movement :-

Of the overwhelming number of Muslims in Bangladesh, the status of the majority of women is influenced by Islamic law and preaching. Islam, though mingled with myriad local customs, rites, beliefs, etc., has been the most important factor in assigning the traditional position to women in Bangladesh. One may take, for example, the practice of *purdah*. Generally in village, '*purdah*' means wearing '*burqua*' which in its turn means covering by a woman of her whole body with a long stitched piece of cloth or dress extending from her hairtip to toe so that she cannot be seen by other people while she goes out of the home. In Islam, *purdah* has religious sanction which implies that women would not come in front of men or mix freely with men except her very close relatives like brothers, father, uncles, grandfather, paternal and maternal uncles. This leads towards segregation of the female sex. Through the observance of *purdah,* the feminine image of a woman, i.e., staying at home, looking after and taking care of the family members and children, restricting her mobility outside her homestead is very much encouraged" (Noman, 1983, p.7).

For the purpose of attaining the objective of *purdah* religious leaders have prescribed the women to wear *burqua*. "*Purdah* and seclusion is essentially a religious prescription of Islam restricring a woman's mobility and participation in activities outsider her '*bari*' or homestead" (Huq,

Jahanara 1979, p. 143-44).

Asfia Duza however points out that "The *purdah*.....the degree of seclusion to which a woman must conform...." depends upon her locality and social class (Duza, 1989 p.126). *Purdah* is usually an index of social status in poverty-stricken Bangladesh where only well-off families can bear the cost of the observance of *purdah*.

"As such though one can argue that *purdah* as a social system does not hamper women's development because the majority of women do not or cannot observe it....*purdah* is still emblematic of the general socio-cultural attitudes about women." (Duza, 1989, p. 127). Seclusion from the outside world results in limited mobility of women, which keeps them ignorant of the world outside home and many practical matters and perpetuates their dependence on men. Their status remains inferior to men's. Since the men are the chief earners and a patriarchal system prevails in the familles in rural Bangladesh, the men have the power to deny the women the freedom to move outside home. In view of the above situation, the study seeks to examine whether the loanee-women who have to interact with the world outside home, in course of performing their income-generating activities, have the power to move outside home. In other words, whether there is an association between the financial contribution made by the loanee-women to the family and the power of women to take decision or participate in decision-making with regard to their freedom of movement outside their homes. The study compares the status of loanee-women relating to this aspect with that of non-loanee-women for a better understanding of the situation of the loanee-women.

9. Participating in decisions regarding freedom to talk to male outsiders :

The seclusion of the female sex because of the observance of *purdah* or because of continuous emphasis on the value of *purdah* in the rural Muslim society of Bangladesh stands in the way of women's freedom to talk to male outsiders. This lack of women's freedom to talk to male outsiders indicates their subservience to their husbands who are the chief earners in the family or the relatives of husbands (who, too, generally subscribe to partiarchal values), that is to say, their inferior status. The study attempts to find out whether there is any alteration of the above situation in case of loanee-women who have an independent income of their own and financially contribute to their respective families. It has collected and sought to scrutinise data regarding the nature of association between the loanee-women who are financially contributing to the family and their power to decide or participate in decisions regarding the freedom to talk to male outsiders. Also, the study facilitates a comparison of the status of loanee-women with that of the non-loanee-women in this respect.

10. Participating in decisions regarding casting of vote in elections in favour of this or that candidate according to one's choice :—

As in most of the countries, women in Bangladesh are eligible to vote as well as to contest and hold office in any publicly elected body. The constitution clearly states that "women have equal rights with men in all spheres of the State and of public life" (Art. 28 (2)). But the existence of the legal right to vote does not necessarily mean the exercise of this right.

Proper exercise of this right depends on many supporting factors like social and political awareness of the voters and favourable social conditions and customs. Noman observes that the voting rights of the Bangladeshi women are, generally, not exercised properly because of the political manoeuvres, lack of, political awareness, lack of mobility due to *'purdah'* agreement to cast vote according to husbands' instructions in regard to the choice of candidate or political party. Women voters are mostly instructed by their male counterparts to act as instructed and normally they tend to do so" (1983, p. 36). Writing in 1991 Alia Ahmad observes, "Although the constitution recognises equal rights for women, *purdah* and the 'paternalistic' attitude women face, prevent them from participating in the political arena. Thus, no women representatives are seen in the local bodies in the rural areas. Women, because of the existing social norms and religious biases, do not have much of a say in decision making areas" (Ahmad, 1991, p. 97, emphasis added). The study wants to examine whether there is any association between the loanee-women on the one hand and their power of taking decisions or participating in decision-making in relation to the exercise of voting right by them.

To have a clearer appreciation of the situation, the status of loanee-women has been compared with non-loanee-women in this sphere.

2

The Status of Women in Bangladesh

As is well known, Bangladesh is one of the most densely populated and poorest countries of the world (Chen, 1986, p. 217). Its area covers only 56,977 sq. miles or 147,570 sq. kms. On the other hand, it bears the burden of a large population of 111.4 million (according to the 1991 census). It means that population density is very high in Bangladesh, i.e., 755 people per sq. kms. Indeed, it is one of the highest in the world. The annual rate of population growth is 2.17 (Bangladesh Statistical Pocket Book, 1994, p. 3).

In Bangladesh women constitute a little less than a half of the population. Of the total population, 57.3 million are males and 54.2 million are females. Of the 89.0 million rural population, 43.9 million are rural women (Bangladesh Population Census 1991, Volume 1, Analytical Report, 1994, p. xi). Sex ratio in the total population is 106 males per 100 females. Thus it is evidently tilted in favour of males. In life expectancy also males enjoy a slightly better lot than females. For the malefolk men it is 57.2 years and for the women, it is 56.3 years (Bangladesh Statistical Pocket Book, 1994, p. 3).

Bangladesh is predominantly a rural society, where eighty-five percent of its population draws its economic sustenance, directly and indirectly, from agriculture. Agriculture is the largest single contributor to the G.D.P. of Bangladesh. It alone accounts for 30.5 of the G.D.P. of the country at the current market price, while the share of manufacturing is only 9.7 of the same (vide Table 1, Bangladesh Statistical Pocket Book 1994, Table. 10.04, p. 238.) Rural Bangladesh is characterised by landlessness, low income and unemployment, resulting in a high incidence of poverty (Palli— Karma— Sahayak Foundation Annual Report, 1990 - 91, p. 26). The majority of the population in Bangladesh (88.3) are Muslims; other minorities belonging to other religions : are 10.5 are Hindus and 0.6 are Buddhist, Christian and others (Statistical Yearbook of Bangladesh, 1994, p. 32).

As exists in other underdeveloped countries, women in Bangladesh also are doubly disadvantaged for being poor as well as for being women.The problems and constraints which affect women's economic and social status in Bangladesh are complex and numerous (BRAC, 1990, p. 5).

In the male - dominated society of Bangladesh, women occupy a status which is, generally, much inferior to that of men. In all spheres of social and economic activities such as education, employment and work, health and nutrition, politics and even life within the family, women have access to very limited opportunities only, if at all. The socio - economic context of the country is such that the male children are desired by almost every couple. As a result, sons almost always get more attention, are more carefully looked after and nourished, while girls are considered a veritable burden on the family. Parents are anxious to get rid of the burden of their daughters, by getting them married as early as possible (Sen, 1991, p.80).

In Bangladesh, women have been relegated, primarily, to the roles of a docile daughter, an obedient wife and a dependent mother. Women, working outside their home, talking with outsiders, deviating from the *purdah* are not favourably viewed by the society in this country (Sen, 1992, p. 1). Accordingly, rural women in Bangladesh are largely confined within the boundaries of their homes. In performing household chores their movements are restricted within the house. Not only are their movement restricted within a prescribed space, but, what is no less important for affecting their status, a clearly and rigidly defined allocation of gender-based responsibilities is the there. It has bred the general powerlessness of women, even though the contribution of women to their families, through their economic activities, is considerable. This subordinate position is further reinforced through various kinds of religious beliefs and cultural practices. The pattern of training imparted to a female child in Bangladesh reinforces her subordinate role within the household (Aziz,1989, p. 56).

A brief description of rural women's life from birth to death may facilitate the understanding of her life style. In the rural areas of Bangladesh when a girl is born, the event is rarely celebrated by parents and relatives, unless she happens to be the first daughter after four or five sons (Jahan, 1975, p. 3). The birth of a male child is usually celebrated by distribution of sweets, whereas the birth of a female child is, by and large, not followed by any such celebrations. In Bangladeshi culture, the distribution of sweets symbolises the expression of happiness.

The idea that women are inferior to men is stressed from the very moment a child is born, and is nurtured by the differential behaviour patterns prescribed for girls and women (Chaudhury and Ahmed, 1980, p. 12 ; Aziz, 1986, p. 55). From early childhood on, girls are made fully conscious of the fact that, unlike their brothers who are assets to the family, they are liabilities. Girls are taught the two virtues– patience and sacrifice– the ideal Bangalee womanhood. Both folklore and religious traditions glorify those women who sacrifice their interests and happiness for their husbands. From the very childhood, a girl learns to accept her inferior and dependent status in the society, and is trained to fit into the few socially acceptable roles available to her, i.e., those of a wife and a mother. By the time she is five or six years old, her mother gives birth to two or three additional children, and the young girl has to take care of them. She also helps her mother in performing other household chores, i.e., cooking, cleaning, sewing, etc. The major share of available food, including the best food, goes to her father, brother(s), male guardian and other male household members (Jahan, 1975, pp. 3 - 4 ; Nur, 1988, p. 8).

Formal education of a girl is not considered as important as her religious education, say, for example, reading the *Quran*. In the rural areas, very few girls are sent to the school. This is reflected in the low enrolment figures of girls in primary schools in the rural areas (Jahan, 1975, p. 4). As soon as a girl reaches her puberty, she is instructed to observe *purdah*, which, in effect, means that she has to leave the school (Nur, 1988, p.8).

How rigidly the rules of *purdah* will be obeyed depends very much on the socio-economic status of the family. An easy index of the rising socio-economic status of a family is the increasing rigidity in observance of *purdah*. Economic status and observance of *purdah* are correlated because only economically well-off families can afford to put their women behind *purdah*.

Observance of *purdah* involves two kinds of restrictions on women's movements (Papanek, 1971, cited by Jahan, 1975, p.7). The first one is spatial, i.e., women have to be confined within the four walls of their homes. There would be a separate women's wing in the house, a separate tank for women's bathing and cleaning activities, and separate toilet provisions for women. The second type of restriction allows a woman to move out of her home, but only if she is veiled in a *burquah* (veil covering the whole body from head to foot) or travels in veiled transports, i.e., carts, boats and rickshaws with heavy curtains drawn around them. To enforce the first kind of restriction, i.e., spatial restriction on women's mobility, the family is required to be relatively wealthy, so that it can allocate enough living space and sink tubewells for women. However, rural women who are mostly poor, have only one or two *sarees* to wear; hence it becomes almost impossible and uneconomical for them to observe the *purdah* rules.

In poor rural families, women have no other option than to move out of their households and go to a rich farmer's house to fetch water and to work as part-time domestic servants. When moving out of their houses, these women cover their heads with their *sarees* to symbolise their observance of *purdah.* While the rigidity in observance of *purdah* varies between families, on attaining puberty all girls are required to start observing some symbols of *purdah*, be it total seclusion at home or imposition of some restrictions on contact with men (Jahan, 1975, p. 6).

In rural areas, girls are usually married between the ages of 12 and 15. Girls are married at an early age because by 11 or 12 years of age they complete all the informal and formal training necessary for assuming their socially ordained roles, viz., those of housewife and mother. Additionally, after a girl reaches puberty, she is regarded as "vulnerable" one who needs "shelter", and the safest course open to her family is to arrange a marriage for her so that she can move into a permanent and secure shelter in her husband's family (Papanek, 1971, cited in Jahan, 1975, p. 7).

Marriage is always arranged and the father and other male members of the family have the dominant say in the matter. As the marriage requires arrangements for a series of negotiations, mostly with the malefolk, it is handled by the male guardian(s) of the girl. In the marriage ceremony of a Muslim girl, her consent is mandatory, but in reality, her consent is hardly taken.

After her marriage a girl moves to her husband's household. In the first few years of marriage, her position is very insecure. In her husband's house, a bride has to observe a stricter *purdah*, her mobility is severely restricted, her work load increases. Moreover, her position is inferior to that of the other women of her husband's house, i.e., her mother-in-law, sister(s)-in-law, and so on. The only way she can earn security in her husband's household is by producing a male heir. The more male children she gives birth to, the greater is her security and acceptance. As women are kept socially secluded and economically dependent, they try to secure their position by giving birth to male children. It becomes economically rational for women to aim at several births (Ahmad, 1991, p.37).

A woman's status degenerates in another way. She has little control over her body; the decision to have children is totally her husband's. Rarely would a rural woman practice any form of birth control. A survey in Comilla district of Bangladesh indicated that after six years of widespread publicity about family planning, only about 4 percent of women practised some measure of birth control (Stoeckel and Chawdhury, 1973, cited in Jahan, 1975, p. 8). On an average a rural woman has eleven to twelve pregnancies. She might have one or two miscarriages, two or three of her children might die at a premature age, and she might have six or seven surviving children.

According to official statistics, the current use of family planning methods among eligible couples is about 33 percent (Bangladesh Bureau of Statistics, 1989, p.335). Contraceptive Prevalence Survey and various micro-studies indicate that a much lower proportion of women use effective methods of birth control (quoted from Ahmed, 1991, p.16). Abortion as a means of birth control is sometimes practised by the poorer sections of the rural population but it is looked down upon as a sin (Jahan, 1975, p. 8). Then, a woman's role and status are closely bound up with motherhood. Child bearing is highly valued, and inability to bear a child is regarded as a grave incapacity on the part of a woman. She has to bear children, preferably male, for her husband. Also she is expected to bear the responsibility for her children for their proper upbringing. If she cannot bear children, or appears unable to bear a male child, she is often deserted by husband or alternatively, is made to accept co-wives. It is not expected that she should go out of her home to earn a living. It is generally believed that a woman's world is her home while the man's world is outside the home. Women perform tasks at home, i.e., cooking, cleaning, rearing children, sewing, collection of fuel and water, caring for other family members, while men negotiate with the outside world.

The curtailment of rights of women, as has been stated in the previous pages, is not the common feature of all the Muslim societies. In some Muslim countries, Indonesia, for example, women work freely in the field and in the market places.Women in Bangladesh are not allowed that much of freedom. However, mostly due to the economic pressure, the rural women of Bangladesh have to undertake certain activities for helping their families financially. Often they are found to husk and dry the paddy, prepare fuel, make sugar, look after poultry and livestock and tend the kitchen garden. But what is most unfortunate is that their economic contribution is never appreciated. Often they help their malefolk in the field (cultivation), but it is unreported and not properly acknowledged (Papanak, 1973, quoted from

Jahan, 1975 p. 6).She is hardly paid for this labour. Consequently, mostly her role in the economic activities remain invisible and therefore unrecognised.

Thus, while the worlds of men and women are interrelated and interdependent, women's contribution is always regarded as inferior to that of men's.Ideally, a woman is under the guardianship of male relations, for example, father, brother, husband or son, and she depends on them for everything she needs. It is generally believed that women are physically weak, intellectually poor, whimsical, timid and emotional, and as such must be under the constant protection and supervision of a man who is supposed to be more physically strong, assertive, intelligent and wise. These beliefs perpetuate another belief that it is undesirable for a woman to live alone in a house or leave the house without a male escort.

The degree of a woman's subordination varies, however, with time and place. When she becomes a mother of grown-up children in a middle income household, she may enjoy considerable respect and authority and may have a say in the family decision making process. If she settles away from the patri-viri-local village, there are fewer restrictions on her movements. Her role is also less restricted in a simple (nuclear) household where she is the mistress of the house and not subject to the control of her husband's kin. Socially she has no individual identity; she is considered a part of her father's or husband's or son's household, and it is believed that her happiness lies in their happiness (Nur, 1987, p. 10).

Divorce and remarriage are frequent in rural areas, especially among the poor farmers (Chowdhury and Ahmed, 1980, p. 14; Jahan, 1975, p. 8). Women of rural Bangladesh have never challenged men's dominance, authority or superiority. They have become so used with this system that unless very positive steps and action programmes are undertaken for elevating their status, the situation will continue to remain the same for decades to come. In this system of family authority and social relations they learn to feel secure in the system and do not find substantial reasons why such situations should be changed.

The state of women's education in Bangladesh is extremely depressing. The overall literacy rate is very low by the international standard. The difference between the male and female literacy rates is even more shocking. The female literacy rate is only 19.5% compared with male literacy rate of 30.0% (Bangladesh Population Census, 1991, p. XII). The literacy rate among the rural women is lower than the corresponding rate for their urban counterparts. While 21.2% of the rural men are literate only 16.3% of the rural women have achieved this status (ibid., p. 123).

The present state of female education in Bangladesh is a good indicator of the low rate of development of the country and relatively lower status of women. Lack of education is one of the main factors which deters women from the equal participation in socio-economic activities side by side with their male counterparts, and helps to perpetuate inequality between the sexes (Khan, 1988, p.3).

Education is recognised as a basic human right, but in reality a woman's right to education has never been considered seriously in Bangladesh until very recently. Table 2.1 reflects it.

Table 2.1
Literacy Rate for Persons of All Ages by Sex in Census Years, 1961-1991, in Bangladesh

Census Years	Both Sex	Male	Female
1961	17.0	26.0	8.6
1974	20.2	27.6	12.2
1981	19.7	25.8	13.2
1991	24.9	30.0	19.5

Source : Bangladesh Population Census 1991, p. 123

Table 2.2
Literacy Rate for Persons of All Ages by Sex and Residence in Census Years, 1961-1991, in Bangladesh

Sex	1961	1974	1981	1991
URBAN				
Both Sex	38.7	37.7	34.8	40.3
Male	47.7	45.3	42.3	46.2
Female	26.1	27.9	25.5	33.3
RURAL				
Both Sex	16.5	18.5	17.0	21.2
Male	24.5	25.7	22.6	25.8
Female	7.8	10.8	11.2	16.3

Source : Bangladesh Population Census 1991, p. 123.

Social attitudes and institutions positively support males over females in every aspect of life including education. Because most families cannot afford schooling for all children, the choice naturally falls on the boys.....for as the proverb goes, 'investment in girls is like watering someone else's garden' (Duza, 1989, pp.128-129).

Most parents in general, and particularly in the rural areas, do not perceive any economic value in educating their daughters. Few village girls go to the school; of those who do, most drop out at the fifth or sixth grade. Only 1.7% of rural women above the age of fifteen are enrolled in the school, as compared to 20.8% of males. Girls discontinue schooling at an early age mainly for two reasons. First, by the time a girl is in the fifth grade, she completes basic training in reading, writing and arithmetic, and any further education is regarded as redundant, if not harmful for a happy married life. Second, after she reaches the age of 12 or 13 a girl has to drop out of the school for *purdah* considerations. Few villages have high schools for girls and the village society frowns upon girls' attending co-educational schools after they reach puberty. Additionally, as many villages do not have boys' schools, girls' enrolment becomes even more problematic. While it is difficult for a girl to study in a boys' high school in her village, it is nearly impossible for her to go for studies in a neighbouring village (Jahan, 1975, pp. 4-5).

According to the 1974 population census, the female population of Bangladesh is slightly less than half of the total population but the ratio of female to male enrolment is only 1 : 2 in the primary, 1 : 5 in the secondary, and 1 : 26 in higher (college) education. It thus appears that the rate of drop out (voluntary or forced) in the case of female enrolment escalates very rapidly from stage to stage, the degree of escalation is, however, more pronounced in the rural areas than in the urban areas (The Report of the Committee on Non-formal Education, Government of the People's Republic of Bangladesh, 1975, p.54).

The degree of literacy is an important factor affecting the status of women. For example, within households where women have some education, decision-making within the family, is more egalitarian (Jahan, 1975, p.). Theoretically, education is a reservoir of skill and knowledge. Thus, a woman having less education compared to her husband, may have little voice in decision-making, and a wife having more education may experience more say in decision-making upon crucial matters (Mizan, 1992, p.92).

Employment is another sector where special interventions by the state are necessary to alleviate women's inferior status (Shahana, 1989, p. 114). It is very difficult to discuss about employment because of the existing ambiguities regarding the definition of employment. Parameters for measuring the employment status or the economic activities of men are still debatable. So these are still inadequate for measuring the employment of women (Quddus, Solaiman & Karim, 1985, p. 33).

According to Labour Force Survey 1991 "employed persons" and "Unemployed persons" were defined as :

Employed persons are those persons of age 10 years and above, who were either :

(*a*) working at least one or more hours for pay or profit or working without pay in a family farm or enterprise,

Or

(*b*) not working but who had a job or business from which they were absent temporarily during the reference period.

Unemployed persons : Persons 10 years of age and over were classified as unemployed if they were involuntarily out of gainful employment during the reference week, but were either :

(*a*) actively looking for employment in the past two months, or

(*b*) willing to work but not looking for work because they were temporarily ill or believed no work was available.

Like activity rate, it is rather difficult to determine the employment status of women from the census documents. Moreover, "in a subsistence agriculture and informal rural and urban sectors where the main areas of employment are characterised by self-employment, even numerical estimation of employment *per se* faces definition and enumeration problem". [The Second Five - Year Plan (1980-85), Planning Commission, Government of Bangladesh, p. VI-14]. According to census estimates, 2.6 million women were employed in 1961, in 1974 the figure came down to 0.8 million and in 1981 again it rose to 1.2 million and 1991 further it rose to 2.2 million. Whereas during the same period the employment rate of males shows a steady rise, the figure being 14.7 million in 1961, 19.2 million in 1974, 22.4 million in 1981, and 27.6 million in 1991 (Bangladesh Population Census 1991, p. 143). The intercensal growth rate of female labour is negative 69 percent from 1961 to 1974, 50 percent from 1974 to 1981 and 83 percent from 1981 to 1991. The figure for male during the later period (1974-1981 and 1981-1991) shows the trend of increase of 17 percent and 23 percent respectively. This is an indication that female labour is increasing at a faster rate than male.

However, in the real sense, the censuses of 1961, 1974, 1981, and 1991 were not of much help for monitoring changes over time because of the difference in concept and definitions. Perhaps, due to changes in definitions, it is observed that a sharp fall in the female employment level from 2.6 million in 1961 to 0.8 million in 1974, which accounts for only 4 percent of rural females (aged 10 years and above) who are engaged in labour force. Census documents report the number of unemployed female in 1974 as less than 50,000 which is a very negligible number (Bangladesh Population Census 1991, Table 9.1, pp. 142 - 143). In other words, it means that nearly all of the remaining 96 percent of women (aged 10 years and above) were outside the labour force and most probably they belonged to the category of housewivese (16.7 million) and inactive persons (4.3 million) (ibid, p. 142).

According to the 1974 census definition, employment status includes persons in categories of :

(*a*) agricultural self-employed,
(*b*) agricultural labour,
(*c*) non-agricultural self-employed,
(*d*) non-agricultural labour,
(*e*) unpaid family helpers and
(*f*) domestic servants

(B.B.S. 1982, Table 4.17., p. 157; quoted Khan, 1988, p. 32). So this 4 percent of female labour includes women belonging to all categories of employed women including unpaid family labour in subsistence agriculture. This estimate not only fails to explain the employment status of 96 percent of the working age female population but also leads one to think that 96 percent of the female working age population are not contributing anything at all to the G.N.P. Next, among the employed females, 30 percent women were recorded as unpaid family labour in 1974. If the working pattern of village women are analysed then it would be obvious that a much higher percentage of women should have been included under this category (Khan, 1988, p. 32).

One of the most important categories under the classification of "not in the civilian labour force" are housewives. The 1974 figure for this is 16.7 million i.e., 76 percent of the working age women are in the group of housewives and 20 percent are inactive. Since this 96 percent women are excluded from any form of employment status, it is understood that they do not participate in any kind of economic activity even as unpaid family helpers. In the context of the Bangladesh productive system, it is hard to believe that 16.7 million women termed as housewives do not directly help their families in the production process. Similarly, as Khan say, "Even if we assume that nearly 50 percent of these women belong to landless families and consequently have no family land to work on, the fact remains that their families are engaged in non-farm activities and depend heavily on their female labour power" (Khan, 1988, p. 33).

Rural women in Bangladesh are major, but largely unrecognised contributors to agriculture and economic activity (Kabir, et. al., 1977, p. 73). Rural women in Bangladesh work long hours of the day on domestic chores which start from gathering the food and fuels to serving the prepared meal, rearing the children, looking after old and superior male members, tending the domestic animals and growing fruits and vegetables besides participation in post-harvest activities. Regarding the total hours a woman has to work in rural Bangladesh, there has been some variation. The amount of time rural women spend on various production activities has been found to vary between 10 and 14 hours a day (Farouk, et al., 1975, p 30). Farouk's (1980) study indicates that men work between 3,138 and 3,700 hours a year, whereas women's productive hours have been estimated at 2,048 hours a year which are devoted to cultivation, livestock raising and kitchen gardening (p. 50). A time allocation study shows that the average peasant women spend 43% of their time on activities related to farm production, about the same on actual household work, and about 11% on child-care and other family matters (Fuglesang & Chandler, 1993, p. 24).

However, landless women have to devote less total hours for work compared to women in medium and large farming households. Women from large farming households retire much late at night compared to others, although they usually take one or two hours rest during the day, which is denied to landless women (Khan, 1988, p. 35).

In general, women do not participate in field activities which are done by men. While, in general, most of the tasks can be performed within the household compound, in certain areas of Bangladesh rural women also work in the field (Mizan, 1992, p. 86). Khan (1988) reports that, in some districts specially Rangpur and Dinajpur area and other parts of North Bengal, women work in the field performing transplantation, line sowing and hand irrigation (Khan, 1988, p. 35).

Tasks performed by rural women in Bangladesh, outside home, are usually of a subsistence agricultural nature and are harmful to the well-being of the household. They include growing family food, processing food grains, preservation and storage of seeds, rearing poultry and livestock and growing vegetables. However, the phrase "economic activity", academically and in general usage, refers to productive activities engaged in, for financial gain and these activities are excluded from official "economic" consideration (Huq, 1979, p.139).

Rural women in Bangladesh always have been active in both "income-generating" and "income-converting" production. For example, following the harvest of rice a woman's typical work consists of winnowing and sieving, drying, parboiling, husking, polishing, milling and storing. People rarely recognise that such activities conserve income and are productive labour. Women are also involved in food preservation and processing of *muri* (puffed rice), *cheera* (pounded rice), *gur* (molasses) (Mizan, 1992, p. 86). But their work has not been quantified in monetary terms, and as such cannot include the full connotation of economic participation (Duza, 1989, p. 130).

As the market for women labour is demarcated both physically and functionally, women have limited choice and earn less than what male labour does for similar kinds of work. An important area of non-farm employment for women is the traditional "specialised family trade" performed by caste or class of people where both men and women of the family are involved in the trades. This includes *kumar* (potter), *tanti* (weaver), *dhopa* (washer-man), etc. Women play an equal role to the men in these occupation, but remain unpaid for their work (Khan, 1988, p. 39) Table 2.3 presents involvement of women in non-farm productions as found by Rural Industry Survey Project (Khan, 1988, Table 12, p. 39).

Table 2.3

Involvement of Women in Non-farm Production in Bangladesh

Product	% of female labour
Ginger preserving	65.6
Gulap oil	46.4
Coconut oil	47.5
Dheki products	53.3
Bidi making	44.8
Chatai	40.0
Mat making	52.2
Kantha	74.6
Woollen products	44.3
Coir mats	69.8
Jute rope	48.3
Coir rope	59.2
Fishing net	51.9
Yarn dying	49.6
Lungi and saree	42.1
Than cloth	40.9
Other handloom	42.8
Silk weaving	44.4
Shika and jute works	62.7
Embroidery	50.4
Paper bag	47.2
Pottery	41.4

Source : BIDS Rural Industries Survey, 1982. (cited in Khan, 1988, p. 39)

Table 2.4

Employed persons 10 years and above by Status in Employment and Sex, 1990

(Percent)

Status in employment	**Bangladesh**			**Urban**			**Rural**		
	Both Sex	Male	Female	Both Sex	Male	Female	Both Sex	Male	Female
All employed persons	100.0	100.0	100.0	100.0	100.0	100.0	100.0	100.0	100.0
Self employed	26.8	40.0	6.5	33.2	41.7	5.2	25.5	39.5	6.6
Employee	47.2	22.7	84.8	24.9	12.7	65.2	51.7	5.5	87.0
Unpaid family worker	47.2	22.7	84.8	24.9	12.7	65.2	51.7	5.5	87.0
Employer	11.7	15.9	5.3	32.1	33.6	27.1	7.6	11.1	2.9
Day labourer	13.9	20.9	3.0	9.1	11.3	1.8	14.8	23.5	3.1
Others	0.4	0.5	0.4	0.7	0.7	0.7	0.4	0.4	0.4

Increasing impoverishment, decrease in farm size, government and non-government organisational efforts, and income-generating opportunities are breaking the age-old cultural norm of absolute seclusion of women, which discourage women from seeking employment outside the home (Mizen, 1992, p. 87). But absence of job opportunities in the rural areas, lack of education and training facilities (skill), poverty and general lack of awareness have forced them to stay outside regular economic activities (Khanam, 1990, p.49).

Official figures in Bangladesh still show a bleak situation:

Table 2.5
Economic Activity Rate (by sex) in Bangladesh

Items	1991 (Enumerated)	1981 (Enumerated)	Growth Decade	Rate Annual
Both Sex	43.05	40.50	6.30	0.61
Male	77.06	73.90	4.28	0.42
Female	6.66	4.30	54.88	4.47

Source : Bangladesh Population Census 1991, p xiii

Income-generating opportunities are opening up with more accessibility to credit and some skill training for women by rural institutions, such as Women's Co-operatives, Mother's Centre, Vocational Training programmes and various projects under Women's Affairs Directorate. However, they still lack the control over their own produce because of normative and cultural conditions. For example, in *hat*s and *bazar*s (village market) it is men who buy and sell. Under such circumstances, women need the aid of a husband, a brother or a son to sell their products, thereby losing control over both the price and the earnings (Mizan, 1992, p. 87).

Further, the traditional skills of women, especially in processing agricultural products by which they earn an income, have been taken over by machines. Although a few organisations have revived the rural women's skill at handicrafts, such as making *kathas* (cotton quilts) and jute products, there is no demand, in the local markets, for such products and these special skills do not bring a steady income for the women. While there has been a proliferation of institutions to provide training on earning an income, not much has been done to create a demand for their products in the market. In other words, in the absence of marketing facilities, whatever traditional skill women have to earn an income, may become obsolete (Mizan, 1992, p. 88).

At the same time it must be noted that a vast majority of these women are employed as unskilled labourer with very low wages. Table 2.6 (Khan, 1988, p. 41; Table 14), which shows the distribution of female labour in establishments, reveals that 75.0 percent women are working as unskilled labourer and only 25.0 percent women are working as professionals and skilled craftsmen. Of the skilled group of women, 12.0 percent are engaged in clerical or secretarial jobs, and only 1.0 percent in administrative and managerial jobs (Khan, 1988, p. 41, Table 14).

Table 2.6

Distribution of Women Employed in Establishments Employing 10 Persons or more by Professional Category, 1982 in Bangladesh

Category	Percent of women among all employees within the category	Percent of women among total women employed in all categories
Administrative & managerial	2.3	1.0
Professional	6.8	2.0
Doctors	0.9	
Engineers	0.003	
Agricultural	0.006	

Teacher		5.2	
Others		0.7	
Technical (Diploma level)	16.6		4.0
Medical		16.4	
Engineer		0.1	
Agricultural		0.1	
Clerical / Secretarial	7.8		12.0
Skilled Craftsmen	2.3		6.0
Construction		0.02	
Textile		1.07	
Automotive		0.04	
Mechanical/ Electrical/Metal works		0.15	
Printing		0.02	
Others		1.00	
Unskilled	17.4		75.0

Source : Establishment Survey 1982, Bangladesh Manpower, Planning Centre, 1984. (cited in Khan, 1988, p. 41)

The labour market in rural areas, is highly unorganised and in the absence of adequate localised employment opportunities, female labour for unskilled jobs is abundant which brings down their wage rate.

Legal Status of Women

The theme of the present chapter is to focus on the nature of change brought about in the status of women in Bangladesh through the legal system. It is common knowledge that the constitution of a state is the fundamental law of the land.

The legal rights of women in Bangladesh have been enshrined in Part III of the Constitution of the People's

Republic of Bangladesh, which are the Fundamental Rights guaranteed by the Constitution.

Article 27 says, "All citizens are equal before law and are entitled to equal protection of law." Sub-Article (1) of Article 28 removes discrimination on grounds of religion, sex, etc. "The State shall not discriminate against any citizen on grounds only of religion, race, caste, sex or place of brith."

Sub-Article (2) of Articile 28 of the Constitution of Bangladesh says "Women shall have equal rights with men in all spheres of the State and of public life."

Sub-Article (3) of the same Article says, "No citizen shall, on grounds only of religion, race, caste, sex, or place of brith, be subjected to any disability, liability, restriction or condition with regard to access to any place of public entertainment or resort, or admission to any educational institution."

Sub-Atricle (4) of Article 28 states, "Nothing in this article shall prevent the State from making special provision in favour of women or children or for the advancenment of any backward section of citizen."

From the above it is clear that on the one hand the Constition ensures the equality of sexes, while on the other hand, it recognises an unequal status of women by reserving for the state the right of making special provisions in favour of women.

The above also make it apparent that women possess some rights in theory or on paper but in practice these rights are overridden by customs, tradition and usage. As Salma Sobhan (1978) observes, "the drafter of the Constitution could not fail to acknowledge tacitly the fact of the inequality present in the status of women" (cited in Khan, 1988, p.16). This inequality is reflected in many other areas of law governing the life of a woman. With the realisation of women's vulnerability, though particular provisions are made for them in the Constitution, the basis of the assumption was, as Sobhan further observes that, "it is women who are backward, not society in its attitude towards women. Women are given the privilege of having reserved seats in the legislature and other public bodies with the same attitude of "paternalism", though they are equally eligible to contest for any public office starting from the President of the Republic to member of Union Parishads (Khan, 1988, p.16).

One interesting thing to note here is that in Bangladesh the most important events in a woman's life—marriage, divorce, custody of children, inheritance, etc. for example, are governed by the personal laws, which in case of Muslims are the "*Sharia*" based on the *Quran* and *Hadith* (sayings of Prophet Muhammad). But civil laws are also exercised in some areas relating to these issues and it is hard to establish the logic regarding the jurisdiction of each. For example, the purchase, sale and any other litigations regarding property is governed by the civil law whereas the inheritance of property is governed by the personal law. Similarly, though marriage, divorce and custody of children are governed by the personal laws, Child Marriage Restraint Act, Dissolution of Muslim Marriage Act, Muslim Family Law Ordinance, etc., are formulated by the civil authority to deal with marital and family affairs. This question is more pertinent to Muslim women because, two most important things of a woman's life are affected, critically, by the exercise of discriminatory personal laws : firstly, the sanction of co-wives and secondly, unequal inheritance right in father's property. Occasionally, proposals for revising these in the light of modern civil laws have been raised but they subsided on the plea that personal laws are based on Quranic injunction : therefore they cannot be changed or modified. Since men are greater beneficiaries under the personal laws, one may think that male law makers find this arrangement more convenient to safeguard their own interests.

Marriage is not a sacrament but a civil contract in Islam. The special rights for women were recognised by the Child Marriage Restraint Act of 1929 in which case a woman below 18 years is considered a minor child. But if a female child under 18 years of age marries a man, the marriage shall not be void, dissolved, only the Marriage Registrar shall be punished for solemnising the marriage of a child under section 50 of the Act. The consequence of it, in reality, has been according to Chaudhury and Ahmed, that "most girls in rural areas are married between the ages of 12 and 15 in complete disregard for the law" (1980, p 28).

Under Muslim law, the consent of the girl is necessary for the marriage to be valid. A Muslim women can even legally renounce her marriage if contracted without her consent (or, interestingly enough, guardian's consent in case of a minor). But this is usually only a formality. A woman's marriage is arranged by her father or some other male guardian, and she usually consents to such arrangments. Only in rare cases, would a girl protest against her guardians decision—and there have been instances where girls have been forced into marriage (Chowdhury and Ahmed, 1980, p. 28.)

All Muslim marriages are required to be registered though in practice more than half of the marriages are not registered (Khan, 1988, p. 19).

Under the Muslim law the bridegroom has to pay *mehr* or dower. It (dower) is a sum of money or other property which the wife is entitled to receive from the husband and in consideration of the marriage.

As per the provisions of Section 10 of the Muslim Family Laws Ordinance 1961, where no details about the mode of payment of dower are specified in the *Nikanamah*, or the marriage contract, the entire amount of the dower shall be presumed to be payable on demand.

But in most cases such demands are not made mainly due to social norms. and partly due to the fear of incurring displeasure of the husband.

There are different forms of dissolution of Muslim marriage. The contract of marriage under the Muslim laws may be dissolved in any one of the following ways :

1. by the husband at his will without the intervention of a court,
2. by mutual consent of the husband and the wife, without the intervention of a court,
3. by a judicial decree at the suit of the husband or the wife. The wife cannot divorce herself from her husband without his consent, except under a contract whether made before of after marriage, but she may, in some cases, obtain a divorce by judicial decree (Ordinance No. 18 of 1985).

When the divorce is issued by the husband, it is called *talaq*; when it is effected by mutual consent, it is called *khula* or divorce, according to the term of the contracts between the parties.

Divorce by *talaq*

Any Muslim of sound mind who has attained puberty, may divorce his wife, whenever he desires without assigning any cause.

Delegation of power to divorce

Although the power to give divorce belongs primarily to the husband, he may delegate the power to the wife or to a third person either absolutely or conditionally, and either for a particular period or permanently. The person to whom the power is thus delegated may then pronounce the divorce accordingly (Dissolution of Muslim Marriage Act, Ordinance No. 18 of 1985).

So a Muslim woman in Bangladesh has the right to divorce only when such power has been delegated to her at the time of the contract of marriage. However, under the Dissolution of Muslim Marriage Act, 1939, a woman is entitled to obtain decree for dissolution of her marriage on some specific grounds like impotency or insanity of husband or desertion, non-maintenance, or imprisonment of husband for a long period, etc. On the other hand a Muslim man has the right to divorce at any time.

Another important aspect of Muslim marriage in Bangladesh is the sanction of limited polygamy to men under certain given conditions (for example, infertility, mental illness, physical inability to perform wifely duties).

Sub-section (1) of Section 5 of the Muslim Family Laws Ordinance, 1961 Ordinance No. VIII of 1961). says, "No man, during the subsistence of an existing marriage, shall except with the previous permission in writing of the Arbitraiton Council, contract another marriage, nor shall any such marriage contracted without such permission, be registered (under the Muslim Marriage and Divorces (Registration) Act 1974."

The other sub-sections of Section are as follows :

(2) An application for permission under sub-section (1) shall be submitted to the Chairman in the prescribed manner, together with the prescribed fees, and shall state the reason for the proposed marriage, and whether the consent of the existing wife or wives has been obtained thereto.

(3) On receipt of the application under sub-section (2), the Chairman shall ask the applicant and his existing wife or wives each to nominate a representative, and the Arbitration Council so constituted may, if satisfied that the proposed marriage is necessary and just, grant, subject to such conditions if any, as may be deemend fit, the permission applied for.

(4) In deciding the application the Arbitration Council shall record its reasons for the decision, and any party

may, in the prescribed manner, within the prescribed period, and on payment of the prescribed fees, prefer an application for revision to the Munsif concerned and his decision shall be final and shall not be called in question in any court.

(5) Any man who contracts another marriage without the permission of the Arbitration Council shall...

(*a*) pay immediately the entire amount of the dower whether prompt or deferred, due to the existing wife or wives, which amount, if not so paid, shall be recoverable as arrears of land revenue; and

(b) on conviction upon complaint be punishable with simple imprisonment which may extend to one year, or with fine which may extended to ten thousand *taka* or with both.

But men often derive advantage from laws without having any valid grounds for doing so. In spite of the above provisions of law putting constratints on polygamy, there are quite a large number of cases where men have contracted a subsequent marriage without the required permission from the Arbitration Council and there has been no case where a man has been made to pay the entire dower or was punished (Quamruddin, K.A.A., 1977, cited in Chaudhury and Ahmed, 1980, f.n. 28 p. 28) According to Khan, "Polygamy is not commonly practised in Bangladesh, but it remains as a constant threat to every married woman, especially in rural areas (1988, p. 20)

Women suffer discrimination also in the field of inheritance. The Law of Inheritance gets different kinds of interpretations in the courts of law. The case of Shah Banu, the divorced wife of Mohammed Ahmad Khan, brought the Indian Muslims to a state of turmoil. The Fundamentalists demanded that a divorced Muslim woman is not entitled to any maintenance from her former husband as provided for in the Muslim Laws. The progressive group led by Mrs. Zoyo Hassan submitted a petition to the Prime Minister of

India that any surrender to the demands of the Fundamentalists would be suicidal and harmful to the Muslim women of India. But Mr. Rajiv Gahdhi, the then Prime Minsiter of India, surrendered to the demands of the Muslim Fundamentalists. The Musilm Women (Protection of Rights on Divorce) Bill 1986 was passed by the members of the Indian Parliament. This was done to invalidate the Provision of Section 125 of the Code of Criminal Procedure.

In Bangladesh though women were given the Constitutional right to enjoy equal rights with male persons under Articles 27 and 28 of the Constitution of the People's Republic of Bangladesh, the said equality clause is not applicable to the right of a woman to inherit her father's property under the Sunni Law of Inheritance.

The constitutional right of equal protection of law or equality before law has been effectively emasculated or in some cases rendered completely negatory by the continued existence of unequal Laws of Inheritance in the case of female persons. The Law of Inheritance does not give equal share to a woman, who receives half of the share of male person, as a residuray with male persons.

Under the Muslim Personal Law the wife (or wives taken together) gets one eighth of the husband's property if there is a child and one fourth if there is no child after her husband's death. A husband, on the other hand gets exactly double (one-fourth or half) from the estate of the wife. A daughter is entitled to get half of the total estate if there is no other brother or sister, and two-thirds among them if there are sisters; and the residue will go to the agnatic relations. Each sister will get half of the brother's share, if there is a brother. If there are only female children then they are deprived of a major share which goes to the brother or father of the deceased; wife and daughters together, in such cases, get two-thirds of the total estate. A daughter is therfore, discriminated against in both cases : if she has a brother, she gets only half of her brother's share, if she does not have a brother, a share of her father's property is taken away by agnatic relations. The mother is entitled to inherit one-sixth of her son's property when he leaves children and one-third when no child is left. The father gets one sixth from the estate of his son if any child is left and entire residue after satisfying other sharer's claim in the absence of any child.

From the above discussion it is clear that, on the one hand, Muslim Personal Laws protect the inheritance rights of the woman as a daughter, mother and wife, on the other hand it prevents inheritance by her of equal shares with her male counterpart or the entire estate of the parents or husband in the absence of surviving brothers or son. The Muslim Jurists explain the reason for this difference of share in terms that "a woman inherits share from her husband, from her father and also dower from her husband and moreover she has no responsibility to maintain anybody" (Bhuiyan, 1984, cited in Khan, 1988, p.18). This is obviously a very weak argument since men also inherit from as many sources and, in many cases, women have to, partly or fully bear family responsibilities. Moreover, it is contrary to Bangladeshi Social custom for a woman to claim her father's property unless it is given to her willingly. Though "every girl knows that she has the right to a share of her father's property, in practice Bangladeshi women do not always claim the property which they legally own through inheritance. The main reason for this is that a Muslim woman often "exchanges" her inheritance for visiting rights to her homestead. This social custom is called *naior*. It must be mentioned here that such "exchange" has no legal validity and she retains the right to claim her share any time, though a woman hardly exercises this right.

The bane of dowry plagues the women in many traditional societies like those of Hindus in the neighbouring country of India or in Bangladesh. The Muslim society was free from this curse. But this evil practice seems to have cast its spell on the Muslims also in the society of Bangladesh which is why Laws like Dowry Prohibition Act, 1980, had to be promulgated. The Act seems to vindicate the fact that the Muslim law does not allow payment of dowry.

Dowry means any property or valuable security given or agreed to be given either, directly or inderectly, during marriage

(*a*) by one party to a marriage to the other party to the marriage,

(*b*) by the parents of either party to a marriage or by any other person to either party to the marriage or to any other persons; at the time of marriage or at any time before or after the marriage as consideration for the marriage of the said parties but does not include dower or *mehr* in the case of persons to whom the Muslim Personal Law (*Shariah*) applies.

By way of explanation of the above provision, the Act. stipulates that for the removal of doubts, it is hereby declared that any presents made at the time of a marriage by any person other than a party to the marriage to either party to the marriage in the form of any articles, the value of which does not exceed five hundred *taka* shall not deemed to be dowry within the meaning of this section, unless they are made as consideration for the marriage of the said party.

The words "valuable security" denote, according to the Act, a document which is, or purports to be, a document where by any legal right is created, extended, transferred, restricted, extinguished or released, or whereby any person acknowledges that he lies under legal liability, or has not a certain legal right.

The Dowry Prohibition Act, 1980, provides penalty for giving or taking dowry. If any person after the commencement of this Act, gives or takes or abets the giving or taking of dowry, he shall be punishable with imprisonment which may extend to five years and shall not be less than one year, or with fine, or with both.

It also prescribes penalty for demanding dowry. If any person, after the commencement of this Act, demands, directly or indirectly, from the parents or guardian or a bride or bridegroom, as the case may be, any dowry, he shall be punishable with imprisonment which may extend to five years and shall not be less than one year, or with fine, or with both.

In spite of legal prohibition of dowry, dowry has become a serious problem undermining the status of women in Bangladesh. It has turned in many cases into a menace for their very existenece. In Bangladesh, a recent trend is to demand dowry not in money or in monetary equivalents but in the form of a renumerative job. There are lots of cases where women are being tortured, killed or burnt to death or divorced by their husbands in collusion with in-laws for dowry. Indeed, it is very difficult to establish a case under Dowry Prohibition Act because of lack of evidence which may be acceptable to and firmly established before a court of law and also because of lacuna in the law. A lacuna has been removed through an amendment of the Act of 1980. But even then many other difficulties originating from the sphere of law and from society at large perpetuate the unfortunate conditions of the women (Bhuiyan, 1985, p. 243).

Hence, it appears from what has been discussed above, that there is a wide gap between the legal status and the actual status of women in Bangladesh. This gap is due, in part, to the prevailing patriarchal system partly reflected in practices like *purdah,* economic dependence of women together with ther ignorance of their rights.

3

The Grameen Bank

I

Most of the countries in South Asia have, in recent decades, undertaken a number of programmes for alleviation of poverty and creation of assets for the poor, and Bangladesh is one of them. These programmes seek to strengthen the capacity of the poor women, in general, and those of rural areas, in particular, to survive. They help the poor women in the countryside engage in income-generating activities and meet their social and economic needs through various measures including provision of credit for them on a very small interest, increase their savings and utilise these savings along with available credit for further improving their socio-economic conditions as well as those of their families.

It is quite pertinent at this stage to look into how these programmes are working for the actual benefit of these poor women. In other words, one may legitimately like to know whether the women,who constitute the target group of these programmes, have been able to utilise the opportunities supposedly flowing from the programmes for enhancing their status vis-à-vis men, particularly, in their families.

It is claimed in certain quarters that the Grameen Bank is a glimmer of hope in the midst of Bangladesh's misery. It boldly flies in the face of judiciary convention by lending money to the illiterate, landless villagers who can offer no collateral. The speciality of the Grameen Bank lies in the fact that it has introduced special programmes for women clients and, what is equally important, it operates, door to door, in remote interior villages, instead of working from the headquarters situated in the capital city or from other urban commercial centres. Being totally disappointed with the latter system of banking, Professor Muhammad Yunus, the founder and managing director of the Grameen Bank, remarks, "We are not standing on our head. We are the right way up. It is conventional banking which is upside down" (Cited by Shehabuddin 1992, p.70, from Todd, 1989).

Grameen is the Bangalee word for rural or something relating to or found or working in village. The Grameen Bank is thus a rural bank. Many people even call it the bareofoot bank, referring to its clientele, the poorest of the rural poor. So far as the goal of assisting poor women of the villages in alleviating their age-old poverty is concerned, the Grameen Bank has been mostly successful. Because, unlike the usual commercial banks, it is based on a fundamental respect for their abilities. Yunus is totally unhappy with and utterly critical of the conventional ideas about the poor : "You will be told with 100% certainty that the poor have to be trained before they can do anything. The poor cannot budget, they have no skills. The influence of religion and custom is so strong on them that they cannot move an inch in any direction" (ibid). In contrast, the reality is that, argues,Yunus, "The poor have been able to survive. They know what to do. All you have to give them is access to capital. Most of them can take it from there" (ibid).

The Grameen Bank has been so designed as it can directly issue credit to the poor. For, it regards that, "Credit is a Human Right" (Yunus, 1987, p.4).

Commercial banks, usually, demand some collateral from the recipients of loan or credit. The Grameen Bank is the first institution to break away from such traditional credit disbursing practices and provides credit to rural people without collateral. Further, to effectively utilise human resources, the Grameen Bank targets rural women below the subsistence level and involve them with its organizational framework for economic and social mobilisation. Through its economic and social programmes, the Grameen Bank has continuously tried to break the interlock of rural women's economic dependency and social practices like purdah, which perpetuate through cultural tradition and religious norms (Cited by Mizan, 1992, p. 9, from Rahman, 1987).

II

The idea of the Grameen Bank was first introduced as a pilot project in Jobra, a village near the Chittagong University Campus (Yunus, 1984 foreword to Joriman of Belton Village and Others : In Search of a Future). In 1975, Professor Yunus, the chairman of the Economics Department of the Chittagong University, came across an old village women, whose occupation was to prepare bamboo tools for making a living. Since she could not afford to buy the raw material—the bamboo sticks—herself, she borrowed some money from a local money lender at an exorbitant rate of interest. The outcome of her whole day's labour was only two cents. Yunus found that there were many such women in the village. He felt a strong sympathy for these poor, helpless souls, and he decided to do something for them. At that time he could only lend a small amount——$28 —to forty three villagers.He charged only a moderate rate of interest for the money which was within the capacity of the people. However small the amount was, it was of a great help to those people who could thereby shake off the middlemen and attain self-sufficiency. Being encouraged with the result,Yunus thought that if these poor villagers could work independently without taking help from the middlemen, they could enhance their income to a great extent. Actually, the middlemen, appropriate a lot of the fruits of their hard labour. Hence, he felt the need for a provision for easy availability of credit at a cheap rate of interest for the rural people. Bankers, however, scoffed at his idea of lending money to the poor. They could not believe that illiterate, poor, landless villagers could meaningfully utilise the money to the benefit of the society and themselves, or they would be able to pay back the loans.

Yunus, however, was undaunted by this attitude of the bankers. He resorted to his personal savings, lent money from the same, and to the surprise of all, got back what he lent out. And this was the beginning of the Grameen Bank. Ultimately, the project of the Grameen Bank was inaugurated in the village of Jobra in 1976. The programme developed over the next few years, and in 1983 it was transformed by a Government Ordinance into the Grameen Bank, a specialized financial institution for the poor. Being convinced that lending to the poor was not a risk, the Central Bank of Bangladesh, the International Fund for Agricultural Development, and the United Nations Children's Fund have provided millions of dollars to the Grameen Bank. The Grameen Bank at present has over 17, 15, 186 members (16,12, 853 women members compared to 1,02,833 men) in more than 33,420 villages (Monthly Statements, 1993, p.2) and has disbursed over $400 million since 1976 (Shams, 1992, p.25).

Yunus criticizes the poverty alleviation programmes being traditionally implemented in Bangladesh which, in effect do not distinguish much between those below and above the subsistence level. As a result, the poor are almost elbowed out, and it is the comparatively well-off villagers who seem to benefit from these programmes at the expense of the poor.Yunus believes that development should be approached as a 'human rights issue' rather—than one of simple economic growth where it is assumed that any enhancement in the national economy (G.N.P.) would surely and automatically benefit the poor. He defines development as a "positive change in the economic status of the bottom 50% of the population in a given society. If an effort fails to improve the economic condition of the bottom 50% of the population, it cannot qualify to be categorized as development effort. In other words, if one is looking for a measurement of economic development, one would be looking for the per capita real income of the bottom half of the population, not the national per capita real income" (Yunus, 1987, p.2). Thus, he includes the concept of distribution as well within development. It is not the sheer increase of income of the country, but the relative status of different situations and distribution of the national income among the various segments of the society are to be considered while measuring the development achieved by the country.

Thus, the Grameen Bank rests on the philosophy that poor people remain poor because an inequalitarian economic base makes them turn to middlemen, thereby ensuring that they do not receive the full worth of their economic contribution. The opportunity to build an asset base, however, could put an end to the dependence on the middlemen. Credit is a liquid asset which the receipient can put to whatever use he chooses as he sets out to build an asset base. "With financial resources at his disposal, an individual is free to build his own fate with his own labour. Nothing can match this spirit of a free human being" (Yunus, 1987, p.4).

As has already been stated, Yunus believes that credit for self-employment is a "fundamental human right", "a powerful weapon" that grants one access to resources previously out of reach and a fair chance to improve one's economic condition. He recognises the availability of credit as a "basic condition for the economic emancipation of the poor, in general, and poor women, in particular, (Yunus, 1987, pp. 4 - 5).

III

The Grameen Bank has an exclusive clientele—it grants credit only to the landless, that is those who own less than half an acre of farm land (Shehabuddin 1992, p. 72). More specifically, it reaches a villager whose family owns less than 0.4 acre of cultivable land or possesses assets whose value dose not exceed the market value of one acre of medium quality land in the area (Ray, 1987, p.1). A recent survey indicates that 2.5 to 3 acres of land are required to maintain an average Bangladeshi family at subsistence level (Singh, not dated, quoted from Shehabuddin, 1992 p.72). Villagers interested in taking loans are required to form groups of five like-minded and unrelated persons (either five men or five women) of similar economic standing. Persons approaching for loans are required to be literate and be able sign their own names.The loans are disbursed at the rate of 16%, to be paid at the end of one year. The loans are not doles because, as says Yunus "if you give something for free, you lose the borrower and the money" (Cited by Shehabuddin, 1992, p.74, from Arab News, 1987).

Smiles of great expectation ?
Loanee Women receiving money (loan) from a G. B. *Kendra*.

In any case, the rate is substantially cheap in comparison to that of 120 percent charged by local **mohajons.** In addition to the regular loans, the Grameen Bank also disburses house-building loans to members who demonstrate a good repayment record over a number of years. These loans extend to Bangladeshi Taka 18,000 ($500), with an interest rate of only five percent and within a repayment period of ten years. The Bank views the house building loans as part of both of their economic and social-development programs (Fuglesang, 1986, p. 123). Members gladly utilise this opportunity to repair their houses. The Bank assumes that a stable shelter increases the productivity of members by increasing storage area and making them less vulnerable to the rainy season.

The Grameen Bank offers several other types of facilities, schemes and programs which are described below :

Group Fund Loan : Every group members deposits one Taka each week as a personal savings. This is accumulated in an account called the "Group Fund Account". The account is managed by the group of five members on a consensus basis (Fuglesang, 1986, p. 122). The Group Fund is a compulsory savings scheme. The borrowers initially have to contribute five percent of the loan amount

Resolve to practise Discipline, Unity, Courage and Hard Work – loanee women repeating the Sixteen Decisions at the start of a meeting in a *Kendra.*

to the group fund (Mizan, 1992, p.10). The "Group Fund" is explained to the members as being their own 'little bank'. It protects them from resorting to the money-lenders when they really need small amounts of money. Any group member can borrow from the Group Fund for any purpose, for investment or for personal consumption, what is required is the consent of the other group members who also decide terms and conditions. It is common that loans are granted for a fixed term at no interest. The 1984 Grameen Bank Annual Report lists 294 different activities for which loans were granted from the 'Group Fund'. The activities are grouped under the following nine headings : social and household needs; health and medical expenses; loan repayment : maintenance, repair and addition of capital equipment; raw materials for manufacturing and processing; new and supplementary investments; trading; farming; and collective enterprise.

Specifically, the Group Fund grants loan for meeting the expenses for cattle-shed, clothes, religious festival ceremonies, medicines, cart-repairing, tools for welding, bamboo groves, bamboo for ice-cream sticks, yarn purchase, goat-raising, betel leaf trading, seeding and a collective enterprise in market leasing. The limited selection reveals the spectrum of needs met by the "Group Fund".

The amount of Group Fund savings programme had accumulated Taka 13,078 lakh of which Taka 7,502 lakh was disbursed as loan (Grameen Bank Annual Report 1992, p. 70).

Emergency Fund : This fund is raised from advances given by the Grameen Bank. An amount equivalent to 25 percent of the interest charged by the bank on individual loans is deposited by the borrowers to the emergency fund. This fund provides insurance against illness, accident, death, disability, theft, damage to crops or livestock etc. (Mizan, 1992, p.11).

The Emergency Fund is managed by the members at the centre level (Vide Figure : 1). To be operational, it requires the joint signatures of the centre chief, deputy centre chief and the branch manager. It would be largely up to the centre's discretion to determine the amount of money to be drawn from the "Emergency Fund". This would require approval by the branch manager. There is an upper limit to the amount that can be approved (Fuglesang and Chandker, 1986, p.121).

Children's Welfare Fund : Recognizing that the growth of the centres and the Bank as a whole is one, staff and members are turning their attention to the welfare of member's children. To maintain this recently established fund, it is mandatory for the members to contribute one Taka per week. The money is used for building or making arrangements for a modest school room, which usually functions as the centre house too, for paying a teacher's salary or purchasing school books from the Grameen Bank. Similar to the 'Group Fund', the 'Children's Welfare Fund' is a source of small loans, but for the specific purpose of promoting small income-generating activities among children themselves which will aid in their continuing education (Fuglesang and Chandker, 1986, pp. 122-123).

Special Savings Account/Joint Enterprises : This is a voluntary savings scheme which operates at the level of the centre. After sucessful proof and assurance that members can save collectively, if they wish to enter into a joint enterprise (Mizan, 1992, p.11), the bank provides loan no more than ten times to the size of the members' savings (Funglesang and Chandker, 1986, p. 122). Such joint enterprise may comprise of buying tube-wells, power-pumps, rice -husking machines; oil mills, etc. Each individual member at the centre becomes responsible for the amount borrowed. Money from the special savings account may be used for other purposes also, such as the purchase of clothes and furniture (Mizan, 1992, p.12).

Shareholding Scheme : As a group's savings reach Taka 600, it becomes compulsory for each member to buy one share of the Grameen Bank in the amount of Taka 100 (total of Taka 500 for the group). These share remain in the members' savings, permanently and cannnot be taken out as loan. This process ensures the ownership of the Bank in the hands of its members. As in 1986, the Grameen Bank members owned 75 percent of the bank's shares while the, Government of Bangladesh owned the remaining 25 percent (Fuglesang, 1986, p.123; Mizan, 1992, p. 12).

Individual Savings Deposits : In addition to the various collective savings scheme, the Grameen Bank is encouraging members to build their economic viability by keeping their income from other sources (income for the generation of which the Grameen Bank has not provided loan) in personal savings accounts. The number of deposits and the amounts are expected to increase as members' standard of living improves and they can accumulate something for the future. The Bank considers deposit banking an important feature of its fund management in the years to come (Fuglesang and Chandker, 1986, p. 123).

IV

Targeting landless women

In situations of extreme poverty and hunger, it is the women who suffer the greatest deprivation. The most disadvantaged persons in Bangladeshi villages generally are the mothers in the landless families with no male support. Women in extreme poverty are the most appreciative of such opportunities as they are the persons who make the best use of the loans extended by the Grameen Bank (Shehabuddin, 1992, p.76).

It is also true that men suffer in times of hardship, but primarily, mothers are traditionally cencerned with family welfare.

Case studies reveal that two things happen once a female client starts earning :

(a) the initial benefit of the income is enjoyed by the women's children. They get clothes to wear or if there is an older child, he starts going to school, (b) the second benefit comes to the whole family with the repairs and improvement of the dwelling place (Yunus, 1991, p. XIX). Yunus belives that "helping the mother to earn an income is the most dependable way to help the children." (Yunus, 1989, P. 8)

He adds that it is not an "emotional or moral compulsion ———but a very strong economic reason" that motivates the bank to help children (Yunus, 1989, p. 8).

The possibility of getting progressively larger amount of loans, which permit even more profitable ventures, has been an important motivation for women to pay back on time. For, it is required that each the Grameen Bank loan is to be fully repaid within a one year period, in fifty weekly instalments of two percent of the sum borrowed,following a grace period of two weeks.

Critics have often argued that poor rural women, lackings formal training and education, would misuse the money. This line of thingking ignores the basic skills of rural Bangladeshi women displayed in various kinds of household productions. In reality "their isn't a single chore, within the household, that they (women) don't know or don't do. The skill which they attain by doing all kinds of work within the home can easily be channelized into income generation (Yunus, 1982, p.XV). A vast range of activities are purchased by the bank's female borrowers. They husk paddy; make earthen pots; raise domestic animals such as poultry, cows or goats; puff rice, grow fruits and vegetables or make handicraft items out of bamboos or canes, like sieves, baskets and mats.

The Grameen Bank has a social development programme which is represented in the "Sixteen Decisions" (Vide Appendix : B) The famous "Sixteen Decisions", were adopted at the second women's workshop organised by the

Grameen Bank from 18 - 22 March 1984. These decisions broadly reflect the four principles of the Grameen Bank i.e. discipline, unity, courage and hard work. The borrowers pledged to improve the quality of their life through hard work, additional income, having small family, educating the children, taking care of health and hygiene. They also pledge dowry-less marriage and group solidarity. Some attention was paid to injustice to women in a broad sense but no reference was made with regard to reformulation of gender ideology, (Afsar, 1989, p. 233).

They are a blueprint for action, arising out of the needs of the landless population it seeks to help. Members are taught and expected to live by these "Sixteen Decisions").

"In ——— the (Sixteen Decisions) social and economic distinctions overlap. Solidarity and mutual help are as much a practical concern as building a pit latrine or drinking tubewell water. Savings and investment in collective enterprises reflect the same spirits as tree-planting or growing vegetables. Abolition of drwry payments is linked with the issues of discipline, physical exercises and courage with the guest for social justice. Environmental sanitation is as important as children's education. The subject matter of the 16 Decisions has become the major focus for a comprehensive process of change (Fuglesung, 1986, p. 128).

V

Workshops

Grameen Bank regularly organises at all levels ——— national, zonal and branch areas. A zone arranges about 85 workshops every year, one at each branch and over a half are for women. The intense branch level workshops, which last seven days form the core of the bank's social development programme. They are attended by 30-35 women, with one or two from each centre under the jurisdiction of that particular branch (Shehabuddin, 1992,

p. 82).

Workshops are held with a view to realising some objectives viz :

(*a*) Exchange of ideas and experiences among the participants;

(*b*) To inform the participants about the principles and rules of the Grameen Bank;

(*c*) To create awareness about the importance family planning, health and sanitation among the participants so that they can take effective measurs in these regards;

(*d*) To give the participants information about nutrition and preservation of food;

(*e*) To impart knowledge about the steps to take care of children, pregnant women and to prevent child diseases/mortality;

(*f*) To inform about the necessity and means to grow more vegetables and plant various trees;

(*g*) To inform the women leaders (centre-chiefs) of their, role, responsibilities and duties in a comprehensive way;

(*h*) To inform about various new ventures undertaken and experiences gained by different social problems.

(*i*) To impart a sense of perseverance, and confidence among the participants so that they can make their groups centres strong.

A comparative training programme has been formulated for the participants of the workshops.

The Grameen Bank also has undertaken some welfare programmes for its members.

For example, the Grameen Bank group members themselves are advised to solve their problems and conflict, without any intervention from outside. Also, they are taught to help solve problems and conflicts of the other group members in and around the centre, (Fuglesang and

Chandker, 1986, pp. 228 - 232). Moreover, Grameen Bank aims to encourage its members not to give and take dowry which is a social evil.

The Grameen Bank apporach depends very heavily on social pressure and constructive criticism at a number of levels; for example, group members are responsible for the regular repayment of loans by their fellow group members, while one centre may force another to admit that it has not followed the rules and regulations of the bank. This concept of social pressure and cooperation may seem oppressive to an observer weaned on individual rights to privacy and freedom; the term freedom should not however be, expaneded to exclude socail responsibility. Landless rural women suffer from both gender and economic subordination; collective action can empower them and allow them to challenge their 'Lot in life' (Shehabuddin, 1992, p.85).

VI

So far we have discussed the structure of the Grameen Bank. Let us look into operations, as viewed and found by different studies.

The Grameen Bank has evidently been able to break the vicious circle of poverty, exploitation and fear in those villages where it operates (Ray, 1987, p. 215). The Grameen Bank has succeeded in helping the rural poor overcome their fear. It has set in motion a process in which the rural poor strengthen and manifest their self-esteem and self-confidence in a variety of ways (Ray, 1987, p. 104).

The social status and solidarity of the Grameen Bank borrowers rise also when they sucessfully challenge the rural rich and win local Government elections. The Grameen Bank borrowers have raised subscriptions to pay for security deposits, etc. The Grameen Bank is, thus, sucessfully chasing the miracle of removing poverty from rural Bangladesh without a rapid and largescale restructuring of social relation (Ray, 1987, p.215).

Studies evaluting the operation of the Grameen Bank have shown that with the help of loans from the Grameen Bank, most borrowers have been able to improve their living conditions considerably. They have acquired substantial new assets. Almost 120,000 families (have now built new homes to replace the dilapidated shacks in which they used to live (Shams, 1992, p.25; Rahamn et.al.; 1991, p.22).

A change in their standard of living can be noted. They are now sending their children to the school for the first time; they can afford better food to eat and better clothes to wear (ibid).

Studies on the Grameen Bank have mostly focussed on its performance, its success in accessing the landless rural poor. Some of them have concentrated on the areas where the Grameen Bank has mostly invested its resources, the rate of the recovery of credit, and so forth. Only a few of them have exclusively focussed on the impact which the Grameen Bank credit has had on women's lives (Mizan, 1992, p. 101).

In the remaining pages of this chapter, an attempt will be made to make a survey of literature on those studies which have looked into the impact that the Grameen Bank has created on women through the disbursement of various types of loans.

Hossain (1984), specifically focuses on the extent of the Grameen Bank's impact on poor women's employment and income as well as productivity.His primary source of data comes from a survey held during 1982 - 83 covering 612 borrowers. The survey was conducted by the Bangladesh Institutes for Development Studies (BIDS). Beside this source, Hossain also uses Monthly Statistics and Annual Reports of the Bank. While commenting on the socio-economic background of the female borrowers, he maintains that a majority (61 percent) of the respondents belonged to an extremely impoverished class. He concludes that the loan enables female borrowers to add to their family budget. The net yearly income of their families are estimated to be 6,000 Takas (Hossain, 1986, p. 18).

More than 80 percent of the women had no productive occupations before joining the Grameen Bank. At present, these women-loanees are found to devote about 28 hours per week to income earning activities. It is true the labour productivity is low in activities in which women are empolyed compared to about 44 hours for the male workers. But considering that women have very little job opportunities, whatever little they can earn, contributes substantially to raise the income of their households (Hossain, 1986, p.22).

Looking at socio-economic status (SES) and mobility of the Grameen Bank's female borrowers measured by indicators such as increase in land ownership, income and gainful empolyment, Ahmed (1985) notes considerable change in all these areas. Thirty-seven percent of the females (N = 120) have said that they own some land, and fifty-eight percent, who had no income earlier, now earn some money after taking loans from the Bank. Further, this study shows that while "entrepreneurial activites" increased by twenty-eight percent for these women, their house-work decreased by forty percent (Ahmed, 1985, pp. 7 - 9, quoted from Mizan, 1992, p. 101).

Ahmed (1985), among others, investigates whether borrowing from the Grameen Bank has had any effect on women's actual as well as perceived status. He assumes that the Grameen Bank's women participants would be more conscious than non-participants about the evil of dowry, repression, divorce, desertion and violence against them. Consequently, they are expected more often to support equal rights for men and women. Ahmed's study reveals that even though awarness about such issues is very high (81 to

100 percent) among the female borrowers, only 48 percent of them support equal rights movements. However, he tests the extent of awereness on variables for the Grameen Bank participants only, there being no control group in his study for comparison (Ahmed, 1985, p. 102).

To find out the extent to which the bank's efforts raise awareness among women, Rahman (1986) gathered data through a survey of female and male members. His findings show that 54 percent of the male and 81 percent of the female respondents have learned to sign their names, and in the process have become aware of the necessity of education (Ahmed, 1986, p. 11; Rahman et. al., 1991, p.22). A majority of the borrowers have said they would provide higher education for their sons, while they agreed that girls should have same education (pp. 11 - 12).

Apart from these quantitative data, Rahman (1986) has further presented some case - studies which depict that those women who have been enabled by the Grameen Bank to earn something, have gained strength in building a collective solidarity which not only challenges the traditional terms and values, but also fight against social evils and injustices to women. Yunus (1982) and Ray (1987) also have got similar findings.

It appears that members are aware of the barriers like purdah, dowry, various types of superstitions imposed on women, as well as the benefits of sanitation, family planning, marriage at an advanced age, and group co-operation —— conditions that provide an opportunity to enhance their quality of life (Rahman, 1986, p 104).

Apart from this, women borrowers have been found to be more conscious about the rules of health, hygiene. and the benefis of cleanliness than their male counterparts (I. Rahamn, 1986). Also the fertility rate has been found to be lower among female-loanees which goes down with the longer period of membership in the Grameen Bank (R. I.

Rahman, 1986, p.66).

The discussion can be concluded with the observation that although the performance of the Grameen Bank is quite promising, it is still mainly involved primarily in economic mobilisation of landless men and women (Rahman, 1986). It does not seem to question social roots of gender inequality, e.g., the sexual division of labour, occupational segregation and discrimination and unequal work load, Although there is a dearth of literature on the empowerment aspect of the famous "Sixteen Decisions" and, unequal work load. Although there is a dearth of literature on the empowerment aspect, the famous "Sixteen Decisions" and, to some extent, the nature of credit disbursed to male and female borrowers may be cited as indications in this direction. The Grameen Bank's recent move to bring women to workshops outside the village is undoubtedly a progressive beginning. But how far it will help to alter the intra-household resource distribution and authority pattern needs to be researched throughly (Afsar, 1989, p. 232).

There are some more studies and reports conducted on and by the Grameen Bank. However, these studies are mainly concerned with the mode and style of operation of the Bank, the evalution of the Bank in various spheres, and the impact the Bank has created on the life style of its members.

Very little systematic investigation has, however, been noted so far on the roles of the women who have become members of the Grameen Bank, in the family power structure, decision-making process and division of labour within the family. The present inquiry will try to fill in this gap in knowledge. Along with the above issues, it will also look into the aspiration level, and level of consciousness about the rights and duties among the women members of the Grameen Bank.

4

Methods Followed in the Study

The present survey attempts to enquire into the association, if any, between the women's economic status and their contribution to the familiy's subsistence, on the one hand, and their participation in the process of decision-making, on the other.

To carry out this objective it was necessary to specify and formulate, precisely and concretely, the topics on which information was needed, and also the method through which this information was to be collected. The design of the study is primarily descriptive in nature. That is, the primary purpose of this inquiry is to describe a specific situation, namely, whether and how far a woman's status is releated to her contribution to the subsistence of her family.

As necessitated in this study design, what is called for here is observation of patterns only, that is, what it is. Scientific descriptions are typically more accurate and precise than casual, haphazard descriptions.

However, neither this research design demands nor has the present researcher proposed testing of any casual relationship among variables or introduction of any 'elaboration model" (Babbie, 1992, p. 91) in data analysis. The application of the elaboration model (the name is associated with a logical model used in the analysis of multivariate relationships in social research and it involves the introduction of a control variable as a mechanism for understanding a relationship discovered between two other variables) has not, therefore, been necessary here (Babbie, 1992, p.410). What the researcher has tried to see here is whether the loanee group of women [i.e., the group of women who were engaged in income-generating activities with loan from the Grameen Bank and financial-contribute to their respective families, enjoy any better status (relating to their participation in the family decision-making process) vis-a-vis their non-loanee counterparts. Of course, if any such association (between the women's economic contribution to the family decision-making process) is found, effort has been made to <u>interpret</u> such association and find the probable rationale behind the same. Also, while interpreting data, attempt has been made to compare the findings of this inquiry with what other researchers have found in comparable situations. The study, however, *never planned* to test any hypothesis stating that the economic contribution of women *leads to* the enhancement of their status. The study never proposed to identify the necessary or sufficient conditions behind any probable enhancement of the women's status. So, multivariate analysis of data, which involves measuring the effects of intervening variables, is not called for by the research objective and design of the present inquiry.

To secure some guidelines, directions and suggestions for formulating the working hypothesis of the research and its appropriate design, a pilot survey among a small number of 20 "loanee" and 10 "non-loanee" women was undertaken. On the basis of the experience gained in the pilot survey specific questions were selected for a more systematic study. It was also necessary to test the feasibi=lity of carrying out such a research project. After the completion of this survey the general pattern of the study took shape and focused on more limited and concrete problems.

An interview guide was used for the purpose, where only the topics which seemed to be relevant to the researcher at that moment were set. The pattern followed may be understood for a perusal of the following questions: To what extent do you participate in the decision-making process relating to different matters or aspects of life in the family? Do you submit to the decisions made by your husband or the senior members in the husband's family and abide by them? While those decisions are made, is your opinion sought and considered? Can you take decision in these matters (i.e., the matters referred to by the researcher in the begining of her discussion with the respondent) on your own i.e., without the opinion or decision of your husband? Do you think that women should agree to and abide by the dicisions taken by their husbands or should the wives also take part in decision-making in relation to a familial matter? A family is made jointly by a man and his wife but is it your husband who takes decision in all the matters relating to the family ? Do you take decisions or just assent to what is decided by your husband?

It was hoped that discussions with both the categories, viz., loanee-women and non-loanee-women, would help the researcher appreciate the nature and extent of participation by the women in decision-making in relation to various familial matters. Also, an attempt was made to form an idea of their perception of the phenomenon under study and other relevant phenomena. These opinions were assiduously collected. In course of the discussions several relevant issues were raised so that interviews should not prove "meaningless", but every attempt was made to let the discussions proceed naturally and spontaneously, allowing the respondent to fit from one topic to another as often happens in ordinary conversions, as has been done by Chakbortty, 1978, p.65). The discussion were held in such a manner as to counter an issue raised by the respondent by another relevant issue and thus "converting the implied content of the informant's question into a cue for further discussion". Notes were taken during the discussions, and thus material for formulating the working hypothesis was collected.

These interviews strengthened the impression that all did not go well with these women, particularly, loanee-women, so far as status in the family, i.e., their participation in the decision-making process in the family, vis-a-vis their husbands was concerned. Though, it was felt there was some differences between the loanee-and non-loanee-women in this respect. All these suggested a number of research questions, one of which was selected for the systematic study on the present occasion, viz., the women do not experience an unqualified improvement in their status or power of decision making in the family even when they financially contribute to the family with the help of their engagement in income-generative activity with the economic support (loan) from development agencies like the Grameen Bank. Even when they report their joint participation with their husbands in decision-making, the experience of all such women are not the same on all occasions and in every case (vide pp. 122-123)

This specific problem viz., the nature of association between the financial contribution made by the women through their independent income from income-generating activities initiated with help from agencies like Grameen Bank and their status or the decision-making power in the family was chosen on grounds of its implications for theoritical interest and opportunities for research. Such research would, it is hoped, provide scientifically grounded knowledge in the place of current uncertainties and ambiguities, and thus may help policy makers too.

Definitions of the Concepts

"Women's economic contribution" in the present study means goods and/or services which a woman contributes to her family's subsistence, out of her income which she earns from the work carried out which the loan taken from the Grameen Bank. This income may be used for meeting the requirments of her family as well as for improving her quality of life situation.

More specifically stated, women can contribute to the family and to the improvement of quality of their life in the following ways :

1. by providing for such bare necessities as food and clothes for the family;
2. by helping their husbands in pursuing their business activities;
3. by sharing a portion of the capital to set up a handloom unit, run jointly with or solely by the husband;
4. by providing money for buying land for the purpose of cultivation;
5. by making monetary contribution for the purpose of housebuilding;
6. by bearing the entire or part expenses for education of their children;
7. by bearing expences on health of family members;
8. by contributing money towards maintenance of sanitary system of their homes;
9. by meeting expenses incurred with regard to the marriage of their offspring.

In this study, 'women's status' has been defined as women's capacity for participation in the family-decision-making process which has been operationalised with the help of following indices (Block letters stand for classes of indices and numerals stand for the consequitive number of indices) :

A. Participation in decisions on family budget :

1. expenses for daily shopping
2. expenditure on guests

3. expenses on festivals
4. daily cuisine
5. expences on food
6. expenditure on children's items, such as clothes, gifts, toys, snacks, and so on
7. buying things for other family members
8. buying sundry articles for the household
9. buing cloths for self
10. expenses on house repair/building

B. Participation in decision on daily cuisine

C. Participation in decision concerning the education of the offspring :

11. admission of children into schools
12. choice or selection of the school for the child's/childern's study
13. appointment of tutors for the children
14. extent of children's education, i.e. to what stage the children should continue their studies.

D. Participation in the making of decisions regarding the marriage of the offspring :

15. negotiating children's marriage
16. expenses on children's marriage

E. Participation in the making decisions regarding the nature of medical treatment to be adopted in the event of sickness or illness in the family :

17. selecting the health institution where children would be treated in case they become ill.
18. selecting the health institution where other members of the household would be treated in case they become ill.
19. selecting the health institution where the respondent herself would be treated in case she becomes ill.

F. Participation in decisions on the mode of expenditure of the family income:

The study has collected information on the following specific aspects of the matter.

20. who controls expenditure of husband's income?
21. who controls expenditure of money earned through sale of poultry and dairy products?
22. who controls expenditure of other sources of income in the family?
23. who is entrusted with safe keeping of husband's income?
24. who is entrusted with safe keeping of family savings?

G. Participation in decisions regarding the mode of expenditure of income earned by one for one's own purpose or according to one's choice

25. their (loanee-women's) control over their own income to the question: who is entrusted with the safe keeping of your income?
26. their control over expenditure of their (loanee-women) own income as revealed in the answer to the question: who controls expenditure of your income?

Besides making an attempt to seek information on the above points, the study also has gathered information regarding their power to dispose of the property acquired with their own income or otherwise, e.g., through gift from their natal family.

28. women's freedom to sell their property

In the pilot study it was observed by the researcher that not a single woman reported that she could dispose of the property earned by her (in the sense mentioned in the preceding para) absolutely independently of her husband. Hence, later on, the study inquired into the following questings only:

(a) can a woman sell the property acquired by her after duly informing her husband?
(b) can she sell it only after due permission from her husband?
(c) is she denied the power to sell it at all?

H. Participation in decision-making regarding the number of children a family should have

I. Participation in decision making regarding the freedom of movement

J. Participation in decision making regarding freedom to talk:

29. freedom to talk to male outsiders
30. husband's and other family members' approval of women's direct conversation with male outsiders
31. freedom from the compulsion to abide by the disapproval of women's family relating to their conversation with male outsiders
32. Participation in decision-making regarding casting of vote in elections in favour of this or that candidate according to one's choice

In all the items mentioned under each of the above A to J broad indices are counted, their total number comes to 32. Of these only two items, i.e., subsumed by broad index 6, viz., loanee-women's control over their income and their control over the expenditure of their income apply to the loanee-women only. Though they do not allow any comparison between loanee and non-loanee-women, they do indicate an important aspect of the status of the loanee-women who have an independent earning of their own.

In addition to these 32 items concerning decision-making process in the family, the researcher gathered information regarding the respondents' opinions or perceptions of several matters since these opinions or perceptions have been viewed for the purpose of this study as indices of women's status. These indices into the following:

1. Respondents' opinion regarding the role of husbands and wives in running the household
2. Respondents' opinion regarding the desirability of taking decisions conjointly by husbands and wives.
3. Respondents' perception of happiness
4. Division of labour within the family

(a) time devoted to household chores and economic activities per-day
(b) help received by women in day-to-day activities
(c) women's (loanee respondent's) perception of their work-load
(d) women's (loanee respondent's) opinion of their work-load

Choice of the Field

The choice of the field for carrying out this study, viz., the villages of Pachdona and Bhatapara in Narsingdi district of Bangladesh, has been made on a purposive basis. That is, the field has been chosen in consonance with the purpose of the study. During the pilot study, it transpired to the present researcher that there was hardly any difference between those loanee-women who received loan from the Grameen Bank only in the recent past, i.e., for two or three years or less, and their non-loanee counterparts in the realm of their status as reflected in their relative extent of participation in the decision-making process in the family and other areas of life. The researcher then collected information from the Head Office at the city of Dhaka regarding those branches of the Bank which had been extending loans to the village women for some length of time. One might expect to find among the clients of these branches of the Grameen Bank the village women who had been carrying out, with loan from the Bank, income-generating activities for some length of time. And the Pachdona branch was found in the list of areas where such branches as referred to above were operating for a relatively greater length of time. Pachdona Branch of the Grameen Bank situated in Pachdona village of Narsingdi District had been extending loan to the women of Pachdona village as well as the villages surrounding it since 1985. And, Bhatapara was village adjacent to Pachdona.

One of the principal reasons why the researcher chose Pachdona Branch, in particular, from among several areas with branches of the Grameen Bank functioning for a relatively long period of time, was that she had access to a few key informants in that area. There is no gainsaying the fact that the key informants help fieldwork in the kind of research in rural areas, which the present researcher undertook, if, of course, the help is utilized with adequate caution and discretion.

Another reason for choosing the area was that the researcher had the expectation that she would find the facility for accommodation in the village there. Staying in the village was very important for the researcher particularly when she was required to observe the activities of the women in the village(s) and establish rapport with them for gaining their confidence and a closer or more intimate view of their life-style. It is a common knowledge that villages in Bangladesh do not have facilities for hotel, hostel or bungalaw. So the researcher must find some suitable alternative accommodation so that she could stay at the village area for a prolonged period to complete her research. The researcher could learn from the Head Office of the Grameen Bank at Dhaka that the Branch Manager of the Grameen Bank at Pachdona at Narsingdi District was a lady. She had the faint expectation that she could find lodging with that Branch Manager, which expectation proved to be true.

That the Branch Manager at Pachdona was a lady helped the present researcher in a special way. Since she herself was a woman, the present researcher could convey to her the researcher's viewpoint as well as the nature of her work and requirment without much difficulty. And, the manager could readily understand the women's point of view shared by the researcher and see the problems and opportunities of village women from that point of view. Now, the researcher might have difficulty in explaining her view point and the problems of her research on women's difficulties and opportunities to a male manager. At the same time, the researcher must admit that a female bias might creep in her inquiry and analysis as a result of her association with and sharing of view with a female researcher. Exchange of ideas with a male Branch Manager would have corrected this female bias, if there were any, in the findings and their analysis by the researcher.

The researcher's stay with the Branch Manager of the Grameen Bank at Pachdona may, however, be viewed with scepticism by some. They may point out that a certain kind of bias in favour of the positive aspects of the Grameen Bank crept in the account of the researcher as a consequence of it. True, the researchre's stay with the chief functionary of the Grameen Bank at Pachdona helped her get an intimate knowledge of the functioning of the Grameen Bank. But who knows that this very fact of the researcher's close association and frequent interaction and discussion with the Branch Manager of the Grameen Bank stood in the way of the researcher to have an objective view of the activities of the Grameen Bank and the loanee-women? Also, it might have happened that the loanee respondents did not disclose all the relevant information regarding their experience with the Grameen bank, when they came to learn that the researcher was residing with the Branch Manager. One may pertinently say that the close association of the researcher with the Branch Manager of the Grameen Bank Branch at Pachdona detracted from the researcher's objective view of the phenomena under study, particularly when they touched the relationship of the loanee-women with the Grameen Bank. To allay this kind of skepticism, the researcher may submit with all humility that she tried her best to mix intimately with the respondents so that the latter should not feel inhibited in narrating their hopes and aspirations, problems and difficulties in connection with the Grameen Bank. Even then she must admit the possibility of a somewhat different view of the relationship of the Grameen Bank and the respondents, if she did not stay with the Branch Manager of the Grameen Bank.

A point or two, other than the ones mentioned above, seem worth-mentioning here. Narsingdi District was, prior, to 1984, a part of Dhaka, the capital of Bangladesh, and experienced what is called modernization which generally characterizes state capitals of recent times. Narsingdi itself is a trading and commercial centre. Also, it houses several textile mills and is an important center for handloom. Such a commercially and, to an extent, industrially advanced area is expected to offer more opportunities for income-generating activities than the areas which are relatively backward. And, it is expected that in such areas women would have a greater scope for income-generating activities then elsewhere. Whether it was the fact specially because of the operation of the Grameen Bank and whether it had some association with difference in the status of women in this areas (as distinguished from the women in other areas lacking in the facilities offered by Narsingdi) were the point of inquiry of the present researcher.

Viewed from a different angle, the area of Narsingdi seems to nurture conservatism in relation to women's behaviour. the custom of *Purdah* is widely prevalent in Narsingdi, i.e., the women here extensively use *Purdah* or *borquah*, i.e., veil covering the whole body from head to foot, the researcher found that because of the predominance of the culture of purdah in this area, women used to come to the Bank (the Pachdona Branch Office of the Grameen Bank where from the loanee-women of the villages of Pachdona and Bhatapara received their loans and organizational and other kinds of help) clad in *borquah*. The area where the study was carried out provided, thus, an intersting example of the interplay of the forces of modernization and conservatism. Since women's status (or more precisely, their power of decision-making) depends to a considerable extent on this interplay, the area under study provided a suitable field for carrying inquiry into the association between women's participation income-generating activities and the domination of the hold of conservation on their status and power.

Further, the present researcher is a female researcher coming of a Muslim family in Bangladesh. And, the movement of a Muslim girl in Bangladesh hardly enjoys totally unrestricted freedom of movement, even if she is not constrained by *purdah* or veil. It might not, therefore, be possible for the present researcher to move freely in an area totally unknown to her. It was not possible for her to commute daily from the city to the village and carry out her fieldwork there.

The above reasons, academic as well as personal, lay behind the selection of the particular field by the researcher for carrying out her investigation.

Method of Data Collection

Interview is the main method of data collection for this study. Interview has been considered here to be the most appropriate method of obtaining relevent data in view of the fact that a large number of respondents were illiterate or just literate.

Moreover, where the primary emphasis is on discovery of ideas and insights, it requires that the research design must be flexible enough to permit the consideration of many diverse aspects of the phenomenon. Hence, to gather as much information as possible and to make the study intensive, the method of personal interviewing was adopted for data collection (Chakrabortty, 1978, p. 68).

The purpose of providing the interview with partly structured schedule is to ensure that all the persons interviewed respond to the questions which the researcher seeks answers to and also to ask the respondents to clarify their answers in case any inconsistency is found.

Experience in the pilot study also suggested that interview would be the most suitable technique of data collection for the purpose. The pilot study revealed two things. First, a considerable degree of rapport with the respondents is necessary for any study on family relations, which involve attitudes and sentiments as well as facts, and where intimate, delicate, complex, emotionally laden and personal information is sought. It is required so that respondents can be adequately persuaded to be frank, honest and candid in narrating their experiences answering and the questions put to them. Interviewing is the most fruitful way for achieving this end. Secondly, if the respondent is allowed to follow her own train of thought, answers to many questions would be obtained automatically and spontaneously and there would be no need of asking each question specifically. For these reasons some time has to be spent while approaching a respondent and while initiating the interview, to establish a kind of relationship through informal discussing. As has been noted by Chakrobarty (1978, p.69) once some degree of rapport has been established, the informal and undirected conversation is to be stopped without the knowledge of the respondent, leaving her confident and at ease. This would, of course, make the interviews lengthy and time consuming and also labourious, yet no other method seemed to be suitable for the present purpose.

This direct, face to face conversation helps the researcher in a varity of ways. Chakroborty observes (1978, p.69) a casual remark, a look or a facial expression of the respondent may serve many purposes and answer many questions more correctly and precisely than mere verbal expressions. Here the interviewer is in a position to observe not only what the respondent says but also how she says it and thus to appraise the validity of what the respondent says, or even cross-question her if it is so required. When the researcher herself interviews her subjects, there is generally speaking no problem of misunderstanding or misinterpreting the questions, nor of questions losing their weight or gaining undue importance. If any bias creeps in, it remains constant throughout. And, this fact ensures a high degree of uniformity.

However, as Chakroborty (1978, p.70) has noted, the main disadvantage of this system is that if the interviewer is also the designer of the research, as in the present case, the very expectations that lay behind the choice of the research topic may assume some of the responses given. To put the matter more specifically, the fact that one and the same researcher has to perform all the different tasks, viz., preparing the schedule, conducting the interviews, collecting the data, and also analysing the same, may lead to a bias generated by assumed inter-relationships among the variables. Chakroborty (1978, pp. 70-71) suggested that it is difficult to avoid or remove completely these defects, but an awarness of the problems together with constant and conscious self-control on the part of the researcher may reduce their incidence and extent.

However, in framing the interview schedule for collecting the facts, the experience gathered by the researcher during the pilot study was utilized. On the basis of experience gained from the pilot study, some question which had been there in the schedule were dropped, while some additional questions were added to the schedule in certain cases, the wording of questions was changed. For example, originally the schedule contained a number of questions on family planning, which the respondents felt ill at ease to answer. Thus when they were asked as to whether they used any contraceptives, many respondents did not give any answer or gave answers which proved to be factually incorrect when the researcher checked them off with the Family Planning Officers or workers.

Accordingly, in the present study the purpose of interviewing respondents was not to 'rate' them in any way, but to elicit additional and useful information from them and to secure classification of their answers on certain points.

Whenever any inconsistency was found between what a respondent observed in response to a certain question at a certain point of time and what she said in reply to another closely related question put to her at a later point of time during the interview, probe question were put to her ascertain facts but in no case was there an attempt to influence the opinions of respondent or to persuade her in any way such that she would agree with the interview on any point contradicting her own views.

In this study, the researcher collected a variety of information of factual and attitudinal types.

It took 2 to 3 days to complete one interview as it was the respondents who decided when and how long they would talk to the researcher. It hardly happened that the respondents talked to the researcher in an uninterrupted manner. They would talk to the researcher intermittently as and when they got an opportunity for conversation with the researcher in the midst of their preoccupation with their household chores or when they got a respite from their daily cycle of household activities. Sometimes it happened that during the conversation between researcher and a respondent, the husband of the latter came back home before the schedule hour of his return or a guest arrived.

In such cases, the respondent would keep the researcher waiting and attend her husband or the guest. It obviously delayed the completion of the interview. The researcher, of course, derived useful understanding of, rather, insight into, the behaviour and verbal expression of the respondent interviwed through her observation of the respondent's interaction with her relative or guests.

Besides, in most of the cases, women and children from the neighbouring families would gather in the courtyard of the hut of a respondent when the researcher went to interview her. That is to say, when the researcher went to interview a respondent, she could, hardly, interview her in isolation from others. The women and children from the neighbouring houses of the respondent would come. Obviously, they hardly kept quiet. They would talk on sundry matters. They would join the conversation between the researcher and the respondent. Many a time they would ask the researcher questions regarding the purpose behind her inquiry into different aspects of their life. They wanted to know whether any benefit would accrue to them from the researcher's inquiry and, if so, what kind of benefit they would get. As a result, a lot of time was required for eliciting answers from the respondent to the queries of the researcher. But this fact of presence of a number of women during an interview helped the researcher in ascertainig the veracity of the statements made by a respondent, observed the reaction of the other women to the statements, of the respondent. Sometimes they felt ill at ease or even contradicted the respondent, if the respondent's statement did not seem to be acceptable to them.

In addition to the collection of primary data through interview, the researcher had to gather secondary data from the Head Office of the Grameen Bank at Dhaka, its Branch Office at Pachdona, Union Parishad Office, Narsingdi Police Station at Pachdona, Statistical Bureau at Narisingdi Sadar (District Headquarter). Information regarding the history, aims and objectives and gamut of activities of the Grameen Bank, the number and locations of Branch Office of the Bank, the number of members (loanees) of the Bank, the working capital of the Bank, the amount of loan advanced by the Bank to the loanees, the Rules and Regulations of the Bank and the *modus operandi* of the Headquarters and Branch Office of the Bank was collected from the Headquarters of the the Grameen Bank. The Branch Office of the Bank at Panchdona gave information regarding the number and names of the villages served by it, the number and names of the kendras or centeres under its jurisdiction, wherefrom the loanees received the loan and where to they paid off the instalments of the amount of loan received and the interest thereon, the number and names of the loanee-women, the period of association of loanee-women with the Branch Office and the *kendras*. Information regarding the population of the two villages under study was gathered from the Office of the Union Parishad at Pachdona. Also, preliminary information regarding the socio-economic conditions of the villagers was collected from the same office. The Police Station at Pachdona provided the researcher with the map of the villages under its jurisdiction. However, the Officer-in-charge of the police station advised the researcher to approch Statistical Bureau at Zila Sadar (District Headquarters) of Narsingdi for more detailed maps of the particular villages which the researcher wanted to study. In addition to these detailed maps, the statistical Bureau provided more recent census data than what were provided by the Union Parishad Office. The Union Parishad Office provided only 1981 census data. But 1991 census data were given by the Statistical Bureau Office.

The Statistical Bureau Office, of course, cautioned the resercher that the data provided by them, at that stage, were not processed data. And the collection of data was incomplete.

Construction of The Survey Instrument

The interview guide used in the initial stage could not, it appeared, focus on significant facts. So the researcher had to prepare an interview-schedule which depended considerably on the information gathered from pilot study. The experience gathered from the pilot study helped a great deal in formulating the interview schedule and in defining the meaning of the indices. Thus all the indices included in the interview schedule were "Operationalized" only after pilot study.

In the interview schedule, some questions were closed and others were open-ended. The interview schedule in this study was to cover four major aspects :

1. Extent of participation of women in the family decision-making process;
2. Extent of freedom enjoyed by women in certain specific respects, for example, freedom to talk to male outsiders, and freedom of movement (outside home);
3. Division of labour within the family;
4. Perception and opinion of women regarding some matters which are supposed to be related to their status such as their perception of happiness, their opinion in relation to the role of husbands and wives in running the household and the desirability of taking decisions conjointly by husband and wife.

In addition, a number of questions were included in the interview schedule to facilitate collection of some relevant socio-economic and demographic information regarding the respondents' age, level of literacy, income, per-capita monthly income of their family, family size, family type, number of children, husbands' education, husbands' occupation.

In addition to the above, information was sought from the non-loanee respondents as to why they did not take loan from the Grameen Bank.

Sample

Selection and drawing of sample is another important phase in the process of data collection.Research economy, in a study like the present one, dictates that respondents in any survey should be carefully selected. Here the aim is to obtain not only an accurate picture of the prevailing conditions but also insight into the nature of relationships among variables.

Selltize and her associates have insisted that in such

survey it is a waste of time and effort to interview people, who have little competence, or little relevant experience, or who lack ability to communicate their experience" (Selltiz *et al*, 1965, p.55).

On another occasion these authors have said, "Morever, there are circumstances in which probability sampling is unnecessary or inappropriate. One such circumstance arises from the fact one does not necessarily carry out studies of samples only for the purpose of being able to generalize to the populations that are being sampled. If one uses samples for other reasons, ablilty to evaluate the like hood of deviations from the population values is irrelevant....... the goal is to obtain ideas, good insights and experienced critical appraisals. One selects the sample a purpose sample with this in mind and not with the intention of assessing the status of opnion among practitioners............ We are sampling, not to estimate some population values, but to get some idea of the variety of elements available in the population". (Selltiz et al, 1965, pp. 538 - 539).

The purpose of the present research was not only to quantitatively describe the reality but also to provide adequate depth and details. Hence the choice of respondents depended more on the possibility of getting in-depth ideas about the problem being studied than on the purpose of making generalization only.

For the purpose of conducting intervies, a sample of 150 women has been drawn following the purposive sample technique. The sample is, however, divided into two subgroups———those who had taken loan from the Grameen Bank (loanee group) and those who had not taken any such loan either from the Grameen Bank or any other development agencies (non-loanee group)——for the purpose of subgroup comparisan. As there is no methodological or statistical requirement that for holding comparisions the subgroups would be of equal size (Babbi, 1992, p. 394), 100 "loanee" women were drawn from amongst the list of beneficiaries of the Pachdona Branch of the Grameen Bank. The sample of 50 "non-loanee" respondents were chosen from amongst the neighbour of the "loanee" respondents.

From among the loanee-women, the researcher has chosen for her study those women who have been found to continue with some income-generating activity with loan from the Grameen Bank at least for four consecutive terms. That is to say, each such loanee-woman received loan from the Grameen Bank and within one year repaid it along with interest (and thus completed one term) and received fresh loan from the Bank for another term of one year. Such continuity in income-generating activity may show some difference in the status of a loanee-woman from that of a non-loanee woman.

Another criterion for choosing the respondents from the loanee-women has been that they would be married and living with husbands. The reason behind it is that the researcher has made an effort in this study to know to what extent the respondents participate in the decision-making process in the family in comparison with their husbands. Because of this the present study has not considered such loanee-women as are widows or separated or divorced (i.e., this who have been given *talaq* by their husbands).

Analysis of Data

The study seeks to examine whether there is any association between women's financial contribution to the family's subsistence and their status.

How the data were collected for the study has already been told. The researcher should now turn to how the data gathered by her have been analysed. In this study the researcher has understood by "women's status", as has already been stated in chapter I p. 2 their capacity for participation in the decision-making process in the family with regard to 33 items. While 28 out of these items pertain directly to issues within the family, 5 of them are related to matters like women's capacity for taking decisions regarding the exercise of their voting right, movement outside home, and conversation with male outsiders. The last 5 items are considered part of the phenomenon of decision - making and hence the status of women vis-a-vis men in the family, since women's ability to take decisions on them depends to a large extent on their immediate environment in the family (particularly in the tradition bound society of Bangladesh). A women having a subordinate status vis-a-vis her husband in the family will hardly enjoy the power of making decisions in these matters independently of their husbands, or share the decision-making power relating to their husbands, or share the decision-making power relating to these items equally with them. That is women's power or making decisions in these matters is most directly contingent on the norms within their families.

In addition to these 33 items concerning decision-making process in the family, the researcher gathered information regarding the respondents' opinions or perception of several matters since these opinions or perceptions have been viewed for the purpose of this study as indices of women's status. These indices have been described earlier (vide).

The extent or intensity of women's participation in the family decision-making process has been measured in this study with the help of 33 items. However, while assigning scores, all these 33 items could not be included. At the time of assigning scores the researcher has considered only those items which have been found to be applicable to all the respondents of both the loanee and non-loanee-women groups. That is, the items, against which respondenses regarding participation in decision-making have been obtained from all the 150 respondents, have been taken into consideration for the purpose of assigning scores. But those items where responses could be obtained from some respondents but not from all or responses are not applicable to all the respondents have been kept out of this exercise to ensure for each of the respondents an equal chance of obtaining scores in all the items considered. In other words, an attempt has been made to see that the scores obtained by each of the 150 respondents are theoretically or logically may be equal. Ultimately, the items considered for the purpose of assigning scores are 22 in number. They are as follows:

1. expenses for daily shopping
2. expenditure on guest
3. expenditure on festivals
4. daily cuisine
5. expenditure on children's items, such as clothes, gifts, toys, snacks, and so on.
6. expenses on food
7. buying clothes for self
8. buying sundry articles for the household
9. selecting the health institution where children would be treated in case they become ill
10. selecting the health institution where other members of the household would be treated in case they become ill
11. selecting the health institution where the respondent herself would be treated in case she becomes ill
12. desicion-making on the number of children
13. control over expenditure of husband's income
14. control over expenditure of money earned through sale of poultry and dairy products
15. control over expenditure of other source of income in the family
16. To be entrusted with safe keeping of husband's income
17. To be entrusted with safe keeping of family savings

18. Women's freedom of movement
19. Women's freedom to talk to male outsiders
20. Husband's and other family members' approval of women's direct conversation with male outsiders
21. Freedom from compulsion to abide by the disapproval of women's family relating to their conversation with male outsiders
22. Nature of women's decisions on casting vote.

The remainig (out of 33) items and the reason for their non-inclusion of the remaing 9 items (given below) for the purpose of assigning scores may be briefly stated below :

1. Buying things for other members of the family : In this study,this item is relevant for the respondents who are members of non-nuclear families, but not for those respondents who belong to nuclear families. In the sample of 150 women under study, only 29 loanee-women and 12 non-loanee-women (i.e., a total of 41 women) belong to the non-nuclear family and the item is relevant for them only. The item has been left out at the time of assigning scores for participation by the respondents in decision - making process in the family as all the women in the sample do not have the chance of getting a score on this account.
2. Expenses on house reparing/building : This item too has not been considered at the time of assigning scores to the respondents for measuring their participation in decision-making. For, this item is not applicable to 11 loanee-respondents and 6 non-loanee respondents. The families they belong to have not either started or completed construction of their houses or undertaken repair of their houses with or without loan from the Grameen Bank. Hence, it is not applicable to all the respondents.
3. Admission of children into schools : This item is not relevant for 12 loanee-women and 7 non-loanee-

women. The children of some of these women are too young to get admitted in a school. In case of the other women, their offspring has crossed the school-going age. Their sons have since entered the job market and their daughters have been married off.

As this item is not applicable for all the respondents, it has not been taken into consideration for the purpose of scoring.

For reasons similar to the ones stated above the following items also have been kept out of consideration at the time of assigning scores :

4. Appointing tutors for children
5. Chosing the school where children would be admitted.
6. Extent of children's education
7. Negotiating children's marriage
8. Expenses on children's marriage

The last two (i.e., 7 and 8) items have not been considered at the time of assigning scores since they have not been found relevant in case of 54 loanee-women and 22 non-loanee-women in the sample.

Negotiations for the marriage of the children of these women have not yet started and /or their children are not yet married. The occasion for participation in decision-making has not therefore arisen in case of these women. These two items have not thus been found relevant for the entire sample.

9. The loanee-women's control over their own income
10. The loanee-women's control over the expenditure of their own income.

The above two items apply only to the cases of loanee-women, since the non-loanee-women have no income of their own. Therefore, these two items too have been left out at the time of assigning scores for participation by the women under consideration in decision-making process in the family as all the women in the sample do not have the chance of getting a score on this account.

11. Freedom to sell their property : This item has not been found relevant for 4 loanee-women and 5 non-laonee women in the sample, who do not have property. As these women do not have any property, the question of their enjoying any freedom to dispose of property does not arise. Since this item is not applicable to all the respondents in the sample it has been left out of consideration for the purpose of assigning scores.

In this context, something need be said about the dimension of scoring. Higher scroes have been allotted to these respondents whose extent of participation in the family decision-making process seems to be higher. Hence, higher the score, higher the participation.

Thus a wife who takes decision-solely or primarily-has been given higher scores than one in whose case husband and/or other members in the family is/are the sole or primary decision-maker. The respondent whose husband takes decision after consultation with her stands midway. All the items have not been uniformly scored, however, depending on the number of answer categories, the items which have 5 point answer categories scores have been assigned from 1 to 5. Similarly, in case of terms having 4-point and 3-point answer categories, some have been assigned from 1 to 4 or 1 to 3 order, respectively. The scoring dimension, known, (higher the particapation, higher the score) has been followed. All the items however, have not been uniformly scored; scoring has depended on the number of answer categories involved or found in any particular items. The items which have 5 point answer categories, scores have been assigned from 1 to 5. Similarly, in case of items having 4 point or 3 point answer categories, scores have been assigned from 1 to 4 or 1 to 3, respectively. Of course, a uniform scoring dimension (i.e., higher the participation, higher the score) has been followed.

In the study there are 11 items all of which have 5 point answer categories viz;

1. expenses for daily shopping,
2. expenditure on guests,
3. expenses on festivals,
4. daily cuisine,
5. expenses on food.
6. expenditure on children's items, such as clothes, gifts, toys, snacks and so on,
7. buying sundry articles for the household,
8. buying clothes for self,
9. selecting the health institution where children would be treated in case they become ill,
10. selecting the health institution where other members of the household would be treated in case they become ill,
11. selecting the health institution where the respondent would be treated in case she becomes ill,
12. women's freedom of movement,
13. women's freedom to talk to male outsiders
14. decision-making on the number of children,
15. control over expenditure of husband's income,
16. control over expenditure of money earned through sale of poultry and dairy products,
17. control over expenditure of other source of income in the family,
18. to be entrusted with safe keeping of husband's income,
19. to be entrusted with safe keeping of family savings,
20. husband's and other family members approval of women's direct conversation with male outsiders,
21. women's freedom from the obligation to abide by the disapproval of women's family relating to their conversation
22. nature of women's decision on casting vote

Thus the maximum possible score a respondent can obtain is 90, while the minimum score is 22, the range being 68 which has been distributed under 3 categories, namely, maximum, medium, minimum, indicating the highest level of participation for those in the "maximum" group and the lowest level of participation for those in the "minimum" category. Women falling in between these two extreme situations have been put in the "medium" category.

Respondents obtaining scores between 22 and 44 scores have been put in the "minimum" level. Respondents obtaining 45 to 67 score from have been included in the "medium" level. Respondents obtaining 68 scores from to 90 have been included in the "maxmium" level.

Chi- square test has been applied for finding association among variables, and 0.05 level of significance has been adopted for determining the statistical significance of association.

Limitation of the Present Study

The present study is a modest attempt to throw some light on whether and how far a women's status is related to her economic contribution to the subsistence of her family. Obviously, the venture, being the first systematic and independent research work of a student who is still under probation, is limited in many respects. This is also to be pointed out that it is the effort of a single person without the support of adequate manpower and fund. The present researcher, however, got a scholarship from the Government of India under the Indian Council for Cultural Relations (ICRR) Scheme and drew a monthly sum of Rs. 2,500/- which is too meagre support as whole time field researcher. It is common knowledge that funds, manpower and time have an important role in any research. Further, the present researcher is a female. And, in field research in rural areas in tradition-bound socieities like the one in Bangladesh a female researcher has to face a series of problems, even today, simply because of her gender.

The study examines women's status mainly in terms of the extent of their participation in the process of decision-making in the family. "Women's Status" is a broad concept. It may be viewed in different ways. There may be variations in the status of a person or a social category or group because of economic, political, educational, demographic and religious factors. These, however, do not constitute the focus of the study.

One may notice a sort of limitation also in the arena of sampling followed in this study. The researcher has resorted to "purposive sampling" for serving the need of the study. It is well known that purpose sampling is a judgement sampling the efficiency of which depends on the efficient and unbiased judgement of the researcher while drawing the sampling units. This kind of sampling does not warrant any large scale generalization. Hence, any large scale generalization is not sought in this inquiry.

The inquiry is limited in many other respects as well. For example, no comparison is made here between the earlier status and present status of the respondents. Such a comparison would have yielded more precise information regarding the changing status of women considered in the study. But because of several difficulties encountered by the researcher, the attempt at gathering data that would help such a comparison was abandoned.

Moreover, the study recorded here may appear to some to be deficient particularly in respect of the validity of the techniques of recording interviews and rating of the respondents used here. The researcher can hardly deny these deficiencies which are, she modestly submits, to some extent inevitable in any descriptive study in areas like the present one where the reports of systematic field surveys are very scarce. However, a venture like the present one can defend itself on the ground that observation and fact-gathering which have been aimed at here must precede policy-framing as well as hypothesis-testing in a rigorous manner. If the design of the present study is found weak in a certain way, it can be said that such associations as have been sought to demonstrate between different variables (although they are frequently inconclusive) are presented in the context of a range of other relevant social, familial and personal and economic variables.

One point should be made clear in this respect. In studying the relationships in the family, the variables are found to be too interrelated and interdependent, and all of them being potentially relevant, one cannot, in testing the effect of any variable, control the others without also measuring them. For such studies the isolation of a single variable - the ideal technique in research - can often be misleading. Yet it was necessary to limit the scope of the study in some respects. For practical reasons it was decided to reduce the number of factors considered for quantitative analysis attempted in this study, and to restrict the main portion of the quantitative analysis to those variables only which seemed to be directly related to the issue.

The present analysis has not described any thing which is very novel and with which the reader is not at all familiar. Nor can it claim to be a contribution in the form of a systematic survey of the status of women or even of the status of the housewives in Bangladesh.

For, it is clear that 150 respondents cannot be treated as representing a large population. Indeed, it should be made clear in the beginning that this study aspires to a very limited extent to empirical generalizations

An attempt has been made to draw inferences and offer interpretations (of cource on a very limited scale) and suggest hypotheses of general relevance, so that they can be applied to and tested on other persons in comparable situations.

5

Findings I

I

The present study was carried in two villages in Narsingdi Zila (District) of Bangladesh, viz., Panchdona and Bhatpara. The present Narsingdi Zila was one of the subdivisions of the former Dhaka district (where in is located the city of Dhaka, the capital of Bangladesh).

It was upgraded to a Zila in 1984. There are different views regarding the origin of the name of the zila. There is a popular belief that about a century ago, there lived in the area an influential Zamindar (landlord) named Narsingha Paul who was well known amongst the people of the locality for his benevolent activities. The zila might have derived its name from the name of that Zamindar.

The zila is bounded on the north by Kishoreganj zila, on the east by Kisnoreganj and Brahmanbaria zilas, on the south by Brahmanbaria and Narayanganj zilas, and on the west by Gazipur zila. The total area of the zila is according to Bangladesh population census 1991-Zila : Narsingdi (August 1995), 1140.76 sq kms. (440.45 sq. miles) of which 78.24 sq kms. (30.21 sq miles) is riverine– [The Bangladesh Census of Agriculture and Livestock : 1983-84 Zila Series: Narasingdi (or BCAL :1983-84) (September 1988) gives slightly different measures of the area of the district]. The

Zila lies between 23°46' and 24°15' north latitudes and between 90°34' and 90°59' east longitudes (Bangladesh Population Census 1991, B.B.S., 1995, p. 1).

River System

The Meghna, the Brahmaputra and the Sitalakhya are the main rivers flowing over the zila. Besides these, the Arialkhan, the Titas, the Haridoa and the Paharia are also important rivers in the zila contributing to seasonal water reservoir system and local transportation. The Meghna, the Sitalakhya and the Brahmaputra are navigable throughout the year. According to BCAL : 1983-84, the length of the rivers is about 74 kms (46 miles) with an area of about 81 sq. kms. It occupies 7.26% of the total area of the zila. The area where the Narsingdi Thana (Police Station) headquarters are situated is not touched by any river. The two villages under the Thana Headquarters, where the study was conducted do not get any benefit from the river water.

Cropping Pattern

According to the Agricultural Census 1983-84, gross cropped area was about 339,000 acres and the net temporary cropped area was about 192,000 acres. The intensity of cropping is thus 176.68%. Rice, wheat, pulses, oilseeds, jute and vegetables are the major crops in the zila. Rice occupies 67.19% and wheat only 2.60% of the gross cropped area. Jute is also produced in the zila. It occupies an area of 36,518 acres which is 10.76% of the gross cropped area in the zila (source : BCAL :1983-84).

Irrigation

In 1983-84, about 57.01% of the farm holdings reported to have used irrigation in a total area of 60,402 acres. This constituted 25.26% of the farm area and 28.81% of the cultivated area. The different size classes of farm holdings show that 53.59% of the small holdings, 75.80% of the medium holdings and 79.37% of the large holdings used irrigation in the zila. The tendency of using irrigation increased with the increase in the size of the holdings. (BCAL : 1983-84, p. 16).

Population Characteristics

Population distribution : the 1991 census shows that 83.98% of the Population live in the rural area and 16.02% in urban area. Thana wise distribution of the population is shown in Table 5.1 :

Table 5.1
Population by Thana and Locality, 1991, in Narsingdi District

Thana	Total Number	%	Rural Number	%	Urban Number	%
Belabo	145,708	8.82	129,893	9.36	15,815	5.98
Monohardi	230,028	13.92	219,855	15.85	10,173	3.84
Narsingdi Sd.	451,335	27.32	346,074	24.94	105,261	39.78
Palash	174,040	10.54	79,607	5.74	94,433	35.68
Rajpura	413,766	25.04	383,805	27.66	29,961	11.32
Shibpur	237,246	14.36	228,254	16.45	8,992	3.40
Total	1,652,123	100.00	1,387,488	100.00	264,635	100.00

Distribution of Household : According to the Population and Housing Census, 1991, total number of households enumerated in the zila was 309,202 of which 302,832 (97.94%) were dwelling, 1,520 (0.49%) were institutional and 4,850 (1.57%) were other households. Urban and rural break-up of dwelling households for the Censuses 1961, 1974, 1981 and 1991 are shown in Table 5.2 :

Table 5.2

Dwelling Households by Locality, (1961-1991), in Narsindi District

Locality	1961*		1974*		1981		1999	
	Number	Percent	Number	Percent	Number	Percent	Number	Percent
Total	157,685	100.00	201,000	100.00	236,272	100.00	302,832	100.00
Rural	155,183	98.41	193,761	96.40	208,729	88.34	256,982	84.86
Urban	2,502	1.59	7,239	3.60	27,543	11.66	45,850	15.14

* Total households.

It can be seen that there was a sharp increase in the proportion of the urban households during the period 1961-1991.

Household Size : In 1991, the average household size for the zila was 5.34 persons. Average size of dwelling households by locality are shown in Table 5.3 :

Table 5.3
Household size of Dwelling Units by Locality, (1961-1991), in Narsingdi District

Locality	1961*	1974*	1981	1991
Total	5.27	5.48	5.53	5.36
Rural	5.26	5.48	5.48	5.35
Urban	5.90	5.41	5.94	5.43

Construction Materials of main structure of household:

In Narsingdi zila 17.78% of households have walls and roofs made of bamboo and straw as the main structure. About 2.44% of the households have cement as the material of wall and roof. In the zila 64.96% of the main structures of the households have their walls made of straw/ bamboo and another 77.17% have their roofs made of tiles/ CI sheet. The main house in rest of the households are semi-pucca, tinshed, tiles or any other combination of construction materials.

Tenancy : Of the dwelling households in this district 91.96% are owned, 5.50% rented and 2.54% are rent-free. In rural areas, 96.67% of households are owned as against 65.60% in urban areas. In urban areas, 29.98% of households are rented compared to only 1.13% in rural areas.

In 1991 census, 62.18% of the households of the zila own agricultural land other than homestead area and 42.42% depend on farming as the principal source of household income. Major sources of household income are shown in Table 5.4 :

Table 5.4
Household Distribution by Main Sources of Income, in Narsingdi District

Source of Income	All Area	Rural	Urban
Agriculture/Farming	42.42	47.14	15.98
Liverstock	0.46	0.48	0.34
Forestry	0.02	0.03	0.01
Fishing	1.40	1.48	0.99
Pisciculture	0.07	0.08	0.05
Agricultural labour	11.37	12.38	5.70
Non-agricultural labour	3.17	3.37	2.05
Handloom	5.83	6.55	1.75
Industry	2.20	2.17	2.36
Business	13.35	11.46	23.92
Hawker	0.33	0.30	0.51
Transport-Non mechanical	0.48	0.39	0.99
Transport-mechanical	1.56	1.34	2.73
Construction work	0.75	0.64	1.33
Religious work	0.20	0.20	0.21
Employment	9.30	5.16	32.51
Rent/Remittances	0.21	0.13	0.63
Other services	0.50	0.47	0.65
Others	6.40	6.24	7.28

The above table shows that in the rural area 47.14% of the households depend on farming as against 15.98% in the urban areas. Including all related sources 61.59% of the rural households depend on agriculture as against 23.07% in the urban area. In the zila, 12.38% of the rural households are agricultural labour household as against 5.70% in Urban area. Proportion of households depending on non-agriculture labour in urban and rural areas are 2.05%, 3.37% respectively. Majority of urban households depend on employment (32.51%) and business (23.92%) for their livelihood.

Tribal Status : In all, 352 households of the zila are tribal which is 0.11% of the total households.

Literacy : The literacy of the population of the zila can be seen from Table 5.5. The literacy figures in 1981 and 1991 for "5 years and over" are shown outside parenthesis and those for "7 years and over" are shown within parenthesis.

Table 5.5
Literacy by Sex and Locality, 1961-91, in Narsingdi District

Locality	Literacy Rate											
	1961			1974			1981			1991		
	Total	Male	Female	Total	Male	Female	Total	Male	Female	Total	Male	Female
All Areas	18.4	26.1	9.8	20.6	27.1	13.00	20.4 (22.3)	26.3 (28.7)	13.9 (15.3)	27.1 (29.6)	32.1 (35.0)	21.7 (23.7)
Rural	18.0	25.6	9.6	19.7	26.1	12.5	18.0	23.4	12.2	24.0 (26.2)	28.6 (31.3)	19.1 (19.1)
Urban	39.1	50.7	24.7	43.9	51.3	31.3	35.9	43.0	26.2	43.1 (46.5)	49.2 (52.7)	35.9 (38.9)

It is seen that literacy has been increasing steadily although the literacy rates of 1981 are smaller than those of 1974 which is due to the use of strict definition of literacy in 1981.

Table 5.6
Economic Participation Rates by Sex and Locality, in Narsingdi District

Locality	1981		1991	
	Crude	Refined	Crude	Refined
Total Area:	29.16	43.16	28.88	43.77
Male	54.01	78.87	52.33	78.80
Female	2.27	3.41	3.75	5.72
Rural Area:	28.47	42.53	28.36	43.39
Male	53.37	79.12	51.81	79.13
Female	2.29	3.45	3.69	5.65
Urban Area:	33.68	47.02	31.62	45.64
Male	57.86	77.53	54.91	77.27
Female	2.10	3.10	4.08	6.08

Note : Persons engaged in household work based economic activity are excluded from computation of activity rate.

It is observed that both the crude and refined patricipation rates of females in economic activity in both urban and rural areas are very low. However, there is significant progress in women's participation rates in the urban areas only during the last decade.

Highest Class Passed : According to 1991 census, 60.92% of the population of age 5 years and over have no formal schooling, 23.34% have primary education, 13.38% have high school education and only 2.35% have higher education.

For administrative purposes Bangladesh is divided into 64 Zilas (districts) and Narsingdi is one of them (see Map Nos. 1, 2 and 3).

The total area of a Zila is placed under the jurisdiction of several Thanas (Police Stations). The villages under the study fall under the jurisdiction of Narsingdi sadar Thana which embraces the Headquarters of District Administration also (Vide Map Nos.). the area under a Thana is further subdivided into several Unions. The village studied fall in the area of Panchdona Union (Code No 89 in Thana and

Union wise code list in BPC 1991 Zila Narsingdi (p. xviii; See Map 4.) The rural area of a Union is divided into *Mauzas* or revenue units or revenue villages. In many cases a *Mauza* may contain more than one village, as it happens in case of Bhatpara *Mauza* which contains the village of Bhatpara (i.e., one of the villages where the fieldwork for the present study was carried out) in addition to nine other villages. In some cases a *Mauza* and a village may be co-terminous as it has happend in case of Panchdona Mauza which contains one village only, viz., Panchdona (i.e., the other village where the fieldwork was carried out).

Information regarding certain socio-demographic characteristics of the population of different Thanas of Narasigdi zila can be seen from the following Table.

Ranking of Thana : Basic Characteristics and Ranking of the Thana can be seen from Table. 5.7 :

Table 5.7
Ranking of Thana in Respect of Basic Characteristics, 1991, in Narsingdi District

	Area		Household		Population		Sex Ratio		Literacy	
Thana Name	Sq.km.	Rank	Total	Rank	Total	Rank	Ratio	Rank	Rate	Rank
Belano	117.66	5	27,802	6	145,708	6	104.0	4	25.9	5
Monohardi	195.57	4	47,397	3	230,028	4	102.0	6	27.3	4
Narsingdi	213.44	2	81,780	1	451,335	1	111.0	2	31.7	3
Palash	94.43	6	31,350	5	174,040	5	115.0	1	42.9	1
Rajpura	312.77	1	76,508	2	413,766	2	107.0	3	22.5	6
Shibpur	206.89	3	44,365	4	237,246	3	103.0	5	32.3	2

* Literacy rate 7 years and over.

Table 5.8

Population 10 years and over by sex, working Status and Main Activity, in Narsingdi District (with detailed information of rural area)

Locality Sex and Working Status	Total	Does not work Total	Does not work Student	Looking for work Total	Looking for work Student	House hold Work	Agri culture	Indus try	Water Gas Elect.	Cons truc tion	Trans port Constru.	Busi ness	Ser vice	other
Narsingdi Zila														
Total	1089993	205469	124979	15238	2326	407428	233533	46766	941	4913	9270	70528	7071	88806
Male	567536	111571	73012	12832	1926	8751	228063	43828	875	4756	9144	69013	5530	73173
Female	522457	93898	51967	2436	398	398677	5470	2938	66	157	126	1515	1561	15633
Rural														
Total	906665	164843	98010	12465	1891	348391	219046	30990	397	3303	6457	50829	5663	64281
Not Employed	177722	164843	98010	12465	1891	84	48	36	-	2	-	58	78	110
Employer	16993	-	-	-	-	2376	10676	878	7	69	113	1439	181	1251
Employee	41338	-	-	-	-	1203	3948	12689	267	914	1091	2062	2184	16980
Self Employed	409351	-	-	-	-	215363	126097	8442	72	969	3310	40051	1703	13344
Family Help	203270	-	-	-	-	126986	49218	3123	28	314	764	6650	1326	14861
Labour	57991	-	-	-	-	2379	29056		5824	23	1035	1179	569	191
17735														
Male	465663	89608	57802	10243	1578	7557	214022	284022	28466	374	3171	6348	49713	4406
51575														
Not Employed	100348	89068	57802	10423	1578	-	47	28	-	2	-	58	77	105
Employer	14402	-	-	-	-	217	10511	810	6	65	109	1411	159	1114
Employee	37546	-	-	-	-	199	3886	12052	251	878	1070	2014	1815	15381
Self Employed	190469	-	-	-	-	2961	123586	7836	71	935	3237	39239	1514	11040
Family Help	70485	-	-	-	-	3923	47452	2534	23	284	719	6438	713	8399
Labour	52413	-	-	-	-	257	28540	5206	23	1007	1163	553	128	15536

Table 5.9

Population (10 years and over) by Source of Household Income and Main Activity, in Narsingdi District (with detailed information of rural area)

Locality Sex and Working Status	Total	Does not work Total	Does not work Student	Looking for work Total	Looking for work Student	House hold Work	Agri culture	Indus try	Water Gas Elect.	Cons truc tion	Trans port Constru.	Busi ness	Ser vice	other
Narsingdi Zila														
Total	1089993	205469	124979	15268	2324	407428	233533	46766	941	4913	9270	70528	7071	88806
own land														
Share Cropping		482044	94184	60530	6171	1154	185396	165975	4768	100	508	734	9068	1817
13323														
Liverstock	4293	646	345	81	8	1975	959	95	1	12	27	162	26	309
Forestry	202	25	8	11	2	82	30	2	-	-	2	10	2	38
Fishing	14291	1821	520	23211	5884	1350	127	8	5	40	1824	69	2931	
Piscirculture	791	117	49	3	329	165	6	-	2	4	68	4	77	
Labour														
Agriculture	109512	14644	6209	1373	116	44669	39848	1328	14	142	326	1311	293	5564
Non-agriculture	29107	3812	1370	602	25	11858	3463	1519	16	463	313	498	81	6482
Handloom	59234	8319	3570	816	89	22867	4835	15406	11	123	115	2827	179	6736
Industry	22805	3423	1723	286	33	1806	790	9091	7	59	40	339	85	831
Business	157022	33197	21141	2236	375	54786	6424	1967	80	274	538	49453	917	7152
Hawker	2894	387	132	40	-	1126	172	34	-	3	209	465	17	443
Transport														
Mechanical	13397	1623	538	113	5	5643	369	195	4	17	4138	130	52	1113
Non-mechanical	4480	746	393	46	5	1772	109	53	9	26	1373	99	14	233
Construction	7865	1358	726	100	5	2837	213	137	15	2741	34	109	17	304
Religious	-	-	-	-	-	-	-	-	-	-	-	-	-	-
Employee	112585	29064	21986	1615	360	34763	4046	13599	622	353	496	2454	1960	23613

Rent/Remittance	2536	823	548	75	18	856	148	131	2	9	41	135	15	301
Service	66935	11230	5191	1456		115247814637	1308	52	176	840	1576	1523	19356	
Others	-	-	-	-	-	-	-	-	-	-	-	-	-	-
Rural														
Total	906665	164843	98010	12465	1891	348391	219046	30990	397	3303	6457	50829	5663	64281
own land														
Share Cropping		453492	88409	56696	5743	1084	174519	157208	4266	83	461	671	8256	1667
12209														
Liverstock	3762	542	281	77	7	1759	835	94	1	11	19	134	24	266
Forestry	184	22	8	10	2	73	30	1	-	-	1	10	2	35
Fishing	12677	1526	430	210	9	5268	1311	113	6	5	37	1482	64	2655
Piscirculture	690	87	36	15	1	294	156	5	-	2	4	57	4	66
Labour														
Agriculture	100785	13309	5556	1260	106	41127	36928	1208	11	122	289	1133	266	5072
Non-agriculture	25819	3350	1173	531	21	19727	3249	1392	12	183	264	372	63	5676
Handloom	56579	7899	3357	783	83	21857	4684	11863	11	112	102	2677	172	6419
Industry	18362	2785	1312	228	24	6532	708	7033	5	47	26	256	77	662
Business	108577	21398	13420	1470	261	39489	5756	1339	42	192	323	33725	694	4149
Hawker	2193	295	94	36	-	831	164	29	-	3	133	336	13	305
Transport														
Mechanical	9846	1171	397	99	5	4196	341	149	1	10	3025	75	482	733
Non-mechanical2963	453	221	30	4	1209	102	30	5	16	904	60	10	144	
Construction	5585	1004	521	84	4	2086	188	96	14	1824	17	65	9	198
Religious	-	-	-	-	-	-	-	-	-	-	-	-	-	-
Employee	50407	13396	10306	771	204	17428	3133	2414	169	201	263	1050	1348	10234
Rent/Remittance	1121	345	227	16	1	457	130	11	-	2	22	49	6	83
Service	53623	8789	3977	1102	95	20491	4123	947	37	112	357	1094	1196	15375
Others	-	-	-	-	-	-	-	-	-	-	-	-	-	-

Table 5.10

Area, Total Households, Dwelling Households by Material of Roof of Main House and Population and Literacy by Sex, at Panchdona Union

Locality Name	Area in Acres	Total House hold	Material of Roof				Population			Literacy Rate (7+year)		
			Total	Straw/	Tile/CI	Ce-	Total	Male	Female	Total	Male	Female
Panchdona Union	3124	3867	3820	700	3099	21	20942	10724	10218	25.0	30.5	19.2
Bhatpara *(Mouza)*	932	677	638	135	500	3	3775	1940	1835	32.3	37.3	27.0
Bhatpara *(Village)*	–	154	149	18	128	3	937	468	469	37.0	42.9	30.8
Panchdona *(Mouza)*	126	152	151	43	107	1	823	419	404	23.6	29.9	17.2
Panchadona*(Village)*	–	152	151	43	107	1	823	419	404	23.6	29.9	17.2

(*Sources:* Bangladesh population census : Narsingdi Zila, 1991, Unpublished).

Table 5.11
Population (10 years and over) by Main Activty at Panchdona Union

Locality Name	Total	Not Working	Looking for work	House-hold work	Agri culture	Industry	Water Electr. and	Construction	Trans Port and Communication	Business	Service	Others
Panchdona Union	13791	2526	223	5337	2831	818	8	136	155	708	59	990
Bhatpara (*Mouza*)	2556	559	44	892	543	99	1	39	59	132	33	155
Panchdona(*Mouza*)	514	96	2	204	63	78	–	34	2	18	–	

(*Source*: Bangladesh population census : Narsingdi Zila, 1991, Unpublished).

Description of the Villages

As one proceeds to further details, one finds the following socio-demographic and economic population and area characteristics of the Panchdona Union and *Mauzas* and villages of Bhatpara and Panchdona, as presented in the Table 5.10 :

It is evident from the tables that in Panchdona Union there is an adverse sex ratio so far as females are concerned. While the total number of males is 10724 that of females is 10218.

A similar pricture prevails in case of Bhatpara *Mauza* and Panchdona *Mauza* (which is coterminous with Panchdona village). In Bhatpara *Mauza* out of a total population of 3775, 1940 are males and 1835 are females.

In Panchdona *Mauza* and Panchdona village (the two of which have the same boundaries) out of a total population of 823, male are 419 in number and 404 are females. In Bhatpara village of Bhatpara *Mauza*, however, the number of females (469) exceeds that of males (468) by one only. There is another village, viz., Lathurbagh, the females 165 are in numbers as against 159 males. But in other eight villages in Bhatpara *Mauza* males outnumber females.

As one comes to consider the literacy rate, one finds the same adverse situation with regard to females. There, at all the levels namely, Panchdona union, Bhatpara *Mauza,* and Panchdona the rate of literacy of females is considerably lower than that of males.

Panchdona Union is comprised of 24 *Mauzas*, of which, interestingly enough, three *Mauzas* bear the name of Panchdona—Chota Panchdona, Nagar Panchdona and Panchdona. Part of the fieldwork for the present study was carried out in the last named *Mauza* which is willy-nilly the village of Panchdona.

It may be noted that Choto Panchdona is a *Mauza* covering 9 acres with household only. Nagar Panchdona *Mauza* has an area of 70 acres supporting 120 households. The households of Nagar Panchdona have developed horizontally, on one side the national highway which comes from Dhaka and touching Nagar Panchdona goes to Brahmanbaria and also to Sylhet. The residents of the Nagar Panchdona are exposed to influences of various external forces because of their proximity to this busy highway. In comparison with Nagar Panchdona the village of Panchdona where the field work was done is a bit interior, though it is adjacent to Nagar Panchdona. The researcher felt that in Panchdona it would be relatively easy for her to assess the association between village women's engagement in income-generating activity and their power of decision-making. The association may not be influenced by such factors as urban influences carried through the commuters passing along the busy highway.

The *Mauza* village of Panchdona covers 126 acres, embraces 152 households. Legend has it that the name, Panchdona, originated in the fact of residence of five (Bengali equivalent of which is *panch*) influential people in the locality who were great benefactors of the common people. People wanted to immortalise them through the naming of the village. The researcher could collect the names of two of these five personalities. One was Kesab Chandra Sen and Sir K.G. Gupta. A High school bearing the name of Sir K.G. Gupta stands on the border between Panchdona and Nagar Panchdona. Students from these two villages as well as many other adjacent villages come to this school for their study. There is a primary school in Panchdona village. There is also a *Madrasa* (traditional Muslim religious school/ seminary) in the village. The walls of the *Madrasa* are brick-built.

Bhatpara is a village very near to the village of Panchdona and it contains 154 households. It is at a distance of fifteen minutes walk from Panchdona. Bhatpara village has been considered specially important for this study, since the office of the Panchdona Branch of Grameen Bank is situated in Bhatpara village. Bhatpara is the most populous of all the villages embraced by the *Mauza* of Bhatpara. The village contains a primary school, a *Swasthya Kendra* (Health Centre), a daily market. There is a branch (sub

Post office) of Panchdona Post office, house within the premises of one teacher (one Dilip *master* — teacher is called *master* by the lay man in the villages of Bangladesh) there is a Hindu temple in the village. The Muslims in the village go to the two masjids in or mosques the nearly Panchdona and Nagar Panchdona villages.

Before concluding this account of the locale of the study brief information regarding Panchdona Branch of the Grameen Bank seems in order. This branch is working since 1985. The office of the Branch works from the premises of a rented house. It looks like a godown (warehouse). It has a long continuous floor bounded by brick built walls supporting a long tin shed which is the roof of the structure. It is situated in that part of Bhatpara village where the daily market operates. One of the special features of this branch is that it has, uptill now advanced loans only to females, upto 31 October 1993, the amount of loan advanced by the Branch was *Taka* 488,10,400. The loan was granted to 1895 members, all of whom were women. The rate of repayment of loan is 99%. In all, 28 villages are being served by this Branch.

II

The study seeks broadly, to examine the nature of association between the economic contribution by women to their families, with the help of income earned from income generating activities carried out by them independently of their husbands, on the one hand, and their status as reflected in their power of decision making in the family on the other. To highlight the nature of the association, the study compares the extent of the loanee-women's power of decision-making with that of non-loanee-women who do not engage in any income-generating activity. But one may legitimately want to know whether there is any siginificant difference between the loanee and the non-loanee-women in other aspects of life than the one concerned with income-generating activities.

For, one may be interested to know whether the difference in the decision-making power of the loanee and the non-loanee-women, if any such difference is found, is linked with differences in the socio-ceonomic characteristies of the two categories of respondents.

It seems, therefore, necessary to give information regarding the socio-economic features of the respondents of both the categories, such as age, education, type of family a respondent belongs to, per capita monthly income of the family, family size, duration of marriage, education of the husband of a respondent, husband's occupation. All this information is presented in Tables from 5.12 to 5.19. Tables 5.20 to 5.21 give information regarding the duration of membership of the Grameen Bank enjoyed by the loanee-women, their monthly income and their occupations. They will give a fuller view of the conditions of the loanee-women. For obvious reasons, no information relating to these aspects is provided in case of non-loanee-women.

Table 5.12

Loanee and Non-loanee Women, by Age

Age (in years)	Loanee Women %	Non-loanee Women %
– 31	28	38
31 – 40	37	24
41 – 54	25	26
55 +	10	12
Total	100	100
	(n = 100)	(n = 50)
Median age	36.9 years	36 years

It is clearly evident from Tables 5.12 and 5.13 that there is no significant difference between loanee-women and non-loance women in terms of their age as well as education. In the higher age groups, viz., 41 yrs-54 yrs and 55 years and above, the percentages of the two categories are almost identical. There are slight variation in percentages of the two categories in lower age group. Similarly, in case of education also, there is no mentionable difference in the percentages of the two categories of respondents at the higher educational levels, i.e., from class V to Matriculation. However, 42% of the non-loanee-women are found to be illiterate, whereas not a single loanee respondent is found to be illiterate. Even then one may say that there is no significant difference between the two categories even at this level For, a closer examination of the data reveals that though it is a fact that not a single loanee respondent is found to be illiterate, 66% of the loanee respondents remain at the level of "just writing their names."

Table 5.13

Loanee and Non-loanee Women, by Education

Level of education	Loanee Women %	Non-loanee Women %
Illiterate	--	42
Just write own name	66	12
Upto Class II	18	26
Upto Class V	9	12
Upto Class VI	5	6
Upto Class X	--	--
Matric (S.S.C.)	2	2
TOTAL	100 (n = 100)	100 (n = 50)

Indeed, one of the requirements of eligibility for membership by the Grameeen Bank is that the intending person must be able to sign his / her name. The difference between such a person and an illierate man / women is very thin. If one looks at the non-loanee respondents one finds that 12% of them can just write their names. If one adds this 12% to 42% (illiterate) the total comes to 54%. So in the lowest educational levels there is not much difference between the two categories of respondents.

A more or less similar picture emerges from the analysis of Tables 5.14 To 5.17.

Table 5.14
Loanee and Non-loanee Women, by the Types of Their Families

Type of Family	Loanee Women %	Non-loanee Women %
Nuclear	71	76
Non-nuclear	29	24
TOTAL	100	100
	(n = 100)	(n = 50)

Table 5.15
Loanee and Non-loanee Women, by The Per-capita Monthly Income of Their Families

Income (In *Taka*)	Loanee Women %	Non-loanee Women %
51 – 150	4	6
151 – 250	11	16
251 – 350	36	46
351 – 450	37	22
451 +	12	10
TOTAL	100	100
	(n = 100)	(n = 50)
Median	348.00	311.00

Table 5.16
Loanee and Non-loanee Women, by Their Family Size

Family size	Loanee Women %	Non-loanee Women %
3	5	10
4	9	16
5	18	26
6	38	28
7	30	20
TOTAL	100	100
	(n=100)	(n = 50)
	Mean = 5.79	Mean = 5.32

Table 5.17
Loanee and Non-loanee Women, by Duration of Their Marriage

Duration of marriage	Loanee Women %	Non-loanee Women %
7 – 15	30	40
16 – 24	38	30
25 – 33	32	30
TOTAL	100	100
	(n = 100)	(n = 50)

The above tables indicate that there is hardly any difference between the loanee and non-loanee-women in relation to the structure of the family, per capita monthly income of the family, their family size and duration of marriage. In cases of both loanee and non-loanee-women there is an overwhelming predominance of nuclear families. The ecomonic condition of women in both the categories as reflected in the per capita monthly income of their respective families is poor, though in case of loanee-women the situation is marginally better. The median per capita monthly income of the family is *Taka* 347.56 in case of loanee-women and it is *Taka* 305.50 in case of non-loanee-women. The difference between the two categories of respondents in terms of duration of their marriage is not at all significant.

Table 5.18
Loanee and Non-loanee Women's Husbands, by Education

Husbands' level of education	Loanee Women %	Non-loanee Women %
1. Illiterate	32	30
2. Upto Class II	21	24
3. Upto Class V	19	22
4. Upto Class VIII	18	14
5. Upto Class IX - X	7	6
6. Matric S.S.C.- H.S.C.*	3	4
Total	100	100
	(n = 100)	(n = 50)

* S.S.C. = Class X Passed and H.S.C. = Class XII Passed.

Table 5.19
Loanee and Non-loanee Women's Husbands, by Occupation

Husbands' occupation	Loanee Women %	Non-loanee Women %
Business	31	30
Shopkeeper	9	16
Petty Service	11	8
Handicraft	18	16
Manual labourer	29	20
Share Cropper	2	6
Religiuns work	--	4
Total	100 (n = 100)	100 (n = 50)

Is there any difference between the two categories of women in terms of education and occupation of their husbands ? Data in Tables 5.6 and 5.7 throw some light on this question.

While tables 5.18 and 5.19 reveal no significant difference between the two categories of respondents so far as the education and occupation of the respondents husbands' are concerned, table 5.18 highlight an interesting fact, viz., 32% of the husbands of loanee-women are illiterate, while none of these women it may be recalled from Table 5.13, is illiterate.

In Table 5.13 the lowest category is illiterate and the next category is those who can "just write her own name". [This category is absent from table 5.18]

While not a single woman is found in the lowest category, 66% of the loanee-women belong to the next higher category.

It means that the husbands of half of these loanee-women (who can just write their own names) are illiterate. The fact is that the requirement that a woman must sign her name for entry into the membership of the Grameen Bank makes the loanee-women earn the ability for just writing their own names. But the line of distinction between illiterate and such a person is very thin. Table 5.20, 5.21 and 5.22 give information regarding the periods of membership of the Grameen Bank enjoyed by the loanee-women, their monthly income and their occupations respectively.

Table 5.20
Loanee Women, by the Period of Their Membership of the Grameen Bank

Period of Receipt of loan (in years)	Loanee Women %
4	49
5	27
6	24
Total	100 (N = 100)

Table 5.21
Loanee Women, by Their Monthly Income

Income (in *Taka*)	Loanee Women %
1–100	2
101–200	7
201–300	10
301–400	30
401–500	17
501–600	11
601–700	10
701–800	6
801+	7
Total	100 (N = 100)
Median	406.0

In fine, a perusal of the above Tables shows no siginificant difference in the socio-economic circumstances of the two categories of respondents considered in the study. The level of education of these respondents is, in general, poor. So is their financial condition (as reflected in the median percapita monthly income of their families.) The husbands of these respondents engage in humble occupation in other aspects also the conditions of both the categories of respondents are more or less similar. As one looks at the income and occupation of the loanee-women one finds that the income earned by these women is in most cases very modest and they find opportunity for earning income from humble occupations only.

Table 5.22

Loanee Women, by Their Occupation

Occupations	Loanee Women%
1. Cattle rearing and/or selling of milk	28
2. Handloom	8
3. Grocery Shop	10
4. Poultry and goatery	4
5. Vending of bananas	9
6. Tailoring	6
7. Sale of timber	1
8. Processing and selling of yarn	5
9. Investment in cycle-rickshaws	7
10. Agricultrue	4
11. Vending of *sarees*	2
12. Raising and selling of sugarcane	4
13. Processing and selling of rice in small quantities	8
14. Selling of seasonal vegetables	2
15. Tea stall	2
Total	100 (N = 100)

Note : *Occupation here means income-generating activity. Since the non-loanee-women are engaged in household chores only and do not engage in any income-generating activity, no separtate table for occupation of non-loanee-women is presented.*

G . B enriches women– How? See the rickshaw and the cow.

A loanee woman busy with the processing of cotton yarn.

Happy faces of loanee women at work with their sewing machines.

6
Findings II

Loanee and Non-loanee Women's Participation in Different Spheres of the Family Decisons Making Process:

With the above background information about the respondents in general and special characteristics of loanee respondents, the researcher now proceeds to present the findings obtained in this study and interpret the same.

In Tables 5.1 to 5.11 responses given by respondents on each individual item intending to measure respondents' level of participation in the decision-making process vis-a-vis other members (their husbands, in-laws, etc.) in the family have been presented in detail.

Next, data have been arranged in such a way as the associations between some social facts like age, education, type of family, duration of marriage, husband's occupation, husband's education, years of membership of the Grameen Bank and respondents' level of participation in the decision-making process may be highlighted. For this purpose, 22 items have been chosen for scoring. Thus, In Table 6.1 the association between the economic contribution of women to their households and the type and degree of their participation in the family decision-making process has been depicted. A comparison has been made here between the 'loanee', (those women who have taken loan from the

Grameen Bank and have utilized the same for any income-generating purposes) and the non-loanee (those women who have not taken any such loan from either the Grameen Bank or any other fund-giving agencies and who are, therefore, purely housewives groups of women in this respect, namely, the role exercised by women in the family decision-making process. Nineteen items have been chosen here in respect of which the extent of participation by women of both the groups in the family decision-making process has been considered. These nineteen items are as follows :-

1. expenses for daily shopping
2. expenditure on guests
3. expenses on festivals
4. daily cuisine
5. expenditure on children's items, such as clothes, gifts, toys, snacks, and so on.
6. expenses on food
7. buying things for other family members
8. buying sundry articles for the household
9. buying clothes for self
10. expenses on house repair / building
11. children's school admission
12. appointing tutors for children
13. choosing the school where children would be admitted
14. extent of children's education
15. negotiating children's marriage
16. expenses on children's marriage
17. selecting the health institution where children would be treated in case they become ill
18. selecting the health institution where other members of the household would be treated in case they become ill
19. selecting the health institution where the respondent herself would be treated in case she becomes ill.

For testing hypothesis, namely, whether there is an

Table 6.1

Loanee and Non-loanee Women, by Their Particapation in the Decision Making Process in Relation to Familiy Budget, Education, Medical Treatment and Marriage of Family Members

Items	Wife solely %	Wife primarily %0	Equally by the wife and the husband %	Loanee Husband Primarily %	Women Husband solely/ along with elderly members/ elderly members %	N.A %	N	Wife solely %	Wife primarily %	Non-Equally by the wife and the husband %	loanee Husb and primarily %	Women Husb and solelt/ along with elderly members /elderly members%	N.A. %	N	X^2	df	Level of Significance at .05 level
1. Expenses for daily shopping	9	13	39	13	26	----	100	2	6	30	24	38	----	50	8.75	4	Not Significant
2. Expenditure on guests	9	12	39	17	23	----	100	2	6	26	22	44	----	50	10.61	4	Not Significant
3. Expenses on festivals	8	11	41	23	17	---	100	4	6	22	26	42	---	50	13.87	4	Not Significant
4. Daily cuisine	10	15	35	14	27	----	100	4	6	26	30	34	---	50	10.32	4	Not Significant
5. Expenditure on children's items, such as clothes, gifts, toys, snacks, and so on	5	9	49	21	16	----	100	4	4	38	21	42	---	50	12.76	4	Not Significant
6. Expenses on fond	9	15	34	17	25	----	100	2	6	26	22	44	---	50	9.60	4	Significant
7. Buying things for other family members	7	7	48	17	21	71	29	---	---	50	25	25	76	12	1.7	4	Not Significant

8. Buying sundary articles for the houschold	7	11	46	23	13	---	100	2	6	34	26	32	---	50	9.93	4	Not Significant
9 Buying clothes for self	25	11	24	17	23	---	100	8	12	22	14	44	---	50	10.14	4	Not Significant
10. Expenses on house repair/building	6	3	56	17	18	11	89	---	2	46	9	43	12	44	11.56	4	Not Significant
11. Children's school admission	3	6	56	15	20	12	88	2	2	28	26	42	14	43	12.25	4	Not Significant
12. Appointing tutors for children	11	9	48	19	13	12	88	2	5	37	26	30	14	43	9.77	4	Not Significant
13 Choosing the school where children would be admitted	3	5	44	19	29	12	88	-----	2	36	26	36	22	39	4.62	4	Not Significant
14. Extent of children's education	7	10	47	19	17	12	88	2	2	33	21	42	14	43	11.95	4	Not Significant
15. Negotiating children's marriage	----	9	56	15	20	54	46	---	----	43	21	36	44	28	5.21	4	Not Significant
16. Expenses on children's marriage	----	11	61	13	15	54	46	---	----	43	25	32	44	28	7.84	4	Not Significant
17. Selecting the health institution where children would be treated in case they become ill	5	4	45	15	31	----	100	2	2	40	10	46	----	50	4.06	4	Not Significant

18. Selecting the health institution where other members of the household would be treated in case they become ill	---	3	35	19	43	---	100	---	2	26	10	62	---	50	5.08	4	Not Significant
19. Selecting the health institution where the respondent herself would go for treatment in case she become ill	2	2	31	25	40	---	100	---	2	24	22	52	---	50	2.79	4	Not Significant

Note: Column headings have been explained at page ----------

For testing hypothesis, namely, whether there is an association between women's economic contribution to their households and the extent of their participation in the family decision-making process, X^2 test has been applied. And,.05 level of significance has been accepted for rejecting the null hypothesis (Ho), that is, for accepting any hypothesis (H_1) as tenable.

As appears in Table 6.1, a statistically significant association (at.05 level of significance) has been found in case of eleven items of the decision-making, namely, (2) expenditure on guests, (3) expenses on festivals, (4) daily cuisine, (5) expenditure on children's items, such as, clothes, gifts, toys, snacks, and so on, (7) buying sundry articles for the household,(8) buying clothes for self, (9) expenses on house repair / building, (10) children's school admission, (11) appointing tutors for children, (15) extent of children's education, and (16) expenses on food.

It suggests that the difference between the loanee-and non-loanee groups of women is tenable so far as these eleven items are concerned. However, as regards the remaining eight items, namely, (1) expenses for daily shopping, (6) buying things for other family members, (12) choosing the school where children would be admitted, (13) negotiating children's marriage, (14) expenses on children's marriage, (17) selecting the medical institution where the children would be treated in case they become ill, (18) selecting the health institution where other members of the household would be treated in case they become ill, and (19) selecting the health institution where the respondent herself would be treated in case she becomes ill, no such statistically significant association has been found. One can infer, therefore, that the difference between the loanee-and the non-loanee groups of women is not striking in respect of these eight items. In the following pages, the present researcher will try to describe her findings in respect of each of these items in decision making.

Also, an attempt will be made here to explain these findings. That is to say, the researcher would try to explain what is the sociological meaning of some associations being statistically, significant and some others, not significant.

So far as item no. 1 (Row 1), namely, participation of women in decision-making relating to expenses for daily shopping, is concerned, no statistically significant difference between the loanee and non-loanee groups is discernible from this study. It appears, however, that whereas 9% of the loanee respondents can take decisions "solely" * i.e., entirely on their own, the corresponding figure for the non-loanee-women is only 2%. Again, while the percentage of women in the loanee category, who enjoy no role at all in the decision-making in relation to expenses for daily shopping is 26, the corresponding figure among the non-loanee counterparts is 38. However, these differences are not large enough to be statistically significant.

One may hazard a guess as to why the difference between the loanee and the non-loanee-women in this respect has not been significant.

Daily market is a rare phenomenon in the village of Bangladesh. Generally, people buy the necessary articles from the weekly markets or *hats*. It is the males who procure the daily needs from outside, according to their means, i.e., daily income, and take decision on the spot.

Note :

**1. "Decision taken by the wife solely" implies those decisions which are made by the respondents themselves, without any participation of their husbands or others.*

2. "Decision taken by the wife primarily" implies those decisions, which are made mainly by respondents themselves but apparently with the participation of their husbands, in the form of offering suggestions by the latter. Such decisions usually carry something like 75% of the respondents' own views along with 25% of the husbands' opinion. As, for instance, a respondent has said : "I have to take decisions even regarding major household matters. However, I always consult my husband before arriving at a final decision" Further, "while buying a plot of land, once, I intended to have the plot registered in my son's name. Initially my husband had objected to this. But later one after some discussion, he conceded to the point made by me and accepted my decision."

3. *"Decision taken equally by the wife and the husband" comprises those decisions which are arrived at by the mutual consent of the respondent and her husband. In such kinds of decision-making, both the respondent and her husband have plausibility equal authority either rejecting or accepting a decision arrived at by either of them, e.g., as regarding decision on the marriage of children. The key characteristic of such a decision is that, both the respondent and her husband participate jointly and with equal effect in reaching the final decision.*
4. *"Decision taken primarily by the husband" involves the decisions made mainly by the husband with the wife (i.e., the respondents) participating in a small way. Such decisions usually carry about 75% of the husband's own views alone with 25% of the respondents' opinion.*
5. *"Decision taken by the husband solely" are those decisions where the respondents have little say and when the respondents' husbands' determine the matters all by themselves, without any participation of the respondents and in such decisions, the husbands' opinion is essentially imposed upon the respondents.*

Or

"Decision taken collectively by the husband and elderly members of the family" are those decision which are made together by the husband and the elderly members of the family, with the exclusion of the respondent. In several non-nuclear families the wife is excluded from the decision-making process and she accepts this position quite easily. Accordingly, the wife, notwithstanding her exclusion from the decision-making process, concedes to the decision arrived at collectively by the husband and elderly members of the family.

Or

"Decisions taken exclusively by elderly members of the family" are essentially those decisions made only by the elderly members, with the exclusion of both the husband and the respondent. In such decision-making processes, neither the husband nor the respondent participates, and therefore, has no control over the decision-making process.

True, women remind their husbands or other male members of their family of the articles which are required in the household. But they do not participate in making the decisions regarding the purchase of the articles. First, it is not known which articles would be available at the weekly market or in the grocer's shop.

Secondly, means of the family are in most cases meager. That is, the earning of the family is so small that money for all the necessities is not readily available. Hence the decision is taken on the spot by the husbands or other male members and women have hardly only scope to share in the decision-making. Nor does their participation matters much.

Let us come to the second item in Table 6.1, namely, women's level of participation in deciding expenditure on guests. The Table shows that while 9% of the loanee-respondents can take decisions solely on their own in this regard, only 2% of the women in the non-loanee group enjoy that capacity. Moreover, whereas 23% of the loanee-women have been found where the decision is taken solely by the husbands and / or any other members of the family, in case of the non-loanee-women such figure is 44%. The difference between the loanee- and non-loanee categories of women in this regard has been found to be statistically significant at.05 level of significance. Hence we can infer that so far as decision-making in relation to expenditure on guests is concerned, loanee-women are in an advantageous position compared to their non-loanee counterparts.

An explanation of the phenomenon may be obtained from what the respondents have confided to the researcher in course of interview. The loanee-women have told the researcher that at present they are in a position to take decisions regarding expenditure for entertaining the guests and relatives including the ones from their natal families. But earlier when they did not pursue any gainful employment, they were abjectly dependent on their husbands in this matter. It was the husbands who took the decision. In a patriarchal system, the women are found to be apologetic about offering hospitality or entertaining guests or relatives associated with their natal families. Since the husbands are the chief earners and since their superiority and domination are an accepted fact, the wives, in general, are incapable of providing hospitality to people related to their own parents or brothers or sisters. But a large number of loanee-women have informed that at present, i.e., subsequent to their initiation to gainful employment and independent earning., they do not hesitate to spend money to entertain the guests and relatives, even when they are related to their natal families.

They can now ask their husbands for the money required for the purpose or request them to bring sweetmeats or other articles for the purpose.

As the researcher meets the non-loanee respondents, the latter frankly admit their inability to take any decision independently of their husbands in the matter. They are totally dependent on their husbands in this respect. Since they do not have any independent source of income, they suffer from a certain kind of tension or powerlessness when the question of entertaining guests or relatives, particularly those connected with their natal families, comes. They are afraid lest their husbands' words should touch a raw nerve, in case the husbands dislike spending of money earned by them by their wives for entertaining the guest or relatives connected with latter's natal families. The earning husbands may sarcastically remind the poor wives of the harsh reality that the money spent by the wives for extending hospility to the guests or relatives, particularly those connected with their (the wives') natal families, is earned by the husbands and the wives do not have any right to play host. Indeed, some of the non-loanee-women have informed the researcher that they actually bore with stinging comments from their husbands on such occasions. They regret that their inability to make any financial contribution to the family and their subservient position to their husbands in this regard.

Some non-loanee-women have observed that it is but natural that their husbands take decision in this matter since husbands take decisions in all other important matters of the family.

What transpires from the above is that the majority of non-loanee-women is denied the power of making decisions solely and primarily in this matter. And, many loanee-women themselves admitted that earlier they could not participate in decision-making in this matter and they could take decisions only after they started contributing economically to the family. An association is thus found between economic contribution by women to the family and their participation in decision-making in relation to expenditure on entertainment of guests and relatives.

Row 3 in Table 6.1 examines the nature of association between economic contribution made by women to the family and their participation in decision making in relation to expenses during the festivals. Festivals occupy a vital place in the life of every community. In a tradition - bound society like the Muslim society of Bangladesh, most of the important festivals are related to or based on religious values and practices. A lot of money is spent during these festivals on clothes, food and entertainment. The poor too, try to buy clothes or sweetmeats according to their means on these occasions. Now, the question is who take decisions regarding the expenses on these occasions ? In a patriarchal society where the males are the sole earners and providers of the family, it is the males or husbands who take decisions and the wives are denied any important role. But if the women too contribute economically to the family, do they get any opportunity for decision-making in relation to expenses on festivals?

In Row 3 of Table 6.1 a comparison is made between the loanee-women and the non-loanee-women in this regard. And, the difference between the loanee and the non-loanee-women is found to be statistically significant. The data clearly show that the percentage of loanee-women is higher than that of non-loanee-women in the category of women taking decision by themselves in this field as well as in the category of women who take decisions in this matter along with their husbands.

Some of the factors associated with the relatively higher participation by loanee-women (who contribute economically to the family) in decision-making in relation to expenses on festivals than the non-loanee-women have been revealed to the researcher by the respondents in the course of the interviews. One of them is related to the stipulation regarding compulsory savings by the loanee-women with the Grameen Bank.

The loanee-women have to deposit a certain sum regularly to the Group Fund Account of the Grameen Bank.They are allowed to withdraw money from the fund. And many loanee-women do withdraw money from their respective accounts with the Grameen Bank at the time of festivals like *Eid* to buy clothes for their children and / or other members of the household. Since the rural families which these loanee-women belong to do not have large savings, the money which they spend on the families from their own accounts with the Grameen Bank counts for much and, as a result, the opinion of these women regarding the purchase of articles on these occasions is given due importance. In other words, with their ability to contribute to the fund of the family for meeting the expenses on festive occasions, the loanee-women acquire importance in the eyes of the other members of the family and have a say on how the money should be spent on such occasions.

Some loanee-women have informed the researcher that

earlier, i.e., when they did not have any independent earning, there were quarrels between them and their husbands during the festivals, since they could not buy for their children any clothes or any other items of their choice because of the reported want of funds. If they criticized the husbands for their inability to purchase clothes for their children, the husbands got enraged and even beat them. And, if the husbands bought any items at all, they did not care to consult their wives. But the situation has altered since the loanee respondents started earning independently. The economic condition of the family has improved in comparison with what prevailed earlier, i.e., when the husbands were the only earners. Therefore, quarrels over the husband's inability to purchase clothing and other articles for the children and other members of the family during the festivals are now a rare phenomenon.

The association between improvement in the standard of living of the family and independent earning by women has been noted by Ahmed also. Ahmed has gathered from interviews with the male informants that since the females in their families started earning money, the families have been better off; i.e., they have been able to eat better and dress better (1980, p. 21).

Women's economic contribution to the family has, it appears in this study also, added to the well being of the family members, and their economic contribution is found to be associated with their ability to participate in making decisions regarding the expenses on festive occasions.

Row 4 presents data regarding the association between economic contribution by the women and their participation in decision-making regarding daily menu. Preparation of food for the entire family commands the major share of the time and energy of women. But in a patriarchal set up, it is the men who have the final say regarding the menu, either in daily life or on festive occasions. Further, though women have to bear the burden of running the kitchen, it is customary to pay special attention to the tastes and nutrition of the males. It is the sign of a good housewife to sacrifice her liking and disliking and considerations of her nutrition for the sake of the nutrition of her husband and other male members of the family. Indeed, the value of giving preference to the male members in the realm of preparation and consumption of food is so deeply ingrained in the minds of the women, that mothers not only themselves sacrifice and suffer but discriminate against their female children and specially favour their male children in distributing food and making provision for nutrition. Undernutrition of female members and girl children is large in the patriarchal socio - cultural system like the one which is found among the Muslims, particularly of lower economic classes, of Bangladesh. Under such conditions, women have the desire of the husbands and male members of the family in the matter of preparing the dishes, even if they face inconvenience for doing it or feel tired. Since the males are the chief earners, their wishes must be honoured.

If the women themselves make some economic contribution to the family, is there any alteration in the situation ? Who decides then what would be the menu for the day — the husband or the wife or both of them acting conjointly ? Is their any difference between the cases of loanee-women and the cases of non-loanee-women in this regard ?

The data in Row 4 of Table 6.1 evince that there is a difference between loanee and non-loanee-women in the matter of women's participation in decision-making with regard to the daily menu, and the difference is statistically significant. The data in Row 4 of Table 6.1 show that in the two categories where women take decisions in the matter, solely and primarily as well as in the category of women who take decisions jointly with their husbands, the percentage of the loanee-women is higher than that of the non-loanee-women. Thus 10% of the loanee-women fall in the first category, i.e., the category of women who take decisions solely on their own whereas only 4% of the non-loanee-women fall in the category. Again, while 11% of the loanee-women are found to fall in the category of women who primarily take the decision, only 6% of the loanee-women are found in that category. Again, 41% of the loanee-women are found to take decisions together with their husbands and the corresponding percentage figure for the non-loanee-women is 26 only. The percentage figures on the other side of the scale, as the data in Row 4 of Table 6.1 show, demonstrate the relatively subservient condition of the non-loanee-women, while 40% of the loanee-women fall in the categories of women whose husbands primarily or solely take decisions in the matter, the corresponding figure for the non-lonaee women is 64%.

The researcher has come to learn from a larger number of loanee-women during the interview that they are at present enjoying a greater share of decision-making power in deciding the menu and the cuisine than earlier, that is to say, when they did not engage in any economic pursuit by taking loan from the Grameen Bank. As they have work now to do in relation to their economic venture, they cook the food according to their convenience, and their husbands concede to what they decide. They have to go to attend the weekly meeting arranged by the local *kendro* of the Grameen Bank. Also, they have to go from time to time to the local branch office of the Bank for collecting money and to the *kendro* for other purposes. On these days, they have to shorten the time for cooking and their husbands generally accept their decisions regarding the number and nature of items to be cooked. On the other hand, a large majority of the non-loanee-women have informed that they hardly get any opportunity to take independent decision regarding the menu and cuisine. Whatever their husbands bring from the market, will have to be cooked by them. Their husbands scarcely seek their opinion in the matter. Of course, a small number of non-loanee-women have told the researcher that their husbands talk to them about the vegetables and other ingredients of food to be brought from the market. But their opinions do not weigh much. A few non-loanee-women have confided in the researcher that their husbands do not hesitate to beat them if the preparation is not to their liking. From the interview it has been evident that the loanee-women participate in decision making in relation to menu and cuisine in daily life to a greater extent than the non-loanee-women. The husbands of the former show greater consideration for their views and conveniences in comparison with what the husbands of the non-loanee-women do in relation to them.

During the interview however, one fact has been very clear. Both the loanee-women and the non-loanee-women show deference to the liking and requirement of their husbands. Women of both the groups try to satisfy the tastes of their husbands. Whatever little amount of tasty and good food becomes available, it is given by women of both the groups to their husbands and other male members in the household. Many loanee-women have told the researcher that it is not true that they always cook and prepare food according to their own choice. They do listen to what their husbands suggest to them regarding the dishes to be prepared. It happens many times that they prepare food with whatever their husbands bring from the market. Of course, their husbands now consider their difficulties and inconveniences. The husbands appreciate the fact that they cannot afford being fastidious regarding the menu or the cuisine, when their wives engage in gainful employment and contribute economically to the family.

A comparison between the loanee and the non-loanee groups of women in terms of their participation in decision-making in relation to expenditure on children's items such as gifts, toys, snacks, etc. has been presented in Row 5 of Table 6.1. A statistically significant (significant at.05 level) difference between the two groups of women have been found in this regard. The data in the Row shows that whereas 49% of the loanee group of women participate in decision making equally with their husbands, only 38% of the non-loanee-women enjoy this capacity. Again, while in the case of only 16% of women of the loanee-group, their husbands (solely or along with members of the family) or other members of the family take the decisions in this matter, the corresponding figure for the non-loanee group is 42%. It means that while 16% of the loanee-women are denied any say in deciding the expenditure on children's items, 42% of the non-loanee-women have no say in the matter.

In their face-to-face interview with the researcher the loanee-women have stated that their economic contribution to their family through gainful employment with the loan from the Grameen Bank has added to the economic well-being of their respective families and has also given a modicum of decision-making power to them in relation to the purchase of different items for their children. The non-loanee-women have, on the other hand, regretted that they hardly get any opportunity to take decisions in relation to buying items for their children.

The data in Row 6 of Table 6.1 suggest that the difference between the loanee-women and non-loanee-women in the matter of taking decisions expenses on food has been statistically significant at.05 level. One may infer from it the existence of an association between the earning of a separate income by the loanee-women and the greater power of decision-making in relation to expenses on food than their non-loanee counterparts.

The interpretation of the phenomenon, as the researcher's interview with the respondents suggests, appears to be similar with the interpretations given in course of discussion of the data in Rows 2, 3, 5.

The data in Row 6 show that so far as loanee-women are concerned in 9% cases the loanee-women take decisions solely on their own in this matter and in 15% cases decisions are taken "Primarily" by them. The corresponding percentage figures in case of non-loanee-women are 2 and 6 respectively.

Further, while in one-fourth (25%) of cases of loanee-women it is the husbands who take decisions solely on their own regarding expenses on food, in nearly half (44%) of cases of non-loanee the husbands take decisions solely on their own.

One may find here some variation between the findings of Row 6 and those of Row 1. The researcher should mention here that the respondents have told her during the interview that most of families of their category live from hand to mouth. They hardly make any budget for purchasing food articles on a monthly or annual basis. And, in such a situation, it is the husbands who go to the market and purchase whatever food they can afford. The families partly engaged in agriculture or having small plots of land which are tilled may get food cereals with which they can maintain themselves for a month or two only. But, beyond that, they just eke out a living. And in such circumstances it is the husbands, who are the only or chief earners, that take decisions regarding the expenses to be made by the family on food.

However, when women have a separate earning, they may, as the loanee-women have told the researcher, have some liquid cash with them. And, with this money they may buy food articles from other village women who sell the same at a relatively cheap price out of financial distress.

Sometimes, they even buy poultry with the money they may have at hand because of their separate income. For obvious reasons, their husbands do not grumble the taking of decisions by the wives in such cases. But the non-loanee-women are denied this kind of power as they do not have any separate income of their own.

Row 7 in Table 6.1 offers a comparative picture of loanee and non-loanee-women in respect of the capacity to take decisions on expenditure for buying things for other members of the family, e.g., parents-in-law, sisters-in-law, brothers-in-law, etc. It is striking to note that the item considered in the row is not applicable in case of an overwhelming majority of the respondents (71% in case of the loanee group and 76% in case of the non-loanee group), since the requirement of buying things for members of the family, other than one's husbands and own children, arises only when the respondents live in a non-nuclear family and most of the respondents in both the groups live in nuclear families (vide Table 5.3, p.141. No statistically significant difference is found between the groups of loanee-women and non-loanee-women in this respect. If the number of respondents is too small,it is generally very difficult to ascertain the existence of statistically significant difference between two groups under comparison, particularly with the help of X^2 test.

Most of the respondents in both the groups have, however, informed the researcher, in course of the interview, that they themselves do not take decisions regarding the purchase of clothes or other articles for other members of the family. Since these members are either the parents, siblings or other relatives of their husbands, and since the husbands are the chief earners and heads of the families, these women leave the matter to their husbands.

It seems natural that the husbands will take most favorable decisions in relation to their own relatives in the matter of buying clothes and other articles for them. And, it is customary for the women to accept their husbands' decision. For, the wives' disagreement with their husbands in this matter may be seriously misunderstood. It may be mistaken for their narrow-mindedness. Of course, the figures in Row 7 show that 7% of the loanee-women who economically contribute to the family fall in the category of wives who take decisions solely on their own in this matter and another 7% of them fall in the category of wives who primarily take decision in this matter, whereas not a single non-loanee woman is found in either of these two categories.

Every family has to buy various articles for daily use, i.e., glassware or china wares, vessels for cooking, bed sheets, pillow covers, etc. In the villages, hawkers go from door to door selling these articles. But who takes decisions regarding the purchase of such sundry articles ? Do the women have any capacity to take decisions in this regard ? Generally, the males are the chief earners and it is the males who take decisions in relation to what is to be purchased. Women are generally denied any effective say in this matter since they cannot earn any money. But if the women or wives have some independent earning and make some financial contribution to their families, do they get the authority to take decisions regarding the articles to be purchased ? Can they buy any article independently of their husbands ? Row 8 in Table 6.1 throws some light on the questions stated above. The data in Row 8 evince a statistically significant difference between the loanee and the non-loanee-women in respect of their ability to take decisions regarding the purchase of sundry articles for the household. The data in the Row show that 7% of the loanee-women take decisions solely on their own and 11% of loanee-women primarily take decisions in this matter and the corresponding percentage figures for the non-loanee-women are 2% and 6% respectively. On the other hand, while 13% of the loanee-women are denied any say in making decisions in the matter, 32% of the non-loanee-women suffer from the denial. All this indicates that the loanee-women exercise a relatively larger degree of discretion in this respect than the non-loanee-women.

The loanee-women have told the researcher at the time of interview that earlier they hardly had any sum at their disposal. They themselves did not have any independent source of income, nor did their husbands keep any money with them. So they could not purchase any commodity independently of their husbands. But now they have an independent source of income and have a small amount of money at their disposal. Also their husbands repose confidence in them and keep a portion of their own earnings with their wives, i.e., these loanee respondents. Now, if a hawker comes to them with an appeal to buy some articles, they themselves take decisions in the matter or they take decisions together with their husbands. Further, if they make a purchase without the prior consent of their husbands, the husbands do not at all take any exception if the purchase made by them bears a semblance of reasonableness.

When it comes to the question of buying articles of a relatively large size and price, e.g., a chair or a table, 46% of the loanee respondents enjoy equality with their husbands regarding the power of decision-making. But the corresponding percentage for the non-loanee-women is lower than that —— it is 34% only.

From these one may infer that there is an association between the separate source of earning of women and their financial contribution to the family on the one hand and their ability to participate in decision-making in relation to the purchase of sundry articles useful for the family.

Item number 9 or, more precisely, Row 9 in Table 6.1 presents information regarding a respondent's ability to take decisions regarding the purchase of clothes for herself. Where the men are the chief earners and where women's position is subservient to them, the men or husbands generally make decisions regarding the purchase of various articles for the family, including the *sarees* for their wives. Women's own choice in this matter hardly gets any due consideration for, who would give the money for buying the *saree* chosen by a housewife ? It is her husband who will have to pay for it. It is, therefore, deemed natural that the males or husbands will take the decision regarding the purchase of the *sarees* for their wives. But a *saree* or a piece of garment is not only an article for use, it has got an aesthetic and emotional appeal. A woman's taste is associated with the *saree* she would wear. But, here too, she is denied the right of taking decision because she herself does not earn any money. What, if a woman herself has an independent source of income ? Is then there any alteration in the situation depicted above ? The data in the Row 9 give some idea about it.

The data reveal that there is a statistically significant difference between the loanee group of women and the non-loanee group of women in relation to a woman's participation in decision making in relation to purchase of clothes for her own self. Whereas 25% of the loanee-women can decide solely on their own in this matter, only 8% of the non-loanee-women enjoy this freedom. Again, while 23% of the loanee-women are denied any voice in this sphere (their husbands and / or other elderly members of their respective families take decision on their behalf), the corresponding figure for non-loanee-women is as high as 44%. One may, therefore, infer from the above that the difference between loanee and non-loanee-women is substantial in this regard.

The association between the gain in the power of the loanee earning women in the capacity for taking decisions relating to the purchase of clothing for themselves and their earning and economic contribution to the family, as is evident from the above, has been explained by the loanee-women during the interview with the researcher in terms of their newly acquired purchasing power after their gainful employment. Earlier, if the hawker or vendor of *sarees* and other dress materials approached them to buy their goods, they could not buy them simply because they had no money with them. Their choices were inconsequential. But now they have some money of their own and their husbands also, in many instances, keep their (husbands' own) earnings at their (wives) disposal. Thus, they can buy the *sarees* or clothes of their choice on cash or on credit. Their husbands do not object much to their purchase of clothes of their own choice.

Certain loanee-women here stated that earlier husbands did not buy them *sarees* even if their *sarees* were old and torn, not to speak of buying them *sarees* of their (the women's) own choice. It is not that their husbands always deliberately ignored their needs but that they could not buy new *sarees* because of paucity of money. But now their husbands themselves try to bring *sarees* for these loanee respondents and even though they themselves buy the *sarees*, they are eager to see that the wives feel happy to get the *sarees* bought by them.

On festive occasions, the husbands buy their wives even relatively costly *sarees*. The loanee-women attribute the change to the better economic condition of the family which has been brought by their separate income and economic contribution to the family.

Another phenomenon which may be interesting for a student of sociology has been revealed by the loanee respondents during the interview. In the Muslim society, there is a great deal of emphasis on women's modesty, decorum and good manners, which is, according to these respondents reflected in the use of *sarees* and other dress materials adequately covering their body and particularly in the use of *burquah* covering the face or *purdah*. These loanee respondents have stated that now with their separate income they can buy adequate clothing including *burquah*. So they are now in a better position than earlier to observe and maintain etiquette and modesty understood in the traditional sense. It is, they think, wrong to suppose that women's engagement in economic pursuits with loan from the Grameen Bank interferes with their dignity and decorum and good manners. The fact is rather the other way round. Because of the gainful employment through the assistance from the Grameen Bank, these women assisted by this particular branch (Panchdona Branch) of the Grameen Bank can afford now the purchase of *sarees*, *blouses*, *petticoats* etc. But earlier in the absence of the economic means for buying these, they had to move out without *burquahs* and this irked the elderly members of the family and the neighborhood. To go to the market area where the Branch Office of the Grameen Bank is situated without *burquah* meant the initiation of serious criticism for their husbands' and themselves.

The Manager of the local Panchdona Branch Office of the Grameen Bank has been perspicuous enough to appreciate the difficulty experienced by the Muslim women to visit the Branch Office situated in the market place and laid down the stipulation that the loanee-women would come to use a *burquah* to come to the Branch Office, so that the women should not face any criticism. The use of *burquah* has, they think, in a sense enhanced their freedom to move to different places, since the use of *burquah* conceals their identity and they can avoid the rustic criticism of their movement outside their families and respective villages.

Mothers have the primary responsibility of looking after the comforts and well being of the children since they are assigned the task of housekeeping. Children's education is considered an important part of their well being in a Muslim family of low income group in Bangladesh. Does a mother have any say in this matter ? Does she make decisions regarding the admission of children into schools ? Or, does the father, who is the sole earner and chief provider of finance in the family, of a child take decision solely on his own in the matter without any consultation with the child's mother ? What happens if a woman has an independent source of earning and makes economic contribution to the family ? Does her economic contribution to the family enable her to take decision solely on her own in the matter? Is there any difference in this matter between the women who economically contribute to the family and the women who do not ? Row 10 in Table 6.1 presents data which throw light on questions like the ones mentioned above.

In a patriarchal system the husband is the chief earner in the family and he is the head of the household. Naturally, it is he who takes decision in all important matters including the building of the house or repair of the same. Though the families to which the respondents belong live, generally, in houses of mud walls and thatched roofs or roofs of tin sheets, the cost of repairing and building such a house seems to be high for the class of people to which these families belong. Obviously, provision of money for building or repairing of the house is an important consideration and it is the male members or husbands who have to think about it. And, the question of consultation with the wives (who do not have any independent source of income) by the husbands generally does not arise.

But if the women economically contribute to the family, does the situation alter ? Row 10 in the Table 6.1 offers data regarding it. The data in Row 10 show that there is a statistically significant difference (at.05 level) between loanee and non-loanee-women in the matter of taking decisions regarding the expenses incurred for repairing or building of their houses.

On examination of the data in Row 10 it becomes clear that while 6% of the loanee-women have the power of taking decisions regarding the matter solely on their own, not a single non-loanee woman has reported the enjoyment of this privilege.

On the other hand, whereas in cases of 18% of the loanee-women, their husbands have made the decisions solely on their own, the corresponding percentage figure for non-loanee-women is 46%, i.e., in case of 46% of the non-loanee-women, it is their husbands who take the decision in the matter solely on their own, or, in other words, without consulting their wives.

From her interview with the respondents the researcher has come to learn several important facts related to the phenomenon above. 25 loanee-women have informed that they themselves are the owners of houses they live in and these houses have been constructed with loan from the Grameen Bank. Their legal ownership of these houses has become possible because of an important stipulation of the Grameen Bank for advancing loans for "house building" the members. The stipulation is that the plot of land on which the house would be constructed with loan from the Grameen Bank must be owned by the recipient of the loan. Loan for house building will not be granted to a woman who herself is not the owner of the site of construction of the house and the house itself. Along with this legal ownership of these houses these women come to experience that their husbands show due consideration to their views at the time of construction of the houses.

Nine loanee-women have informed that they have received loan from the Grameen Bank for repairing the houses they live in. All these loanee-women have told the researcher that they get a lot of useful construction and detailed information and suggestions regarding the construction of houses from the Manager and other employees of the Branch office of the Grameen Bank, to which they are attached. Their husbands show keen interest in information and suggestions of this kind. They, therefore, eagerly listen to what they (i.e., these loanee-women) say. The latter get a lot of importance in the process of making decisions regarding the construction of houses. Further, while a loanee woman goes to the meetings held in the *kendra* of the Grameen Bank to which she is related, she gathers from her information talks with those ladies whose houses have been constructed or under construction many useful tips regarding the ways how to reduce the cost of construction of or best utilize the available resources. They convey these tips to their husbands who seem to be deeply interested in them. The husbands of the loanee-women want to share the information and views which they offer.

By contrast, a good number of non-loanee-women have deplored the fact that they hardly make any contribution towards the cost of construction or repair of the houses. And, their husbands do not in general attach much importance to their views at the time of construction or repair of the houses. Also, they do not, like the loanee-women, get the information and opinion from any source outside home regarding the ways of reducing costs of construction or repair of the houses or of better utilization of the available resources. They do not have, like the loanee-women, the opportunity to go to places outside their homes.

One may note here the experience of some of the loanee-women in this matter. They themselves have told the researcher that earlier, i.e., when they did not have any contact with the Grameen Bank, they did not know a lot of facts regarding the construction or repair of the houses. They could learn those things from the Branch Office or the *kendra* of the Grameen Bank.

The data in Row 11 show that there is a statistically significant difference (at.02 level) between the loanee-women and the non-loanee-women in the matter of making decisions regarding the admission of children into schools.

So far as the question of women's taking decisions on the matter solely on their own is concerned, there is hardly any difference between the loanee and the non-loanee-women. But in case of taking decisions by women jointly with their husbands in this matter there is a striking difference between the two categories. Whereas 56% of the loanee-women take decisions regarding the admission of their children into the school, only 28% of the non-loanee-women take decisions jointly with their husbands in this matter. When one views it from the other side, one finds that in case of only 20% of the loanee-women, their husbands take decisions in the matter solely on their own, i.e., without consulting the respondents. The corresponding percentage figure for non-loanee-women is 42%, i.e., in case of 42% of the non-loanee-women, their husbands take decisions solely on their own in the matter.

One may note here the findings of the study by I.Rahman who has found in her study that in terms of their vision of education of their sons and daughters, "Few women from the loanee group expected that their sons or daughters, would remain illiterate or would leave school before completing the primary level. Among the non-loanee landless group a much larger percentage thought that their sons and daughters would not go above primary level (I. Rahman, 1986, p. 71).

Raj Mohini Sethi, however, finds that women's "dominant participation in economic activities does not give them a dominant role in decision making. The data on Sethi's survey of Indian women show that "in taking decisions on education and admission of children in schools, in selecting an occupation or a mate for children, expenditure on children's marriages, and the observance of ritual and social ceremonies, women participate along with other men in the household; *only seven to ten percent women take such decisions independently of men*" (Shethi, 1989, p. 228, emphases added).

Many loanee respondents of the present study have informed the researcher during the interview that earlier, i.e., when they did not have any independent source of earning and therefore could not financially contribute to the family, they could not think of sending their children to the schools because of poverty. They could not insist on their husbands' initiative and action in getting the children admitted in some school. Quite a few of them mention, with a note of regret, the cases of the elder children in the family, who could not get the opportunity for admission in a school. True, poverty was a major reason behind it. But at the same time, these loanee-women admitted, they could not then appreciate the importance of education.

Nor did they have the idea that education could be provided to the children at a cost which they could afford, and that there were several avenues for education of the children of the poor people.

After their contact with the Grameen Bank they came to appreciate the significance of children's education. One of the conditions of eligibility for receipt of loan from the Grameen Bank is that the person desirous of taking the loan must have the ability to sign his / her name. The Grameen Bank does not provide loans to someone who cannot write his / her name in the application form. Many of these women were illiterate and they could learn how to write their names, with the training offered by the workers of the Bank.

While organising the group of prospective clients, the Bank workers train them how to write their names. At that time the women realized their infirmity. They had regrets for their inability and resolved to do something for their children so that the latter should not suffer from the same handicap as they had to. They decided to send their children to school so that the children could learn the three R's and, if possible, to advance further.

The rules, and regulations, of the Grameen Bank contain what is known as Sholo Siddhanta or Sixteen Decisions which the loanee-women pledge to observe. One of them is that, the seventh resolution states, "We shall educate our children————" (See Fuglesang and Chandler, 1986, p.127; Afsar, 1989, note 12 in p.233). Women in different *kendras* prepare and repeat *slogans* in tune with the Sixteen Decisions. For instance, the loanee respondents considered in the sample repeat in their weekly meetings the following *slogan*, "I shall get my children educated up to class XVI [i.e., M.A/M.Sc].

This, probably, has strongly motivated the loanee-women to take steps for sending their children to schools. That if the children acquire formal academic qualification, they will get better job opportunities. The Grameen Bank also may help them in getting employment or self employment.

Earlier these loanee-women were eager to get their daughters marry off as early as possible and were not at all interested in their education. But from their association with the Grammen Bank and its staff, they now appreciate the importance of school education in a girl's life. Once girls have education, they may find some opportunity for employment and face the threat of *talaq* by their husbands. Also, these women expect that the problem of dowry (payment of money and / or valuables by a bride's parents in her marriage) would not be that severe, if the girls have some educational qualification. All these facts and ideas have been learnt by these women from their association with the Grameen Bank and are conveyed by them to their husbands. These ideas have also been new to the husbands. They, therefore, listen to these loanee-women and discuss the problems of children's education with them. The husbands duly consider the views of the wives at the time of taking decisions on the matter, and in many cases make the decisions jointly with the wives. This has happened after the loanee-women started their independent earning with loan from the Grameen Bank. For, the loanee-women themselves point out that they were devoid of any power in this sphere when they did not have any income of their own. If they have insisted that the children should be sent to the school, their husbands either paid no heed to them, or pleaded their inability to send the children to the school, because of poverty. These loanee-women mention the cases of their grown - up children whom they could not send to school. But now they have some earnings and contribute a little of it towards the cost of education of their children. Also, they now know that the government has taken many steps for the education of the children of the poor. Besides this, if the family of a loanee woman cannot afford even the minimum cost of education of children, the Grameen Bank has arrangements for imparting lessons to the children.

In spite of all this, one fact, which has already been noted, remains. The percentage of loanee-women as well as non-loanee-women, who takes decision solely on their own on this matter, is negligible. Of course, there is a substantial difference between the percentages of loanee and non-loanee-women enjoying the privilege of making decisions jointly with their husbands. A greater number of the former get considerations of their views by their husbands than the latter. And, the former have informed the researcher that they enjoy this privilege more at present than earlier, i.e., the time when they did not have any independent earning of their own.

In countries like Bangladesh, it is not generally possible for the teachers in schools, even at the primary stage, to give individual attention to the learners. The teacher-student ratio is highly unfavorable for extending attention by the teacher to the individual needs of a particular student. A teacher has to look after a large number of students in a class. What is possible, under the circumstances, is, at best, to encourage parroting of the lessons by the students. Even this cannot be done properly because of the noise and lack of congenial atmosphere, which are created by the sheer presence of an unmanageable number of children in one room. Lack of equipment like blackboard, etc., irregularity in attendance of the teachers, etc., make the situation more problematic. Hence whatever little is learnt in the school requires reinforcement by repetition of the lessons at home. But if the guardians themselves are illiterate or very poorly educated, it may not be possible for them to help the children in this process. If they themselves do not have adequate knowledge, how would they detect whether the children's spelling of words is correct or whether the answers they have found to the sums worked out by them are correct. Indeed, it is a very serious problem for the literate in the first generation, which is really quite large in Bangladesh. Under these circumstances the children may require private tutors to guide their study at home. But do the mothers, even if they appreciate the need for private tutors for their children, have any power to take decisions on the matter ? Row 12 in Table 6.1 offers the data relevant for an answer to the question.

The data in the Row show that the difference between the loanee-women and the non-loanee-women in the matter of taking decision on the question of appointing private tutors for the children has been statistically significant at.02 level.

A closer look at the data reveals that 11% of the loanee-women take decision on the matter solely on their own. But only 2% of the non-loanee-women take decisions relating to this matter solely on their own. From the reverse side, i.e., enjoyment of the power of making decisions on the matter by the husbands solely on their own, in case of 13% of the loanee-women the decisions are taken by the husbands independently and in case of 30% of non-loanee-women this fact of decision-making by the husbands independently or any body else, is observed. Further, nearly a half (more precisely, 48%) of the loanee-women take decisions on the matter jointly with their husbands. But the corresponding percentage figure for the non-loanee-women is 37. An association between the women's independent earning and economic contribution to the family on the one hand, and their ability to take decisions on the question of appointing private tutors for children's studies at home, is thus clearly visible.

There is a similarity between what the loanee-women have told the researcher during the interview in detailing their experience in the matter with what they have pointed out in course of discussion of the issue highlighted in Row 11. Regarding decision-making in relation to appointment of tutors for children's studies at home these loanee-women observe that with their economic contribution to the family, there has been an improvement in the economic condition of the family. Earlier they did not properly appreciate the importance of the education of the children. And, even if they felt the need for children's education and also the need for engaging private tutors for helping them in their studies at home, their husbands pleaded inability because of poor financial condition of the family. But now they appreciate the need for children's education. They also feel the necessity of appointing private tutors for helping the children's studies. They do not have the capacity to detect the errors committed by their children while preparing their homeworks. If the children do not properly complete the "homeworks", they cannot control them. They cannot answer many questions raised by their children. So they now try to impress upon their husbands to engage tutors for helping the children prepare their lessons properly and correctly. They now contribute a little to the funds of the family and can pursuade their husbands to accept their suggestions.

If it is not possible for a woman and her husband to appoint a private tutor who would come to their residence to help their children, in that case they find alternatives on those neighbours who are comparatively well informed and look after the studies of their own children and along with them the studies of the children of others. The parents of the latter pay a small amount for their service.

The loanee-women have another advantage. If they do not find anybody to help the studies of their children at home, they get help in the matter from the teacher who is available in the *kendra* of the Grameen Bank, to which she is attached.

The non-loanee-women have, on the other hand, informed the researcher that they do not have any independent source, of income. Even if they feel that their children require tutors to help their studies at home, they cannot insist on their husbands' appointing the same. The husbands would simply express their inability to do so because of paucity of money. And, the loanee-women have, therefore, hardly anything to do in the matter.

Mothers may try to retain the daughters in the school nearby since, in that case, they can have the service of their daughters to perform the domestic chores. Thus even if the options are limited, there is a scope for choice by the parents for the school where the children should be admitted into. But the question is who takes decisions on the matter. Is it the father irrespective of the fact that the mother? too, contributes economically to the family ? Or is it the mother, particularly, when she makes financial contributions to the family ? Do the husband and wife take the decision jointly? Is this joint decision by the couple in any way associated with wives' independent earning and economic contribution to the family ?

Row 13 in Table 6.1 presents data which are relevant to the questions above. The data show that the difference between the loanee-women and the non-loanee-women has not been statistically significant in the matter of taking decisions on the selection of the school to which the children should be admitted. The percentage of women who take decisions on the matter solely on their own is negligible.

The respondents of both the groups——loanee and non-loanee ——have informed the researcher that they do not enjoy as much freedom of movement outside home as their husbands do. Since the husbands have contacts with the world outside home, it is easy for them to get information as to the schools where good teachers are available and / or the students who have access to different equipment necessary for learning various subjects as well as other facilities. The relatively restricted movement of women stands in the way of their getting information on several aspects of school education, available for the children. Hence, they depend on their husbands rather than take decisions solely on their own in the matter. What is noteworthy is that there is a statistically significant difference between the loanee and non-loanee-women in the matter of taking decisions on the question of sending children to the school. The loanee-women economically contribute to the family and they can pursuade their husbands to send the children to the school, if the latter plead inability to meet the cost of education of the children. But decision (by a man or woman) on the particular school in which a boy / girl should be admitted requires a lot of information which may not be readily available to one whose movement is restricted or who enjoys freedom of movement to a limited extent only. Most of the loanee-women have told the researcher at the time of interview that they enjoy less freedom of movement than their husbands.

There are other issues also on which mothers alone

cannot take any decision. For example, if the question of getting a girl admitted into a school which is at a distance from her home and / or is situated in a place which is in close proximity to a market place or business center the girl's father will not leave the matter to the girl's mother. Though he may consult his wife, he will at the same time consult his relatives who may or may not reside with him, his friends and neighbors, and then take a decision on the issue. The data in Row 14 of Table 6.1 reveal that the difference between the loanee-women and the non-loanee-women in the matter of taking decisions regarding the extent of children's education has been statistically significant at.05 level. More precisely, the difference is found to be statistically significant at.02 level).

A closer look at the data shows that while only 2% of the non-loanee-women claim to take decisions solely on their own in this matter, 7% of the loanee-women report that they take decision solely on their own, i.e., the percentage of loanee-women is three times higher than that of the non-loanee-women.

On the other hand, in case of 17% of the loanee-women, the husbands are reported to be taking decisions solely on their own (i.e., without caring for the opinion of the women). But in case of non-loanee-women, the corresponding percentage is 42%.

The finding in Row 14 is in consonance with what is revealed in three preceding rows, viz., Rows 11, 12 and 13. The loanee respondents have informed the researcher during the interview that earlier, i.e., when they did not have any separate income, they were dependent on and subsequent to their husbands who only earned the means of livelihood of the family. But now, when these women have started making a separate income, they have a say in how for a child will prosecute its studies.

The husband in such a family does not have to bear the sole financial responsibility for running the household and the wife shares the responsibility to a certain extent. Concomitantly with this phenomenon, the husband no longer enjoys the monopoly of the power to take decisions regarding the extent to which the children in the family should pursue their studies in educational institutions and the wife has come to have a much greater say in the matter than before. The loanee-women have further pointed out that earlier, when their husbands were the only earners in the families, the families could not afford the luxury of spending money for children's education. Engaging the children, particularly the male children, in petty jobs of all sorts where from some income would be earned for the family was more important. Education for girls was not at all considered, since girls were regarded as a veritable burden.

But women's contribution to the income of the family has lessened to an extent the burden of want in the family. Now, a family, where the wife also has a separate income can afford to spend some money for children's education. And, the loanee-women have told the researcher, there is a two-ofld change in the aspiration of the family regarding the future of the children. First, children with a better education will be better placed in life and therefore they should be allowed to study as far as practicable and the family should spend for their studies. Secondly, the wives making financial contribution to the family have come to appreciate the potentialities of girls for attaining a much better status in life than what is granted to them by the hide-bound gradation of the patriarchal society. They themselves try to do what they can for their daughter's education and also can pursued their husbands to do the needful.

And, the earning wives or women have a much greater say in decisions regarding the extent of education of children-male or female in the family because they can a to degree financially support their decisions.

Marriages, in tradition bound societies like the Muslim society of Bangladesh, are almost invariably arranged marriages or negotiated marriages as distinguished from those marriages where the prospective bride and the prospective groom themselves choose each other and take decision on marriage. In the former variety of marriages, negotiations regarding the wedlock of a girl with a man take place between the respective guardians of the girl and the man. It is the guardians who discuss the pros and cons and take the decisions. The prospective partners themselves do not have, in most of these cases, any important role. The guardians' decisions are final. And, in a male - dominated society, it is the male guardians who take the ultimate decisions. Since the males are the chief providers of the family, they claim the monopoly on decisions regarding the well-being of the children, their present and future affairs including their marriage. The female members of the family, the mothers, do a whole lot of things for the comfort and well-being of all the members of the family including the children, though they do not make independent earnings and economically contribute to the family. But in matters vitally affecting the interests of the children including their marriage, mothers often demand the power of making the final decisions.

Now if the wives economically contribute to the family, is there any alteration of the situation ? That is to say, do they then enjoy any significant role in negotiating children's marriage - can they take decisions in such matters ? Row 15 in Table 6.1 presents data regarding this phenomenon. It reveals that there is no statistically significant difference between the loanee-women and the non-loanee-women in the matter of negotiating children's marriages. What is interesting is that not a single woman in either the category of the loanee-women or in the category of the non-loanee-women who takes decisions solely on their own, in negotiations on their children's marriage. Of course, while 56% of the loanee-women have participated along with their husbands in deciding the final outcome of the negotiations, the corresponding percentage figure for the women of the non-loanee group is 43%.

As to the relative incapacity of the women (of both the loanee and the non-loanee groups) in comparison with the husbands and / or male members of the family in conducting negotiations on children's marriage or taking final decisions thereto, a good number of respondents have informed the researcher during the interview that the father of the children or other elderly members in the family, related to the children's father, e.g., grandfather or elderly uncles of the children, are considered the *murubbi* or guardians of the family. It is they who make decisions regarding the families to which the daughters or sons should be given in marriage. And, women themselves think that this is only natural in view of the constraints on the free movement of women. In many cases proposals come from villages which are situated at a great distance from the natal village of the prospective bride or groom. Women generally cannot and do not visit the families in villages situated at a distance. Obviously, for relevant information regarding the prorspective bride or the groom or her / his family, women have to depend on their husbands or other male members of their family, who actually go to the place of the prospective bride / groom. It is the male members who actually go to call on or interview that would-be daughter-in-law or son-in-law and the female members hardly accompany them.

As a result, they cannot participate in negotiations and they have to depend on the information provided by the male members and also the decisions made by the latter. There is hardly any scope for women for making decisions independently of their husbands or male members. Of course, many of these women are consulted by their husbands and / or other male members of the family at the time of taking final decisions. Further, many loanee-women have told the researcher that they can veto the decision of the husbands / other male members in this matter, if the decision is not to their liking. And, a number of non-loanee-women also have stated that they, too, have this power to veto. In fine, as it transpires from the interviews, in decision-making in this important aspect of life in the family, the males dominate and the women are denied any independent power irrespective of their ability to economically contribute to the family and an important fact associated with it lies in women's inability to move freely.

A matter related to the above phenomenon is manifested in the sphere of making decisions regarding expenses on children's marriage. Row 16 of Table 6.1 focuses on that. As it is evident from the data in Row 16, there is no statistically significant difference between the loanee and non-loanee-women in the matter of taking decisions regarding the expenses on children's marriage. Since the males are the chief earners or even sole earners in a family, their dominant role in making decisions regarding the expenses to be incurred during the marriage of a child of the family, is hardly questioned. For, ultimately, it is the husband or male earners who will have to provide the necessary sum. But, if women, too, economically contribute, they will, it is expected, have the power of taking decisions in the matter.

The data of Row 16 of Table 6.1 however, show that not a single loanee woman has the capacity for taking decision in the matter solely on her own and the picture is the same with the non-loanee-women.

The data evince that whereas in case of 61% of the loanee-women, decisions are taken jointly by the husbands and the wives, it happens in case of only 43% of non-loanee-women. Further, in case of only 15% of loanee-women, husbands take decisions in the matter solely on their own, i.e., without any consultation with their wives. In case of 32% of non-loanee-women, husbands do not consult their wives regarding this matter and take decisions solely on their own.

A sizable section of loanee-women has informed the researcher during the interview that now they make some economic contribution to the family and their husbands consult them regarding the expenses to be incurred during the marriage, as well as the amount of dowry that is to be offered to the groom's party (in case of marriages of daughters) or the amount to be demanded from the bride's party (in case of marriages of sons).

However, the majority of women of both the categories of respondents have told the researcher that it is the husband / male members who conduct the negotiations and take final decisions regarding the marriages of the children of the family. As a result, expenses to be incurred by either the groom's side or the bride's side are decided on by these male members. Though in some cases the women are consulted, the final decision lies, for all practical purposes, with the husband / other male members of the family.

Use of health care services for self and the family is a very important aspect of family life. It involves the expenditure of money, time and energy. A certain kind of gender-bias is reflected in the actual behavior of the families dominated by males and patriarchal values. Generally, the females' need for health care is undermined. In case of children, male children enjoy a better treatment than female children in this regard. Gender-bias is reflected also in women's lack of power to take decisions in relation to the selection of health institutions where children, other members of the family, and women themselves would be treated in case of their sickness. Since women's role is limited mainly to that of a housewife and since they are denied any contact with the world outside their families, they presumably lack in the knowledge of the available people in the profession of medicine or the types or varieties of medical care available. So they have to depend on the males/husbands for the decisions regarding the medical man or institution to whom or where the children, or the women themselves or other members of their families will go for treatment in the eventuality of their sickness or illness. But, if the women themselves start earning independently and economically contribute to the family, does the situation become different ? Do, then, the women themselves get the power of taking decisions in the matter? Rows 17, 18 and 19 in Table 6.1 throw light on the question.

Row 17 presents the data relating to the taking of decisions regarding the type of medical personnel and institutions to be approached for the treatment of their sickness. Looking after the household and particularly the children, is the responsibility of the women or the mothers. Child's health is one of the major concerns of a mother. It is the mother in the family who more than anybody else in the family feels concerned with the ailment of the children. They have the best knowledge of the tastes and habits and normal health of the children as well as the deviation, if any, from them. And, information of these is vital in medical treatment of a child. Hence, it is expected that mothers' views would get importance in selecting the medicine man or medical institution for the treatment of sick children.

The data in Row 17 show, however, that in case of loanee-women only 5% of them take decisions solely on their own in this matter and the corresponding percentage figure for non-loanee-women is only 2%. In case of 31% of the loanee-women, it is their husbands who take the decision in the matter solely on their own, i.e., without any consultation with their wives. The percentage of non-loanee-women having a similar experience (i.e., the husbands take decisions in the matter solely on their own, or, in other words, without any consultation with them) is 46. The percentage figures of the loanee-women and the non-loanee-women who have the experience of taking decisions jointly with husbands regarding the issue under consideration are 45% and 40% respectively. In both the cases less than a half of the women enjoy the power of decision-making jointly with their husbands, and the proportion of women taking decisions solely on their own is very meager (5% and 2% respectively).

What is most important here is that, as the data in Row 17 demonstrate, there is no statistically significant (at.05 level) difference between the loanee and non-loanee-women in this matter. That is to say, women's economic contribution to the family is not accompanied by any significant difference in the above-mentioned situation which is marked by relative male domination.

Respondents of both the groups have informed the researcher at the time of interview that it is the father of the children who takes them to the medical practitioner in case of their illness. In most of the cases he goes to a Homeopath or a *Kaviraj* (an indigenous medicine man who administers herbal medicine prepared by himself in accordance with the principles laid down in the *Ayurveda*), since Homeopathic or *Kaviraji* medicine is much cheaper than allopathic medicine. The husband of a woman may consult his wife but in most of the cases his decision is final. Many a time it happens that a woman insists on her husband's consulting a medicine man for the treatment of her sick child. But if her husband favourably responds to her urging and decides to go to a medical professional, it is he who will take the child along with him to the doctor, the child's mother does not accompany the child. The child's father will collect information regarding the symptoms of the illness from the child's mother and will select medicine from the medicine man of his choice.

Row 18 of Table 6.1 seeks to examine whether there is any statistically significant difference between the loanee and the non-loanee-women in the matter of taking decisions regarding the selection of health or medical institution and / or the medicine man for the treatment of the members of the family, other than the children and the respondents themselves.

The data in Row 18 show that the difference between the loanee-women and non-loanee-women has not been statistically significant in this sphere.

A further scrutiny of the data reveals that there is not a single woman, in either the loanee group or the non-loanee group, who takes decision regarding this matter solely on her own. That is to say, a woman, whether she makes any independent earning and makes economic contribution to the family out of her independent earning or not, cannot take decision solely on her own regarding the place or person for the treatment of illness, her husband or any other member of the family, save her children and herself becomes ill.

Whereas in case of 35% of the loanee-women decisions are taken jointly by the wives and the husbands, it happens in case of 26% of the non-loanee-women.

Further, in case of 43% of the loanee-women, it is the husbands who take decisions solely on their own in this matter and the corresponding percentage figure for the non-loanee-women is 62%.

A sizable number of respondents have told the researcher during the interview that the husbands themselves take decisions regarding the medicine man to be consulted or regarding the institution they will go to in case they become ill. Some women have, of course, admitted that they are consulted by their husbands in cases like this.

In case of other members (i.e., members other than the

husband and the wife and their children) of a non-nuclear family it is the husbands or other members of the family who take the decisions. The opinions of the respondents hardly get any importance.

Row 19 of Table 6.1 explores whether there is any difference between the loanee-women and non-loanee-women in the matter of taking decisions regarding the selection of the medicine man or health institution to be approached for the treatment of their own sickness or illness. If a person who has attained majority falls sick or becomes ill, he / she will normally have the power to take decisions or power to which medical / professional or which medical / health institution, he/she should approach. Do the women in Muslim families in Bangladesh, which are dominated by patriarchal values, have this power ?

If the non-loanee-women who do not economically contribute to the family, are denied the power of decision - making in this matter do the loanee-women, who make economic contribution to the family, have this power ?

The data in Row 19 reveal that there is no statistically significant difference between the loanee-women and the non-loanee-women in the matter of taking decisions regarding the choice of medical personnel and health / medical institution for treatment of their illness.

The data further show that only 2% of the loanee-women take decisions solely on their own in this matter, while not a single woman in the non-loanee group enjoys this power of decision-making.

Only 31% of the loanee-women take decisions jointly with their husbands in this matter, whereas 24% of the non-loanee-women enjoy this power of taking decisions jointly with their husbands in selecting the appropriate medicine man or medical / health institution for the treatment of their own ailments.

40% of the loanee-women have reported that their

husbands take decisions solely on their own, i.e., without any consultation with the respondents, regarding the physician or medical / health institution for treatment of their illness, i.e., illness of the respondents. In 40% cases in the group of loanee-women, the loanee-women themselves are deprived of any say in the selection of the medicine man or health / medical institution for the treatment of their own illness. The corresponding percentage figure for the non-loanee-women is a bit higher than this, i.e., 52%.

The respondents of both the groups have confided in the researcher during the interview that they, generally, ignore their sickness and they do not go in for a physician or a health / medical institution until and unless their illness becomes serious. Many of them regretted that their husbands neglected their difficulties or ailments. They hardly give any importance to their sickness or illness. The women bear with even acute physical discomfort. When it becomes unbearable then and then only, they tell their husbands to bring medicines after consulting a medicine man.

But they have hardly any say as to which physician or which health clinic should be approached. They themselves do not, in most of the cases, go to a physician. It is the husbands, who decide the matter and go to the physician or institution / clinic. The wives tell their husbands the kind of difficulties they have and the husbands pass on that information to the physician and collect medicine from him. The husbands do not, generally, take their wives to the physician or health institution / clinic. The wives admit that that they lack in adequate information regarding the available physicians and medical or health institutions or clinics because they do not have sufficient contact with the world outside. Some of the loanee-women have told the researcher that they have a little bit of knowledge regarding the physicians or medical institutions that may be approached. But even then they themselves do not have the privilege to choose the physician or health / medical institution. They will have to approach their husbands for a decision in the matter and in most of the cases the husbands have the final say, though the latter may consider the views of the women and whatever information they may provide.

The findings presented in Rows 17, 18, 19 have a certain degree of similarity with the finding in Mizan's study (1992). Mizan's study, too, suggests paucity of significant association of the use by the women of health care services for self and the family and participation by them in the Grameen Bank. Her hypothesis that the Grameen Bank participants will have greater use of medical care when they are sick than the women who do not participate in the Grameen Bank, has not been borne out by the data of her study (1992, p. 189).

Table - 6.2

Loanee and Non-loanee Women, by Their Decision-Making on the Number of Children

Decision - making on the number of children	Loanee Women %	Non-loanee Women %
Entirely wife's	5	—
Equally that of husband and wife	44	42
Husband's sole prerogative	51	58
Total	100 (n = 92)	100 (n = 45)

X^2 = 3.72; df = 2; Not significant at.05 level.

Note : *Information in this regard has not been obtained from 8 loanee and 5 non-loanee-women.*

Table 6.2 examines the nature of association between the status of women as loanee-women (who are capable of making economic contributions to the family) and as non-loanee-women (who lack in the capability of making economic contribution to the family), on the one hand, and their participation in the decision-making process relating to the number of children they would like to have on the other. The researcher wants to find out the nature of this association because decision-making process in the family has been found to be an important factor influencing family size or the number of children. It has been observed that in families where division of labour or role relationships between the husband and the wife is of such a nature as the business of looking after children or daily shopping, or helping the children in preparing the home tasks given to them by their school teachers, can be done by either of the spouses, fertility tends to be lower. In a study carried out in the USA, it was observed that "women in joint relationships, where several tasks were performed by either spouse, had lower fertility than those in segregated relationships "(Social work Education and Population Planning Projects, The Status of Women and Fertility, New York, 1975, p. 12; Cited in Noman, 1983, p.50). That is to say, in former cases, the women enjoyed a say regarding the number of children they would have. Hence it is hypothesized that gainful employment of women which was obtained because of the Grameen Bank and the economic contribution made by them to the family by virtue of it, may give the women more authority in deciding on the desirable family size, i.e., the number of children the women would like to have.

The researcher, therefore, hypothesizes, that there is a difference between the loanee and the non-loanee-women in decision making regarding the number of children they would like to have. Indeed, Mizan, too, tested the hypothesis that the greater's participation of women in Grameen Bank loan programme, the higher will be their control over fertility decisions. If economic participation accrues more power to an incumbent than to one who does not have such participation, then, Mizan imagined, the Grameen Bank group should show a higher proportion of wives who would exercise active decision-making regarding fertility issues than the non-Grameen Bank group. And, in Mizan's study "the hypothesis is generally confirmed" (Mizan, 1992, p. 184).

However, as Table 6.2 makes it evident, in the present study there is no statistically significant difference between loanee and non-loanee-women as far as decision making in relation to the number of children is concerned. Indeed, a perusal of the figures in the Table shows that in the majority of cases in both the categories, the decision in this matter is husband's sole prerogative. Of course, a few loanee-women, though their number is very insignificant, have been found to enjoy the power of decision-making entirely on their own in this regard, while not a single non-loanee woman is found to enjoy the similar autonomy.

Though this finding of the present study differs from that of the study by Mizan, it is, in a way, corroborated by the observations of scholars like Ahmad (1991) and Noman (1983). "The right and the ability to control reproduction are", observes Ahmed, "limited for the majority of women (in Bangladesh) because of their dependent socio-economic status, as well as the inadequacy of the health and family planning services" (1991, p.72). According to Noman, in husband-dominated families, where women live in a segregated manner and with specific roles prescribed by tradition, the number of children is generally decided by the husband, even if that number exceeds what a wife actually desires. "This is a common phenomenon in our rural communities". (1983, p. 50) Noman mentions another important factor behind the perpetuation of male predominance in this field. The vast majority of rural women are, according to her, hardly able to communicate freely about family planning, childbirth or anything related to sex with their husbands. "This inhibition has developed from their early life and affects family relationships........... social inhibition has developed centering around sex, reproductive system, child procreation, child bearing process and child delivery" (Ibid, p. 51).

Further, a number of respondents confided to the present researcher that in their milieu male children are always preferred to female children and the desire for male children is very very strong. This desire for male children is prompted by traditional values as well as by the feeling that in their old age security will be provided by their male children. The male children will look after their parents, while the female children will go to their respective husbands' families, leaving their natal families. The husband of a respondent would always, therefore, long for male children and if the first child is a female one or the first couple of children is female, he will not allow his wife any respite until he gets a male child. And, the husband gets strong support from his relatives on this issue. In such cases the women, no matter whether they make economic contributions to the family, do not have any other option than to submit to the desire of their husbands and / or the relations of their husbands.

Table - 6.3

Loanee and Non-loanee Women, by Their Control over Family Income / Expenditure / Savings

Control over family income / expenditure/ savings	Loanee Women				Non-loanee Women				X2	df	Level of Significance at .05 level
	Wife %	Both %	Husband %	N	Wife %	Both %	Husband %	N			
Q.1. Who controls expenditure of husband's income?	15	45	40	100	6	44	50	50	3.01	2	Not Significant
Q.2. Who controls ex-penditure of money earned through sale of poultry and dairy products?	32	48	20	100	18	44	38	50	6.65	2	Significant
Q.3. Who controls expenditure of other sources of income in the family?	17	43	40	100	8	44	48	50	2.43	2	Not Significant
Q.4. Who is entrusted with safe keeping of husband's income?	45	31	24	100	24	48	28	50	6.71	2	Significant
Q.5. Who is entrusted with safe keeping of family savings?	25	37	38	100	20	58	22	50	6.31	2	Significant

In a society where patriarchal value predominates, Bhasin rightly maintains, most property and other productive resources are controlled by men and they pass from one male to another, usually from father to son. Even where women's right to inherit such assets is legally recognized, an entire gamut of customary practices, emotional pressure, social sanctions, and sometimes, naked violence obstruct them in acquiring actual control over them. In other cases personal laws curtail their right rather than increase them. In all cases, the women are at a disadvantage. This is well borne by UN statistics : "Women do more than sixty percent of the hours of work done in the world, but they get ten percent of the world's income and own one percent of the world's property" (cited in Bhasin, 1994, p. 9).

When the women get the scope for independent earning through some form of gainful employment, i.e., when there is a scope for making productive work of women visible and recognizable, one may expect a certain kind of change in the prevailing situation. As Banerjee observes, along with an increase in women's contribution to family income, the probability of their managing the family funds, independently or along with others, would increase. Zarina Bhatty also thinks that an important consequence of women's having a source of income is the increased say they have on how the money in the family will be spent. In her sample, seventy-two percent of the respondents "thought that their views on spending decision had acquired greater weight" (Bhatty, 1987, p.46).

The present researcher wanted to know whether and how far there has been an alteration in the over-all male control over the management of the funds in the family and expenditure of the same, insofar as the loanee-women, who have an independent source of income, are concerned. Though a positive association has been noticed by Fuglesang and Chandler (who worked on women participating in activities assisted by the Grameen Bank) between a woman's status in the household and community and her personal income and control of assets, a woman's personal earning may not, necessarily, lead to her control of the assets of her own or of the family she belongs to.

The women may earn a sum and contribute the same to the family. But does it necessarily mean that such a woman would have control, either independently or along with her husband, over the safe keeping and/or spending of the income of the family she belongs to? Does her independent earning enable her to gain the confidence of her husband in the matter of handling as safe-keeping of the income of the family?

Table 6.3 presents data which throw light on the above questions. Row 2 of the table rereads that there is a difference between the loanee-women and the non-loanee woman in the matter of control over expenditure of money earned through sale of poultry and dairy products (cf. Q. 2 in the table). The difference has been found to be statistically significant at.05 level.

The data show that the category of women who control the expenditure of the sum earned through the sale of poultry and dairy products raised by the family independently (wife alone controlling) as well as in the category of women who do it along with their husbands (both the wife and the husband controlling) the percentage of loanee-women is much higher than that of non-loanee-women. In the first category, the percentage of loanee-women is thirty-two as against that of non-loanee-women, e.g., eighteen. And in the latter category, (both the wife and husband controlling) the percentage of loanee-women is forty-eight while that of non-loanee-women, is forty-four. While in case of twenty percent of the loanee-women the husbands exercise control over the family income from sale of poultry and dairy products, thirty-eight percent of the non-loanee-women have to accept their husbands' sole exercise over family income from their source. It may, therefore, be inferred that with independent earning by women (and thus economic contribution by them to the family) there has been an increase in their control over family income from the sale of poultry and dairy products. Similarly, the data in the fourth row (relating to Q.4 : Who is entrusted with safe keeping of husband's income ?) reveal that there is a difference between loanee and the non-loanee-women in this matter and the difference is found to be statistically significant at.05 level. In this case also the percentage of loanee-women is higher (i.e., forty-five percent, i.e., almost twice as much as) than that of the non-loanee-women (i.e., twenty-four percent) so far as the category of cases where wives are entrusted with safe keeping of their husbands' income is concerned. Similarly, in the category of cases where husbands alone have control over the safe-keeping of their own income, the percentage of loanee-women (i.e., 24%) is lower than that of the non-loanee-women. One may draw the inference from these data that those women who contribute to the income of the family enjoy a greater amount of confidence of their husbands in getting the responsibility for safely keeping their husbands' incomes.

A similar picture arises also in relation to the query posed in Row 5 of Table 6.3 (concerned with Q No. 5 : Who is entrusted with the safe keeping of family savings ?), The data in the said Row suggest that there is a difference between the loanee-women and the non-loanee-women in the realm under consideration. And, the difference is found to be statistically significant at.05 level. The data in Row 5 of Table 6.3 clearly indicate that in the category of cases where wives are entrusted with the safe keeping of family savings, the percentage of loanee-women (i.e.,45%) is more than double the percentage of the non-loanee-women (i.e.,

20%). And, the percentage of the loanee-women is lower than that of the non-loanee-women (i.e., 22%), so far as the category of cases where the husbands alone are entrusted with the safe keeping of family income is concerned. From this set of data one may draw the inference that when women have their separate earnings and separate contribution to the income of the family, they enjoy greater confidence of their husbands in the matter of safely keeping the savings of the family.

During the interview, a number of loanee respondents have told the researcher that the income from the sale of poultry and dairy products raised by the family is often small and their husbands do not, in general, interfere with the way in which they (the loanee respondents) spend the sum earned through this source. They think that their husbands know that they (the women) have an independent source of income and contribute to the income of the family and allow them freedom in this matter. Of course, they spend the sum mainly to meet the needs of the family and so far as the principal income of the family is concerned (which is still earned by the male members), it is their husbands who control it.

Similarly, a good number of the loanee-women have expressed the view that as they now earn independently and contribute to the income of the family, they have come to enjoy greater confidence of their husbands in the matter of safely keeping of the husbands' income in comparison with the non-loanee-women. A large number of the loanee-women have told the researcher at the time of interview that they have come to enjoy the trust of their husbands in the matter of safely keeping the savings of the family than before (i.e., when they did not have any independent source of income). Indeed, quite a few of them have informed the researcher that earlier their husbands never kept any money at their disposal. Their husbands did not have any confidence in their ability to handle money. These women have, of course, admitted that earlier they themselves lacked in self-confidence. But their experience with the Grameen Bank has given them a measure of self-confidence into handling even large sums of money. They now learn how to keep and maintain accounts. They, therefore, are now entrusted with the safe-keeping of the savings of the family.

But the enhancement in the status of loanee-women as reflected in their control of small incomes of the family or in the enjoyment of the trust of their husbands in safely keeping the incomes of the latter or the savings of the family is only partial. They are lacking in any substantial control over the expenditure of their husbands' incomes or the income from other sources (than the husbands' occupation or sale of poultry and dairy products). This is revealed through the data presented in Row 1 and Row 3 of Table 6.3.

The data in Row 1 (relating to Q. No.1: Who control expenditure of husband's income?) make it clear that there is no statistically significant difference between the loanee-women and the non-loanee-women in the matter of controlling expenditure of husband's income. It suggests that independent earning by women (as is the case with the loanee-women) and their economic contribution to the family do not, in any significant measure, empower them to control the expenditure of their husbands' income. What is important to note is that in most of the families in a patriarchal society like that of Bangladesh, it is the husband's income which is the principal source of income for the family. A major share of the needs of the family is satisfied with this principal means. And, if husbands themselves retain control, which they actually do, over their incomes, it means that the husbands have (willy nilly) the final say over how the income of the family will be spent. The husbands have thus control over the budget of the family and they decide the priority of the needs of the family and the nature of allocation of sums of money for meeting the different needs. As a result, their wives have a subservient role. They have to, in general, abide by the decisions of their husbands. And, there is hardly any significant difference in this respect, even if women make some economic contributions to the family.

A similar picture is discerned in case of income of a regular nature (round the year or periodic) from other sources which are controlled by the family. The data presented in Row 3 (relating to the question : Who controls expenditure of other sources of income in the family ?) of Table 6.3 reveal that there is no statistically significant difference between the loanee and the non-loanee-women in this regard. One may infer from it that independent earnings by women is not significantly associated with an enhancement in their status, as is revealed in the very common exercise control over the expenditure. As such, earnings of the family as the earnings from husbands, subsidiary or secondary occupation and earnings which are of a regular nature and which are in most cases larger than the incomes earned from such sources as sale of poultry and dairy products raised by the family.

Other sources of income here mean sources like orchards (which yield fruits and vegetables that may be sold in the market), ponds (where fish may be grown for sale in the market), an additional room (which may yield a small amount in the form of rent), a rickshaw purchased by the family and given to some outsider, on contract, in exchange for a definite sum of money per day or per month). The families, like the ones of the respondents of this study, try for augmenting their income in different ways. And, it is the males who decide how that subsidiary income would be made and it is they who have control over this subsidiary income. The voice of the wives, whether they economically contribute to the family or not, does not count for much in this case. Though women, with some gainful employment, have in some cases, control over the expenditure of very small earnings coming irregularly from such sources as sale of poultry and dairy products, they are, in general, denied any important role in deciding matters relating to the expenditure of the money coming from the principal sources of income (which is almost invariable, the primary occupation of the husband and/or other male members of the family) as also of the income which comes from other subsidiary but regular sources of income.

It is a reflection of the continuance of patriarchy or male authority in the sphere of control of principal income of the family. (As also of the income regularly accruing to the family). Women's economic contributions to the family have not significantly altered the situation. A similar finding is obtained from Nirmala Banerjee's study of Women's Work in the Unorganized Sector in India. She observed, "As a woman's contribution to the family income increased, the probability of her managing the family funds independently or along with the others also increased". Nevertheless, Banerjee pointed out, "even among women earning fifty percent or more of the family income, a third were not consulted about this important decision" (1985, p. 100).

Table 6.4
Loanee Women, by Their Control over Their Own Income

"Who is entrusted with the safe keeping of your income?"

Keeping of women's income by	Loanee Women%
Self	48
Both husband and wife	33
Husband	19
Total	100 (N = 100)

Table 6.5
Loanee Women, by Their Control over Expenditure of Their Own Income

"Who controls expenditure of your income ?"

Control of expenditure of Women's income by	Loanee Women %
Self	31
Both husband and wife	29
Husband	40
Total	100 (N = 100)

The loanee-women earn some amount of money from the economic ventures started with the loan from the Grameen Bank. Usually, a person who earns money can keep the sum he / she earns with himself / herself. But is it invariably the case with the loanee-women who make some earnings? Or, is it a fact that they give their earnings to (the hands of) their husbands because of the patriarchal value generally prevailing in the society ? Table 6.4 throws some light on queries like these. The figures in the table show that (in case of) nearly half (i.e., 48%) of the loanee-women keep their earnings in their own custody. A large section of these women has informed the researcher at the time of interview that earlier they did not have the skill of keeping accounts, since they hardly got any money to handle. They had neither the opportunity nor the courage for handling even such a small sum as Taka 500/-. But now they have to interact with the Grameen Bank and handle their accounts with the Bank. They have to interact with the suppliers of raw materials as well as the buyers of what they produce. As a result, they have now developed the skill of keeping accounts and they are not afraid of keeping their earnings in their own custody. And, in case of one-third of the loanee-women, their earnings are kept in the joint custody of the husband and the wife, whereas in case of nineteen percent of the loanee-women, the earnings of these women are kept in the custody of their husbands. Thus, more than fifty percent of the loanee-women cannot exclusively keep their earnings solely in their own custody.

When it comes to the question of loanee-women's control over expenditure of the money earned by them, the picture seems to be still less optimistic for them. Table 6.5 presents the data regarding the nature of control exercised by the loanee-women over the expenditure of the sum earned by them. And figures in Table 6.5 show that less than one-third of the loanee-women have exclusive control over the expenditure of the income earned by them (though according to Table 6.4 nearly half of them can keep their earning in their own custody). And, what is still more interesting is that the percentage of loanee-women the expenditure of whose income lies in the hands of their husbands is higher than the (which is 31) percentage of those women who themselves take decisions regarding the expenditure of their income and also than the percentage (which is 29) of those loanee-women who take decisions in the matter jointly with their husbands. Thus, at least in this case independent earning by women has not enhanced their decision-making power to any significant extent. And, it is very important to note that the percentage of the loanee-women whose husbands exercise control over the expenditure of the sum earned by them (i.e., 40) is higher than the percentage of women who themselves take decisions regarding the expenditure of the income earned by them (i.e., 31) as well as the percentage of women who take decisions in the matter jointly with their husbands (i.e., 29). Thus at least in this case independent earning has not enhanced their decision-making power or their status to a significant extent.

Table 6.6
Loanee and Non-loanee Women, by Their Freedom to Sell Their Property

Extent of freedom exercised	Loanee Women %	Non-Loanee Women %
Can sell after due intimation to husband	10	2
Can sell only after due permission from husband	42	22
Can not sell anyway	48	76
Total	100 (n = 96)	100 (n = 45)

$X^2 = 9.93$; df = 2; Significant at .05 level.

Note : *Information in this regard has not been obtained from 4 loanee-women and 5 non-loanee-women.*

Table No. 6.6 examines the nature of association between the status of women as the loanee-women (who can economically contribute to the family) or as the non-loanee-women (who lack in the ability to contribute economically to the family), i.e., economic contribution made by the women, on the one hand, and their power to take decisions regarding disposal or sale of their property, on the other hand as and when the need arises other. The researcher has felt the need for examining the nature of this association because in a male-dominated society like the one in Bangladesh, women are kept out of the orbit of decision-making in relation to the major interests in the life of the family. The authority of taking decisions remains concentrated in the hands of the males or husband, since they are the chief earners or providers of finance for the families. And, the women or wives merely follow the decisions made by their husbands. This practice has been institutionalized to such an extent as decision making by the males and submission of women to the decisions taken by the males, have become an important element of the value-system of the society. Because of this value-system carefully nurtured by the male-dominated society of Bangladesh, the women have been marginalized in the sphere of decision-making. In many cases, the women themselves are afraid of taking decisions in any important matter (Begum, 1987, p. 41). If women economically contribute, they would, one may expect, experience some change in this regard. They may at least take decisions to sell their property in case any need arises for that.

Table 6.6 reveals that the loanee-women are in a relatively better position than the non-loanee-women in the matter of taking decisions to dispose of their property, when any need for that arises. The difference between the two groups is statistically significant at.05 level. And, it is evident that while the overwhelming majority, i.e., 76% of the non-loanee-women cannot and do not at all take any decision in this matter, less than a half of the loanee-women fall in this category. On the contrary, 10% of the loanee respondents can sell their property after due intimation to their husbands, the corresponding figure for the non-loanee respondents is only 2%. As one comes to the category of the respondents who can sell their property after permission from their husbands, the percentage of the loanee-women is almost twice (i.e., 42%) as much the percentage of the non-loanee-women (i.e., 22%).

A large number of loanee respondents have told the researcher in course of the interview that they have earned some property through the small savings they have made from their own-earnings. And, they, therefore, can sell that property, of course, with intimation to and permission from their husbands. Intimation to and permission from the husbands can hardly be dispensed with because of the tradition prevailing in this area, though their husbands do not object to their proposal for selling their properly.

It should, however, be mentioned that the need to sell property does not arise frequently and thus the answer relevant to the question posed by the researcher is mostly based on women's supposition and not so much on actual occurrences. Although, some women have informed the researcher of actual sale of property by them.

On the other hand, most of the non-loanee-women have expressed the view that it is their husbands who would take decisions to sell property, if any need arises for that. For, they, i.e., the non-loanee-women, have not added to the property of the family by their own earnings. A few of them have, of course, got some property which has come as a gift from their natal families. But even for the disposal of that property, the husbands would take the decision. In some cases, they have been consulted by their husbands at the time of selling the property but the frequency is not, the researcher has noticed, as high as in the case of loanee-women.

Table 6.7
Loanee and Non-Loanee Women, by Their Freedom to Talk to Male Outsiders

"Do you talk to males who do not belong to your family ?"

Freedom to talk	Loanee Women %	Non-loanee Women %
Yes, and talk directly always	12	4
Yes, and talk directly, but not always	19	12
Yes, and talk directly but only in the presence of my husband	36	28
No, my husband does/Yes, but talk through a mediator	33	56
Total	100 (n = 100)	100 (n = 50)

$X^2 = 8.25$; df = 3; Significant at .05 level.

In Table 6.7 an attempt has been made to examine if there is any association between the capacity of a woman to economically contribute to the family [as a loanee woman]on the one hand, and her participation in decision making as reflected in her freedom to talk to male outsiders, on the other.

The researcher has made this venture since in the Islamic society of Bangladesh, women are, in general, denied the freedom to talk to any male outside the circle of members of their respective families. It is their husbands or other (usually male) members of their families who will decide whether women will talk to any male outsider. And, in most of the cases they decide against women's interactions with the male outsiders. The value of observance of *purdah* by women in relation to the people who do not belong to their families or to the circle of primary or secondary kins is still honoured by the patriarchal. Muslim society of Bangladesh. Hence, women are not usually allowed to talk to male outsiders. They have a subordinate position in relation to men. Since husbands or male members in the families are the chief providers of food and other articles and services needed by their families, wives or women have to submit to the decisions of the former. One may, therefore, like to know whether the situation alters when women themselves economically contribute to their families and are required to interact with male outsiders, particularly in matters related to their occupation or job. In other words, one may legitimately feel interested in learning if their is any association between the economic contributions by women to their families through earning from outside with the help of loans from the Grameen Bank and their freedom to talk to male outsiders or their capacity to participate in making decisions in relation to conversation with male outsiders.

Table 6.7 reveals that there is a difference between loanee and non-loanee respondents in this regard, and the difference is statistically significant at .05 level. The figures in the table show that 12% of the loanee-women talk directly and always, i.e., whenever the need arises, with the male outsiders, whereas only 4% of the non-loanee-women enjoy this freedom. That is to say, the percentage of women having the freedom to talk to and the freedom for conversing with male outsiders is three times higher in the category of loanee-women than in the category of the non-loanee-women.

Contrary to this, more than a half, i.e., 56% of the non-loanee respondents fall in the category of women who do not have the freedom to talk to male outsiders directly; their husbands do it on their behalf. In case they have to communicate anything to any male outsiders, they will do so through an intermediary. However, one-third or 33% of the loanee-respondents fall in this category.

In the other two categories also, i.e., where the women can talk to male outsiders directly but not always, and where the women can talk directly to male outsiders in the presence of their husbands, the percentage of the loanee-women is higher than that of the non-loanee-women. There is thus, no doubt, a positive association between the loanee-women's economic contribution to the family and their capacity to take decisions relating to verbal communications with male outsiders or their freedom to talk to male outsiders. However, this capacity is not enjoyed even today by a section of women in spite of their economic contribution to their families. As it has already been noted, in case of 33% of the loanee-women, even economic contribution by the loanee-women to the family has not empowered them with the power of taking decisions on their own to talk to male outsiders.

Indeed, women's freedom to talk to male outsiders is hamstrung by customs and values in the Muslim society of Bangladesh. A number of respondents have reported to the researcher that in the rural milieu the elderly people do not at all like that female members, particularly the young among them in the families, will talk to any male outsiders. It is a milieu characterised by patriarchal values and male domination. A few loanee respondents have informed the researcher that in their life it happened that their husbands even beat them just on the basis of adverse reports from certain elderly (and mainly male) neighbours who saw them talking to certain male outsiders, though it was purely business-talk, and there was no malafide intention on their (the women's) part.

As has been reported by the respondents, the situation has, of course, changed after they started contributing to their families with the help of loans from the Grameen Bank. Now the husbands have come to accept that the loanee-women are required to communicate to male outsiders so that they can profitably transact the business initiated with the loan from the Grameen Bank. These women make tangible economic contributions to the family. They are required to talk to the male officers and other male functionaries of the Grameen Bank. Similarly, they may have to talk to the male suppliers of raw materials or the male buyers of finished products of their small ventures.

There are several other factors leading to the greater freedom enjoyed by the loanee-women in comparison with the non-loanee-women in the matter of talking to male outsiders. Quite a few loanee-women reported to the researcher that the male personnel from the Head Office of the Grameen Bank as well as male foreigners visit the local *kendra* of the Grameen Bank of the rural habitat of the loanee-women.They enquire with the women into the nature of uplift experienced by them in their standard of living and their socio-economic status. Meeting with them has emboldened the women to shed their inhibitions to talk to male outsiders.

No attempt has been made here to gauge with accuracy

the extent of change in the power or capacity of women in this regard, but a rough idea can be formed from the comments like the one below made by some loanee informants, "Dear sister, had it been the earlier times, we would not have the opportunity of talking to you in such details regarding our family matters as we discuss at present. But because of many contacts with the world outside our families, necessitated by our association with the economic activities initiated with the loan from the Grameen Bank, we have now gathered the courage to talk to even male outsiders; we have obviously no difficulty in freely conversing with a female outsider like you. Those days of beating of wives by their husbands, for the former's lack of modesty alleged betrayed in their talking to male outsiders, are gone. Now the husbands have to accept the fact that we will talk to male outsiders out of necessity, since they find our economic contribution to the family useful. If a husband, now, is reported the fact that his wife has been found to talk to a certain male outsider or if he himself finds her talking to a male outsider, he will enquire with his wife as to what she has been discussing with that male outsider." Further, a few loanee respondents have observed that because of their position as *kendra pradhan* (leader of a group of women in a *kendra* of the Grameen Bank), members and workers of political parties come to their residence, particularly, at the time of election with the request to act in favour of their respective candidates. Earlier, these party workers or candidates would not have even made any direct communication with them. Obviously, such contacts break down the barriers in the way of communications between these women and people, male or female, outside the circles of their respective families.

When the researcher discussed this point with the non-loanee respondents, they informed that they usually did not enjoy any such opportunity of direct conversation with male outsiders. A few non-loanee respondents observed, "We are talking to you the matters and discussing different matters with you since you are a woman. Were you a male outsider, we would not have dared to talk to you without a mediator. Our husbands would not like it. Maybe, the husbands of the loanee-women also do not like any direct and free conversation between their wives and any male outsider. But they have to accept the fact, since these women are contributing economically to their families."

Table 6.8

Loanee and Non-loanee Women by, Their Husbands' and other Family Members' Approval of Their Direct Conversation with Male Outsiders

"Do your husband and other family members approve your talking directly to male who does not belong to your family?"

Approval	Loanee Women %	Non-loanee Women %
Does not object	12	4
Does not approve always	50	46
Never approves	38	50
Total	100 (n = 100)	100 (n = 50)

$X^2 = 3.54$; df = 2 ; Not significant at .05 level.

Table 6.8 seeks to examine the nature of association between the capacity of women to contribute economically to the family and their freedom to talk to the male persons, outside their families from a slightly different angle. To put it precisely, Table 6.8 seeks to examine the nature of association between the capacity of a loanee woman (and concurrently the lack of capacity of a non-loanee woman) to economically contribute to the family on the one hand and the approval of her husband and other male members of the family regarding her direct conversation with male outsiders. It may happen that a respondent informs that she can talk directly to a male outsider. In that case it will be presumed that the informant has the freedom to talk to male outsiders directly . But this freedom may actually be contingent on her husband's permission. That is, she may talk or will talk to male outsiders with the permission from her husband. Her freedom to talk to outsiders becomes, to that extent, limited and is certainly narrower than the freedom of a woman who does not require her husband's permission to talk to male outsiders. Table 6.8 presents data from which one may have a clearer idea about this aspect of the phenomenon of women's freedom to talk to male outsiders. The table reveals that the difference between the loanee-women and the non-loanee-women has not been statistically significant in this respect. It suggests that in both the cases of loanee and non-loanee-women, the husbands or other male members of families, do not approve of women's direct conversation with any male outsider.

In Table 6.7 it was found that a number of loanee-women (and a fewer number of non-loanee-women) enjoy in varying degrees the freedom to talk to male outsiders.This freedom may, however, seems to be associated with the compulsion of actual circumstances ——— the husbands of women or other male members of their families have to accept the fact. But at heart, the husband or other male outsiders they may not like it because of the prevailing value of *purdah* segregating the women from the world outside. And Table 6.8 shows the incidence of the value and fact of male domination of a patriarchal society in cases of both those women who economically contribute to their families and the women who do not.

However, in the category of females, with husbands or other male members of the families, not objecting to their direct conversation with male outsiders the percentage of loanee-women is much higher than that of non-loanee-women. Similarly in the category of women with husbands or other "male family members" never approving of their direct conversation with male outsiders, the percentage of loanee-women is lower than that of non-loanee-women.

But the finiding that the difference between the two groups of women has not been statistically significant is an indicator of the fact that economic contribution by women to the family (which has been made possible in case of the loanee-women in this study through the loan from the Grameen Bank) has not been successful enough to alter the value premises of the patriarchal, male - dominated society of Bangladeshi Muslims.

Table 6.9

Loanee and Non-loanee Women, by Compulsion to Abide by the Disapproval of Their Family Members of Their Conversation with Male Outsiders

"Do you have to abide by the disapproval of your family in this regard" ?

Compulsion to abide by	Loanee Women %	Non-loanee Women%
Yes	31	50
Yes, only in instances	49	42
No	20	8
Total	100 (n = 100)	100 (n = 50)

$X^2 = 6.57$; df = 2 ; Significant at. 05 level.

Table 6.9 further highlights the issue presented in Tables 6.7 and 6.8. Table 6.9 examines the nature of association between the ability of women to economically contribute to the family on the one hand and their compulsion to abide by the disapproval of their families regarding their direct conversation with male outsiders.

The data presented in Table 6.9 indicate that the difference between loanee-women and non-loanee-women with regard to the women's compulsion to abide by the decision of their families disapproving their direct conversation with the male outsiders has been found to be statistically significant at.05 level. The figures in the table suggest that in the category of respondents who have reported that they have no compulsion to abide by the disapproval of their families in this matter, the percentage (20%) of loanee-women is significantly higher than that (8%) of the non-loanee-women. Similarly, less than one-third of the loanee-women have reported that they have a compulsion to abide by the disapproval of their families, whereas a half (50%) of the non-loanee-women have admitted that they have such compulsions.

During the interview with the researcher, the loanee-women reporting the absence of compulsion to abide by the approval / disapproval of their families, have told her that their husbands, have come to accept the fact of their direct conversation with the male outsiders, since it is a concomitant feature of the economic venture of the women, out of which these women make economic contributions to their families. But earlier, when these women did not set out for any such economic venture with loan from the Grameen Bank, their husbands or other members of the husbands' families did not approve of their direct conversation with male outsiders, and these women had to obey that disapproval.

A very large number of non-loanee-women have informed the researcher that they have to abide by the decisions of their families (husbands or other members of husbands' families) approving or disapproving of their direct conversation with male outsiders. And, in most of the occasions their families do not approve of their direct conversation with the male outsiders.

Table 6.10
Loanee and Non- loanee Women, by Their Freedom of Movement

Nature of freedom	*Loanee Women %*	*Non-loanee Women%*
Yes, permission is required and an escort is compulsory	45	70
Yes, permission is required but an escort is only a matter of choice and is not compulsory	39	22
Yes, intimation is provided but can move alone, without an escort	11	6
Do not have to seek permission or the necessity of doing so does not arise. An escort is only a matter of choice	5	2
Total	100 (n = 100)	100 (n = 50)

X^2 = 8.44 ; df = 3 ; Significant at .05 level.

Table 6.10 presents the data regarding the association between the capacity of the loanee-women to economically contribute to their family on the one hand and their freeom of movement, i.e., their participation in decision-making in relation to movement outside the precincts of their houses. The table reveals that there is a difference beteen the loanee and the non-loanee-women in this regard and the difference is statistically significant at .05 level. The figures in the table show that the loanee-women enjoy relatively greater freedom in moving outside their homes than the non-loanee-women.

The factors relating to this greater freedom of the loanee-women than their non-loanee counterparts are more than one. In course of their detailed conversation with the researcher, the loanee-women have informed her that they have to go regularly to the Bank at the local *kendra*s for various reasons, viz., to pay off the instalments of the money borrowed from the bank. They have to attend the weekly meetings which are held in the respective *kendra*s of the Bank. Further, they have to move out of their homes in order to carry out the economic activities in which they engage themselves with the loan borrowed from the Grameen Bank. And, their husbands or other (male) members of their husbands' families have come to accept their freedom to move outside their home. Otherwise, the economic activities of these loanee-women will be hampered. Some women who buy cattle with the money borrowed from the Grameen Bank, tend and milk the cows, supply the milk at the doorsteps of the buyers. Similarly, there are certain loanee-women who deal in *saree*s and sell the *saree*s from door to door. In these and similar other cases, the loanee-women are bound to step out of the premises of their houses, and their husbands or other (male) members of their families cannot help conceding to the fact. Through all these activities the women have mustered courage to move relatively freely outside their homes. A few loanee-women have informed the researcher that they now even go to the market independently for buying clothes for their children and enjoy the confidence of their husbands in this matter, which confidence they did not enjoy earlier, i.e., before they started their economic venture with the loan from the Grameen Bank.

In contrast with the loanee-women, a very large majority of non-loanee-women do not enjoy the confidence of thier husbands in relation to moving freely outside their homes. Nor do they themselves have much confidence in their ability to move independently outside the arena of their homesteads. Not a single non-loanee woman has reported to the researcher that she has gone to the market independently to buy cloths for her children. In fact, most of these respondents have admitted to the researcher that they lack in the courage and self-confidence to move outside their homes independently of their husbands or other male members of their families. They feel that the loanee-women have acquired the strength of mind to move outside independently of male escorts because they have to move outside for the pursuit of thier economic activities, and they are accustomed to moving outside independently. But the non-loanee-women have not, they say, got any such opportunity of moving outside independently.

One fact, however should be mentioned here, though it is not clear from the table. It has transpired to the researcher from conversation with the loanee-women that the freedom enjoyed by the loanee-women to move outside home, is relative in comparison with the condition of the non-loanee-women and not absolute. They move outside but cannot freely interact with the outsiders, particularly the male outsiders. There is generally a certain kind of social control over their social intercourse with the outsiders. They cannot freely mix with the outsiders. It is more strictly applicable to the cases of the non-loanee-women.

Table 6.11

Loanee and Non-loanee Women, by the Nature of Decision on the Casting of Vote

"Who decides whom you will cast your vote for ?"

Nature of decision	Loanee Women %	Non-loanee Women%
Wife alone decides	8	2
Husband and wife together decide	25	19
Others than the respondent decide	67 8	79
Total	100 (n = 100)	100 (n = 50)

X^2 = 2.9 ; df = 2 ; Not significant at .05 level.

Note : *Information in this regard has not been obtained from 3 non-loanee respondents.*

Table 6.11 seeks to examine the association between the ability of a woman to economically contribute to the family and her autonomy in taking decisions relating to the casting of vote in favour of a candidate for election to a democratically constituted public body. One may wonder as to why this matter is included in the list of items relating to the participation by women in the decision-making process in the household. Anybody who is familiar with the socio-cultural system prevailing in Bangladesh will appreciate that women there are denied opportunities for making contacts with the world outside their homes and families. They, therefore, do not have the opportunity and privilege to take decisions regarding the matters vitally affecting their life. And, the exercise of the right to vote is a vital matter in the life of every citizen of a country. The Constitution of the Peoples' Republic of Bangladesh recognises equal franchise of men and women. Also, women can contest the elections. But if women are dominated by their husbands or male relatives in the family in all matters, how can they exercise their right to vote freely, without the interference by their male relatives in the family ? When women economically contribute to the family, one may expect that their subservience to males, who have so far been the only providers for the family will diminish and they will be in a position to freely vote for candidates in elections to various public and political bodies. Scholars and researchers like Mizan (1992), Islam-Rahman (1986) have deemed it fit to examine the nature of association between women's participation in economic activities and their participation in decision-making on the choice of candidates in elections.

This study reveals, as Table 6.11 indicates, that there is no statistically significant difference between loanee and non-loanee-women with regard to their freedom to cast their votes according to their own preference. The figures in Table

6.11 indicate that an overwhelming majority of both the loanee and the non-loanee-women (that 67% of the loanee-women and 79% of the non-loanee-women) do not take decisions on their own or even in consultation with their husbands regarding the exercise of franchise. They rather leave the matter to be decided exclusively by the husbands and/or other male members of the family. Only 8% of the loanee-women and 2% of the non-loanee-women take decisions on their own in this matter. One more fact is to be noted here. While one hundred percent of the loanee-women are found to have cast their votes, 6% of the non-loanee-women have not exercised their franchise at all. The over-all picture, therefore, indicates the dependence of the women on their men in the exercise of franchise irrespective of their capacity to economically contribute to the family.

Mizan's study (1992) indicates that participation by women in the economic and other kinds of activities initiated with financial and other kinds of assistance from the Grameen Bank has not been accompanied by an increase in the participation by these women in voting. Though one might legitimately assume that factors like employment, income or education would raise women's consciouness of their rights and privileges in society and therefore of their political rights as well, her study did not confirm the assumption : She observes, "Any motivation or skill gained through Grameen Bank does not translate into exercising of voting rights" (1992, p. 214).

Islam - Rahman has observed that a larger percentage of women in the loanee families have cast vote (1986, p. 70). But in the absence of any table or further discussion of her data, no definite idea can be formed regarding the comparative picture of borrowers and non-borrowers.

What are the factors related to the lack of capacity of the women who make economic contributions to their families for taking decisions regarding the choice of candidates and casting of votes in favour of candidates of their own choice ? Women in both the groups, viz., the loanee and the non-loanee-women, have observed, in course of their interview with the researcher, that they are usually debarred from moving outside their homes. They are not allowed to talk to the outsiders, particularly, the male outsiders. The custom of *purdah* is still there. As a result, women have hardly any knowledge of the world outside their homsteads or their immediate vicinity.

Also, as the level of education of rural women is very low (Table, 5.5, p.143). They can hardly form any idea of what is happening outside the narrow confines of their immediate milieu. They do not understand the political process and, therefore, leave the matter to the decisions of the male members in the families. It is the latter who take the decisions and the women simply abide by them.

II

Table 6.12

Loanee and Non-loanee Women, by the Level of Their Participation in the Decision-Making Process

Level of Participation in the decision-making process	*Loanee Women %*	*Non-loanee Women%*	*Total %*
Maximum	13	6	19
Medium	50	36	86
Minimum	37	58	95
Total	100 (n = 100)	100 (n = 50)	200 (n = 150)

$X^2 = 6.3$; df = 2; Significant at 0.05 level.

Table 6.12 seeks to offer an over-all view of the levels of participation by loanee and non-loanee-women in the decision-making process within the family. In other words, it presents a comparative estimate of the scores obtained by the two groups of women in different arenas of decision - making. The scores have been arranged into three categories : "Maximum"; "Medium" ; "Minimum" (vide chapter : methodology, p. 96)

Table 6.12 examines if there is any statistically significant difference between loanee and non-loanee-women in terms of scores obtained by them relating to their levels of participation in the family decision-making process.

The table shows that the difference between scores obtained by the loanee-women and those obtained by the non-loanee-women has been statistically significant at .05 level. As one looks at the figures in the table, one finds that the level of participation in decision making is higher in case of the loanee-women than in case of the non-loanee-women.

It is evident that 13% of the loanee-women in the sample fall in the category of "maximum" level of participation in decision making, while only 6% of the non-loanee-women belong to this category. So for as the categoty of "medium" level of participation in decision-making is concerned, 50% of the loanee-women belong to this category, whereas only 36% of the non-loanee-women fall in this category. As one comes to the category of "minimum" level of participation in decision-making, one finds, in contrast with the above, that 37% of the loanee-women fall in this category, whereas the corresponding figure for non-loanee is as high as 58%.

It may, therefore, be said that participation in decision-making is positively associated with economic contribution (which is made by the loanee-women and which is not made by non-loanee-women in the sample) to their families through their independent earnings.

The factor related to the positive association between economic contribution by women and their participation in decision-making within the family has been discussed in the preceding tables.

Table 6.13 seeks to examine the nature of association between the age of the respondents (in both the categories of the loanee and the non-loanee-women) and their level of participation in the decision-making process in their families. The whole exercise is prompted by the prevailing

Table 6.13
Loanee and Non-loanee Women, by Their Age and the Level of Their Participation in the Decision - Making Process

Age (in years)	*Level of Participation in the Decision Making Process*							
	Loanee Women				*Non- loanee Women*			
	Max	Med	Min	Total	Max	Med	Min	Total
– 31	1 (4 %)	13 (46 %)	14 (50 %)	28 (100 %)	—	2 (11 %)	17 (89 %)	19 (100 %)
31 – 40	5 (4 %)	17 (46 %)	15 (40 %)	37 (100 %)	1 (8 %)	6 (50 %)	5 (42 %)	12 (100 %)
41 – 54	5 (20 %)	14 (56 %)	6 (24 %)	25 (100 %)	1 (8 %)	7 (61 %)	5 (31 %)	13 (100 %)
55 +	2 (20 %)	6 (60 %)	2 (20 %)	10 (100 %)	1 (17 %)	3 (60 %)	2 (33 %)	6 (100 %)
Total	13	50	37	100	3	19	28	50

X^2 = 7.12 ; df = 6; Not significant at 0.05 level.

X^2 = 14.95 ; df = 6; Significant at 0.05 level.

idea and findings of certain studies by social scientists that a Bengali woman gets a wider opportunity for participating in decision-making affairs within the household (Mizan, 1992, p. 80). However, the concomitant recognition and gain in status come to a woman usually first on her becoming a mother, and later on her becoming a mother-in-law. For example, "In a joint family, the daughter-in-law does not have any independence unless she becomes the mother of two or three children" (Dube, 1967, p. 145). Age is thus found, generally speaking, to be an important life-cycle factor which affects a woman's status in the family. In the Bangladeshi society, while a daughter-in-law may have to face the drudgery of the household chores, it is the mother-in-law who is found to wield and extend her authority in the family-even over the young bride's husband. With growing maturity and experience conferred by an increasing age, a woman may gain in her supervisory capacity and come to look after different aspects of the material well-being of the family (with the resources provided by the husband) such as buying and dispensing of food and clothings of the members of the household and even managing property (Mizan, 1992, p. 81).

According to Quddus and others (1985, p. 47), age is the most important factor for gaining recognition in rural families in Bangladesh. They go to the extent of inferring that in both male and female headed-households, the higher age of women overrides the influence of such factors as literacy and employment in determining decision-making in the family. Sen, too, found in her work that among the gainfully employed Muslim women studied by her "the degree of participation in decision-making increases along with age siginificantly" (1991, p. 362).

From these findings one may draw the inference that (higher) age provides a woman with much leverage in the realm of decision making in the household. The findings of the present study, as reflected in Table 6.13, do not however, fully endorse the above inference. They only partially bear it out.Table 6.13 shows that the association between age and level of participation in decision making has not been statistically significant in case of loanee-women.

Although, looking at the percentage figures, in the column concerning the minimum level of participation in decision-making, one finds that these figures become increasingly low along with the increase in the age of the loanee respondents.

In case of non-loanee-women, the table reveals that the association between age and the level of participation by these women in decision-making has been statistically significant.That is, the level of participation by non-loanee-women in decision-making in the household has increased along with their increase in age. As the percentage figures evince, not a single non-loanee respondent in the category of the lowest age belongs to the box of maximum level of decision-making, whereas 89% of such women found in the box indicating the minimum level of decision-making.

Thus, the non-loanee-women stand in clear contrast with the loanee-women so far as this aspect (association of age and level of participation in decision-making) is concerned. One may wonder as to why this difference is observed between these two categories. One plausible suggestion is that advancement in age is usually accompained by accumulation of experience and practical knowledge of a person (a woman in this case). Experience and knowledge lead to a larger share of the decision-making process and/or authority within the family.

Since, among the non-loanee-women of young age category (upto 31 yrs. in the sample) there is no such way as engaging in a gainful employment for acquring experience, they are denied any

significant share in the decision-making process. They are almost taken for granted. They hardly have any command over what happens in the family. But as they mature in age, they accumulate more and more experience of worldly matters. This maturity then provides them with a certain kind of influence over the affairs in the household. They get gradual recognition from their respective husbands and other members, if there is any, of the household and enjoy an increasingly larger share of the power of decision-making.

In case of the loanee-women, the matter is a bit different. In this category, even young women *per force* come into contact with the world outside the family, mix with a number of men and women outside the family. They come to know a lot about worldly matters and gather a lot of information. And this gives them a modicum of power or at least influence over what goes on within the household. They do not have to depend so much on advancement in age as their non-loanee counterparts for accumulation of experience. Advancement in age is not the only source of experience and influence for them. There is at least one alternative source of experience (and consequent influence) than age, so far as the loanee-women are concerned. Hence all the age-groups in this category of women (viz, loanee-women) have a chance of gaining experience and participating in the decision- making process in their households. The same is not the case with the non-loanee-women (in the sample).

Table 6.14

Loanee and Non-loanee Women, by Their Education and the level of Their Participation in the Decision - Making Process

Level of education	Level of Participation in the Decision Making Process							
	Loanee Women				Non- loanee Women			
	Max	Med	Min	Total	Max	Med	Min	Total
Illiterate	–	–	–	–	1 (5 %)	6 (28 %)	14 (67 %)	21 (100 %)
Just write own name	5 (8 %)	31 (47 %)	30 (45 %)	66 (100 %)	–	2 (33%)	4 (67 %)	6 (100 %)
Upto class II	3 (17 %)	11 (61 %)	4 (22 %)	18 (100 %)	–	5 (38 %)	8 (62 %)	13 (100 %)
Upto class V	3 (33 %)	4 (45 %)	2 (22 %)	9 (100 %)	1 (17 %)	3 (50 %)	2 (33 %)	6 (100 %)
Upto class VI	1 (20 %)	3 (60 %)	1 (20 %)	5 (100 %)	–	2 (67 %)	1 (33 %)	3 (100 %
Upto class X	–	–	–	–	–	–	–	–
Matric (S.S.C.) *	1 (50 %)	1 (50 %)	–	2 (100 %)	1 (100 %)	–	–	1 (100 %)
Total	13	50	37	100	3	18	29	50

Loanee Women: $X^2 = 11.5$; df = 12; Not significant at 0.05 level.

Non-loanee Women: $X^2 = 20.96$; df = 12; Not significant at 0.05 level.

****Note** : (S.S.C), Secondary School Certificate, i.e., Class X passed.

Table 6.14 gives us an idea of the nature of association between education of the respondents (in both the loanee and the non-loanee categories) and their participation in the family decision-making process. The generally prevailing idea regarding the efficacy of education in promoting individuals' sense of identity and arousing in them the consciousness of their rights and duties (Noman, 1983, p. 27 and Mathew, 1989, p. 204) has prompted the researcher to examine this point. According to Kazi, "educational attainment and even literacy have been regarded as —— pertinent measures of relative status [of women] across and within societies. Access to schooling seems to capture, to quite an extent, access to resources, to higher status occupations, *autonomy*, etc." (1989, p. 20; parenthesis and emphasis added). Kazi goes as far as to say that "employment *per se* is not a good indicator of women's status in the South Asian context but education of females certainly is. Education, even if it is just one year of schooling or more amongst mothers, is usually found to influence fertility and most definitely infant mortality negatively" (ibid, p. 49). Kazi finds support for her inferences in the works of Casterline and Alam (1984) and Ruskin (1983). Writing in the same vein, Jahan (1975) observers, "The degree of literacy is an important factor affecting the status of women. For example, within households where women have some education, decision-making within the family is more egalitarian". In the present study, as Table 6.14 reveals, no statistically significant association is found between education of women and decision making by them in both the categories of loanees and non-loanees. It may, however, be noted, in the same table,

that in terms of percentage figures, 28.57% of the loanee-women with education between the levels of class VI and S.S.C. belong to the category of maximum scores in decision making (that is, their level of participation in the decision-making process is the highest in the present sample), whereas the corresponding percentage figure for loanee-women with education at the lowest level, i.e., the capacity for signing one's name, is 7.57 only. As one looks at the column of medium scores in decision- making, one finds that 57.14% of loanee-women at the highest level of education, as recorded in case of the sample of the study, belong to this category, i.e., if the category medium scores in decision making, while 46.95% of loanee-women with the lowest level of education recorded in the sample belong to this category of medium score in decision making. By contrast, 14.28% of the loanee-women with the highest level of education belong to the category of minimum score in decision making, when the corresponding figure for women with education at the minimum level is 45.45%.

As one looks at the case of the non-loanee group, one gets a more or less similar picture. 33% of the non-loanee-women with the level of education between class VI and S.S.C. (Secondary School Certificate) belong to the category of maximum score in decision-making and the corresponding percentage figure for non-loanee-women showing illiteracy or lowest level of education is 3.84 only. Similarly 66.66% of the women with the highest level of education in the sample belong to the category of medium scores in decision-making and only 30.76% of the non-loanee-women with *illiteracy* or *education* at the lowest level belong to this category of medium scores in decision-making. By contrast 33.33% of the non-loanee-women with the highest level of education in the sample lie in the category of minimum scores in decision-making and 69.23% of the non-loanee-women with the lowest level of education fall in this category.

However, there is no consistency in the trend of increase in the scores in decision-making with the rise in the level of education of the respondents, in both the categories of loanee-women and non-loanee-women, throughout the sample.

This lack of correspondence between educational attainments of women and their capacity for participating in the decision-making process has been noted by other researchers also. Mizan, for example, in her study (1992) observers that theoretically, education is a resource for skills and knowledge and power of women. But in her study the association between women's education and their power of decision-making has not been found statistically significant.

In Sen's study (1991) of the Muslim women of the poor class in two slums in Calcutta and Chittagong, it has been found that the impact of gainful employment of women on their participation in decision-making has been more or less equal for all the categories of respondents, viz., the illiterate, the literate, and the educated. That is, in Sen's study, too, the association between the women's level of education and their participation in decision-making has not been found to be statistically significant.

One may hazard a guess regarding this absence of statistically significant association between women's education and their participation in the process of decision-making. In case of poor women, level of education is not, generally speaking, very high, i.e., beyond the level of proficiency in School Leaving Examination, i.e., S.S.C. (Secondary School Certificate).

And, in the majority of cases the educational attainment is only minimal. This poor level of education does not expose women to the qualities of education and, consequently, hardly adds to the real power of women. In the partriarchal culture, which prrvails in countries like Bangladesh, education of women, particularly at the lower level, is hardly given any recognition by the society. It **may make the women conscious of their rights but it as such does not empower them.**

Table 6.15

Loanee and Non-loanee Women, by The Types of Their Families and the Levels of Their Participation in the Decision - Making Process

Type of the family	Level of Participation in the Decision Making Process							
	Loanee Women				Non- loanee Women			
	Max	Med	Min	Total	Max	Med	Min	Total
Nuclear	10 (14 %)	41 (58 %)	20 (28 %)	71 (100 %)	3 (8 %)	17 (47%)	18 (45 %)	38 (100 %)
Non-nuclear	3 (10 %)	9 (31 %)	17 (59 %)	29 (100 %)	—	1 (8 %)	11 (92 %)	12 (100 %)
Total	13	50	37	100	3	19	28	50

Loanee women: $X^2 = 8.29$; df = 2; Significant at.02 level.

Non-loanee women: $X^2 = 8.16$; df = 2; Significant at.02 level.

An attempt has been made through Table 6.15 to see whether there is an association between the type of the family (viz., nuclear and non-nuclear) of the respondents and their participation in the decision-making process within the family. Structural complexity of family types may be assumed to affect women's exercise of power. In the non-nuclear families, that is to say, where a couple lives with other relatives, viz., the husband's parents or brothers and, in some cases, even sisters, a wife is assumed to experiences reduced power in decision-making in the household. It may be mentioned that nuclear families in Bangladesh are not comparable with those in Western societies. In spite of the nuclear structure of a household, its members may have interactions or functionl relationships with their kinsmen in different ways and these are expected to have a sort of influence on the members of the nuclear household, particularly, the women. Even then the women in nuclear families have been said to enjoy a relative large share in the domain of decision-making. (Ahmed, 1991, p. 65). Hence the researcher seeks to examine whether and this assumed association is supported by empirical observations.

Among the landholding households, there is a tendency for young couples not to form their own households immediately after marriage when a girl comes to her husband's family. She enjoys very little power and influence. It is the elderly women who, having gained power through becoming mothers of sons and acquiring experience of family matters, exert control over the young wives in the family (Chowdhury and Ahmed, 1980; Cain and Khanam, 1979; Aziz, 1979). Ross, while studying the urban families in India, has noted the clear preference of young women and also their mothers for nucler families (1961, p.50). Kolenda (1967), in her analysis of family power in India, maintains that customs that support joint-family-living tend to curb the power of women within the family. In the same vein,

Dube (1967,p.144) also notes the greater power exercised by women in nuclear families. Similarly, Conklin's (1981) study in India notes the negligible share in internal decision-making enjoyed by the wives in joint families.

In recent times, the proportion of nuclear families has increased in Bangladesh (Mizan, 1992, p. 93). Among several factors,poverty and increasing landlessness in rural Bangladesh are the overriding causes of the breakdown of the joint family structure leading to the increase in the number of nuclear families. In a nuclear family, women may manage household work with little intervention from other family members. This freedom leads to an increase in a woman's decision-making power. Of course, among the poor women this enhanced exercise of freedom occurs sometimes at the cost of insecurity posed by the threat or actuality of frequent divorce resorted to by their husbands or caused by their death or disability. In some cases they, however, may receive some assistance from their kinsmen, with whom their connections are never completely severed.

The preceding discussion shows that different family types may have differential impact on women's status and power of decision-making in the family (cf. Mizan, 1992, p. 93).

Table 6.15 indicates that in both the cases of loanee and non-loanee groups of respondents in the sample, the association between the type of family they belong to and the level of their participation in decision-making has been found to be statistically significant. So far as the loanee-women are concerned,while 59% of the women belonging to non-nuclear families are found to remain at the minimum level of participation in decision-making, only 28% of the women belonging to nuclear families are seen to exist at that level. 31% of the former category of women are found to enjoy the medium level of participation in decision-making whereas 58% of the latter category (i.e., women in nuclear families) are found to enjoy the medium level of participation. At the maximum level of participation in decision-making also, the percentage of the former is lower (10%) than that (14%) of the latter.

The finding is almost the same in the case of non-loanee group of women. That is to say, in their case, the association between the type of their families and their level of participation in decision-making has been found to be statistically significant. From amongst the non-loanee-women in the sample not a single woman belonging to the non-nuclear family is found to enjoy the maximum level of participation in decision-making [in case, of the loanee-women at least 10% of the respondents have been found to enjoy the maximum level of participation in decision-making], wheras 8% of the non-loanee-women belonging to nuclear families have been found to enjoy the maximum level of participation. As high as 92% of the non-loanee-women belonging to the non-nuclear type of family are found to enjoy the minimum level of participation and the corresponding percentage for the non-loanee-women of the nuclear type of family is 45% only, i.e., less than a half. So far as the medium level of participation in decision-making is concerned, the percentage of non-loanee-women belonging to the nuclear family is much higher (47%) than that of their sisters (8%) who belong to non-nuclear type of family.

Thus, in this study, the findings show that in nuclear families women enjoy a relatively high degree of participation in decision-making in comparison with women belonging to non-nuclear family have been buttressed. And, the factors related to it may be the same for the respondents of the study as they are for the respondents of other studies.

Table 6.17 deals with the nature of association if any, between the length of the period of the loanee-women's connection with the Grameen Bank and the level of their participation in the family decision-making process. The

Table 6.16

Loanee Women and Non-loanee Women, by Duration of Their Marriage and the Level of Their Participation in the Decision Making Process

Duration of Marriage	Level of participation in the Decision- Making Process							
	Loanee Women				Non-Loanee Women			
	Max	Med	Min	Total	Max	Med	Min	Total
7–15	3 (10%)	12 (40%)	15 (50%)	30 (100%)	–	3 (15%)	17 (85%)	20 (100%)
16–24	6 (15.50%)	20 (52.63%)	12 (31.57%)	38 (100%)	1 (6%)	7 (47%)	7 (47%)	15 (100%)
25–33	4 (12.50%)	18 (56.25%)	10 (31.25%)	32 (100%)	2 (13%)	8 (53%)	5 (44%)	15 (100%)
Total	13	50	37	100	3	18	29	50

$X^2 = 3.31$; df = 4 ;

Not significant at .05 level

$X^2 = 9.93$; df =4 ;

Significant at .05 level.

Table 6.17

Loanee Women, by the Period of Their Membership of the Grameen Bank and the Level of Their Participation in Decision-Making Process

Period of Receipt of loan (in year)	Level of Participation in the Decision - Making Process			
	Maximum	Medium	Minimum	Total
4	3 (6 %)	22 (45 %)	4 (49 %)	49 (100 %)
5	3 (11 %)	14 (52 %)	10 (37 %)	27 (100 %)
6	7 (29 %)	14 (58 %)	3 (13 %)	24 (100 %)
Total	13	50	37	100

$X^2 = 13.07$; df = 4 ;

Significant at.02 level.

length of the period of association has been calculated iterms of years for which the loanee-women are enjoying and utilizing the loan from the Grameen Bank. The researcher has sought to examine the nature of the association, since several researchers (Mizan, 1992, Rahman, 1986) have found a significant and positive association between the length of engagement of women in gainful employment and the corresponding exposure to the world outside on the one hand, and the level of their participation in the decision-making process in the family on the other.

Mizan (1992, p. 200) has, for example, noted that period of association of a loanee woman with the Grameen Bank leads to her greater exposure to the outside world and gives her a wider experience of the same. Indeed, a client of the Grameen Bank receives loan from the bank as a member of a group. Generally, five or six groups collectivelly participate in the activities of one *kendra* of the Grameen Bank. Every member is required to participate in group meetings of a *kendra*. A loanee woman gets a lot of information and gather experience of different aspects of life, various problems and their solutions through their participation in group meetings and other kinds of collective activities held at the *kendra*. They come in contact with the officers and trainers of the Grameen Bank who come from outside and discuss with them and among themselves different matters like the problems of how to best utilize the loans and how to realize the *Sixteen Decisions* in arenas of social and family life (the chapter of the Grameen Bank p.) as well as solution to those problems. Through such interactions amongst themselves as well as with officers and experts from outside, the loanee-women learn how to articulate their views. Hence, greater the lenth of duration of a woman's association with the Grameen Bank, greater is the scope for her to enhance the ability to form opinions and take decisions in different matters. And, it is reflected

in the arena of taking decisions within the family as well. Experiences gathered by a loanee woman through different programmes held at a *kendra* of the Grameen Bank contribute to an increase in her self-confidence and competence in decision-making, i.e.,making wise and timely decisions.

Huq (1985, p. 72) finds that among the participants in the Grameen Bank "greater mobility and wider scope for association as a whole has resulted in general elevation of self- confidence. The self-awareness itself has led to an increased female participation in decision-making within the household".

In a different setting, Blood and Wolfe have noted that "the continued participation of the wife in the occupational world accelerated her maturity toward decision-making resourcefulness" (1960, p.42).

All these observations have prompted the researcher to examine whether there is any statistically significant association between the Grameen Bank membership, i.e., the period for which a loanee woman has been utilizing the loan from the Grameen Bank, on the one hand, and the level of their participation in the decision-making process in the household, on the other.

Table 6.17 reveals that the association between the length of the period of the Grameen Bank membership of the loanee-women and the level of their participation in decision-making in the household has been statistically significant (at.02 level) in this study. It is evident from the table that 29% of those women who have remained members of the Grameen Bank for six years (the longest period of membership in the sample) enjoy the maximum level of participation in decision-making, whereas, only 6% of the loanee-women who enjoy the membership for four years (the minmum period of membership in the sample) are found to enjoy maximum level of participation in decision making. The percentage of women who have been members of the Grameen Bank for five years and enjoy the maximum level of participation in decision-making is lower than that of the first group (having membership for six years) but higher than that of the second group (having membership for four years) mentioned above.

A similar trend is noticed in relation to the medium level of participation by these women in the decision-making process.In cases of the minimum level of participation in the decision-making process, the trend noticed earlier is buttressed by the fact that longer the duration of their membership of the Grameen Bank, lower is the frequency in the minimum level of participation by the loanee-women in the decision-making process.

Table 6.18

Occupations of Husbands of Loanee Women and Non-loanee Women and Levels of Their (the Respondents') Participation in the Decision-making Procss

	Level of Participation in the Decision-Making Process							
	Loanee Women				Non-Loanee Women			
Occupaion	Max	Med	Min	Total	Max	Med	Min	Total
Petty business	4	15	12	31	1	4	10	15
Shopkeeper	2	4	3	9	–	2	6	8
Petty service	1	6	4	11	1	2	1	4
Handicraft	3	7	8	18	–	3	5	8
Manual labourer	3	17	9	29	1	6	3	10
Share Cropper	–	1	1	2	–	1	2	3
Religious Work	–	–	–	–	–	–	2	2
Total	13	50	37	100	3	18	29	50

$X^2 = 2.98$; df = 12 ; Not Significant at .05 level.

$X^2 = 7.33$; df =12 ; Not Significant at .05 level.

An attempt has been made to show in Table 6.18 whether there is any statistically significant association between the occupation of the husbands of the respondents and their level of participation in the decision-making process. Occupation of a person is an important part of his socio-economic status which again is associated with his values and attitudes to persons and things around him. Variations in occupations of the husbands of the respondents may be related to variations in their ideas and attitudes toward the quantum of autonomy to be permitted to their wives. That is to say, respondents belonging to a particular socio-economic status which is associated with a particular occupation of the male members may have a level of participation in decision-making on different matters relating to family life which may be different from the level of participation in decision-making enjoyed by respondents whose husbands have an occupation different from the husbands of the former group. People of different occupations and socio-economic status may have different kinds of relationships with their wives, and this in turn may be associated with the level of participation by wives in the decision-making in the family.

As has been observed in this study, the husbands of respondents are engaged in a variety of occupations. For the purpose of putting the data regarding all these occupations in a tabular form, the occupations have been classified into seven categories. An important fact to note here is that though the sample for the study is a rural one, there is not a single respondent whose husband may be called a farmer. Those husbands who earn their livelihood from agriculture are mere share croppers, i.e., they till the land of others and get only a share-of the crop raised in that land. Indeed, one of the conditions of eligibility of a woman for getting loan from the Grameen Bank is that the family to which such a woman belongs owns less than 0.4 acres of cultivable land or possesses assets whose value does not exceed the market value of one acre of medium quality land.

The data in Table 6.18 show that there is no statistically significant association (at.05 level) between the occupations of the husbands of the respondents and levels of participation by the respondents in the decision-making process in the family in either the category of the loanee-women or the category of the non-loanee-women.

As one looks at the occupations listed in Table 6.18, one finds that these occupations are related to a, more or less, similar socio-economic status. All of them reflect a rather low socio-economic status. And, the similarity in socio-economic status of these occupations may have been reflected in the lack of variations in the levels of participation in the decision-making process by the views of men having these occupations.

Education is an important variable associated with the values and attitudes of persons receiving education. Education gives men ideas and information which may change his outlook on life and social relations. An educated man may have an attitude towards the enjoyment of power in decision-making by his wife different from the attitude of an uneducated or illiterate man towards the same issue or phenomenon. Further, a similar difference may be found between a more educated man and a less educated man regarding the extent of power to be enjoyed by their respective wives in the decision-making process in the family. An attempt has, therefore, been made in Table 6.19 to examine if there is any association between the level of education of the husband of a woman in the sample and her level of participation in the decision-making process in the family.

The data in Table 6.19 show that there is no statistically significant (at .05 level) association between the level of education of the husbands of the respondents and the levels of their (i.e., the respondents') participation in the decision-making in the family. And, the lack of statistically

Table 6.19

Education of Husbands of Loanee Women and Non-loanee Women and the Levels of Their (the Respondents') Participation in the Decision-Making Process

Husbands' level of education	Level of Participation in the Decision-Making Process							
	Loanee Women				Non-Loanee Women			
	Max	Med	Min	Total	Max	Med	Min	Total
Illiterate	4	18	10	32	0	6	9	15
Upto Class II	2	10	9	21	1	4	7	12
Upto Class V	3	9	7	19	1	2	8	11
Upto Calss VIII	1	9	8	18	1	2	4	7
Class IX- X	2	2	3	7	0	2	1	3
S.S.C. and H.S.C*.	1	2	–	3	0	2	0	2
Total	13	50	37	100	3	18	29	50

$X^2 = 5.27$; df = 10 ;
Not Significant at .05 level.

$X^2 = 6.08$; df = 10 ;
Not Significant .05 levle.

* Note : S. S. C. = Class X Passed and H.S.C. = Class XII Passed

significant association between the two above-mentioned variables is evident in both the groups of the loanee and the non-loanee-women.

A closer scrutiny of the data in Table 6.19 shows that the levels of education of the husbands of the respondents are very poor. 32% of the husbands of loanee-women are illiterate and 30% of the husbands of non-loanee-women have reported illiteracy. If one considers, in addition to it the percentage of husbands who have read up to class II only, one finds that in, both the loanee and the non-loanee groups of women, more than 50% of the husbands are either illiterate or have read up to class II only.

Thus the differences among the husbands in relation to education are not at all striking. And, this lack of any great riation in educational levels of the husbands of the respondents may have been associated with lack of any significant difference respondents' in the levels of participation in the decision-making.

III

Table 6.20

Loanee and Non-loanee Women, by the Time devoted by Them Per-Day to Household Chores and Economic Activities

Time devoted	Loanee Women %	Non-loanee Women %
8 - 9	5	6
10 - 11	20	42
12 - 13	47	38
14 - 15	28	14
Total	100 (n = 100)	100 (n = 50)

X^2 = 9.37, df = 3; Significant at .05 level.

There is a certain kind of division of labour between men and women in tradition-bound societies like that of

Bangladesh. Women are assigned the role of housekeeping and men engage in work in the world outside. The women have to bear with the drudgery of household chores and they provide all kinds of services to all the members of the household. But their contribution is never recognised. Men's work is recognized since it can be measured in monetary terms and translated into profits, salaries or wages, as the case may be. The backbreaking load of household work has to be borne by women only and men do not share their burden. Women remain subordinated to men. Now, if women engage in activities which yield income in monetary terms, if they go to the world outside their homesteads for the pursuit of some gainful employment recognized by the society, an alteration in the situation depicted above may be legitimately expected. Is there any sign of such an alteration ? Tables 6.20 and 6.21, present the data which may offer certain answers to the question.

Table 6.20 seeks to examine if there is any statistically significant difference between loanee and non-loanee-women with regard to the time spent by them for carrying out the entire gamut of their daily activities. The exercise has been made, since the loanee-women are now performing a dual role : first, the traditional role of a housekeeper, and second, the role of an earner. For the performance of the new role of earner, which they carry out through economic activities made possible with loan from the Grameen Bank, they have to put in time and labour. Wherefrom do they get the time and energy necessary for performing their role as earners of income from economic activities ? Do they enjoy some respite from their duties within the household because of their newly assumed responsibilitity for income-generating activities ? If it is found that the length of time spent for work by women of both the groups is more or less, similar, one may presume that the loanee-women are compensated for by the labour put in by them for the pursuit of economic or income-generating activities with some relief from the burden of household work. Table 6.20, however, reveals that there is a difference between the loanee-women and non-loanee-women in this regard, and the difference is statistically significant at .05 level.

The figures in Table 6.20 show that in the category of women who have to work for 14-15 hours a day for performing their duties, the percentage of loanee-women is 28 whereas the percentage of non-loanee-women is 14 only. Similarly, in the category of women who have to work for 12-13 hours a day, the percentage of loanee-women is 47 whereas the corresponding percentage figure for the non-loanee-women is 38. In contrast to this, in the category of women who work for 10-11 hours a day, the percentage of non-loanee-women is higher than, rather, twice as much as, the percentage of the loanee-women. Similarly, so far as the category of women who work for 8 - 9 hours a day is concerned, the percentage of non-loanee women is higher than that of the loanee-women. In other words, the figures in Table 6.20 clearly indicate that in the categories of women working for longer hours there is a higher incidence of loanee-women than that of non-loanee-women. One may infer from it that the loanee-women, who are engaged in certain economic activities for making an earning, have, in general, to work for longer hours in comparison with their non-loanee counterparts. It implies that loanee-women have to perform their economic activities in addition to the performance of their household chores. As there has been some addition to their roles and responsibilities, there has been some corresponding increase in their burden of work as well.

Table 6.21

Loanee and Non-loanee Women in Terms of Help Received by Women in Day to Day Activities

Help received	Loanee Women %	Non-loanee Women %
No help received at all	26	24
Help received	74	76
Total	100 (n = 100)	100 (n = 50)

$X^2 = .05$; df = 1 ;

Not significalnt at .05 level

Housekeeping is mainly the responsibility of the wives. In actual practice, women may get assistance from their daughters, sons, and even husbands. In non-nuclear families, the in-laws too may help them in performing the household chores. The assistance may, however, be marginal only in many cases.

Now, is there any distinction between them and the non-loanee-women in receiving assistance from others in the performance of household chores ? It the loanee-women's work outside home is given due consideration by the others, it is expected that they will receive a larger amount of assistance from others in carrying out household chores than what is received by the non-loanee-women who perform household chores only.

The data in Table 6.21 reveal that there is no statistically significant difference between the loanee and the non-loanee-women in this regard. In other words, the loanee-women do not receive any special consideration from others in doing the household chores in comparison with their non-loanee counterparts. The findings in Table 6.21 buttress the findings in Table 6.20.

It should however be mentioned here that a few loanee-women have informed the researcher during the interview that part of their household duties, like feeding the children, etc., is shared by their husbands particularly on the days when they go to attend the weekly meeting in the *kendra.* True, their number is very small but what is noteworthy is that not a single non-loanee respondent has reported that she receives similar help from her husband.

Table 6.22

Loanee Women, by Their Perception of the Quantify Their Work-Load

Perception	Loanee Women %
Work-load has much increased	35
Work-load has increased	44
Work-load has not increased	21
Total	100 (n = 100)

Table 6.22 has a sequential link with table 6.20 and table 6.21. From table 6.20 one finds a higher incidence of loanee-women then non-loanee-women in the category of women working for longer hours. It implies that loanee-women have to perform their economic or income-generating activities in addition to carrying out of their household chores. Since the data presented in table 6.21 do not show any statistically significant difference between loanee and non-loanee-women in the matter of receiving any help from their husbands and other members in the family in performing the household chores, one may presume that the loanee-women who remain busy for long hours with income-generating activities with the help of which they financially contribute to the family do not get any special consideration from their husbands or other members of the family. The latter do not seen to show any interest in an equitable division of labour necessary for performing the household activities. Now, the question is how do the loanee-women themselves perceive the phenomenon? A perusal of

Table 6.21 may suggest an answer to the preceding question. It is interesting to note that 21% of the loanee-women have expressed the opinion that their work load has not increased. It is equally noteworthy that 79% (i.e., more than 3/4) of the loanee-women have reported an increase in their work-load. More precisely, 44% of the loanee-women have said that their work load has increased, and 35% of the loanee-women have said their work has increased to great extent.

Table 6.23
Loanee Women, by Their Opinion of Their Workload

Opinion	Loanee Women %
Extra work	91
Over-burden	9
Total	100 (n = 100)

Tables 6.20, 6.21 and 6.22 taken together suggest that most of the loanee-women express the opinion that the hours which they spend for doing work, at home and outside, have increased but there is no equitable division of labour between them and their husbands for performing the household chores and their work-load has increased. But table 6.23 reveals that an overwhelming majority of the loanee-women do not regard the additional hour and labour they put in for simultaneously carrying out household activities and income-generating activities outside home as an excessive burden. Indeed, 91% of them consider the additional work they have to undertake after their engagement in income-generating activities as merely extra work. And only 9% of these loanee-women have described the additional work as an "excessive burden". Thus all the 4 tables from 6.20 to 6.23 reveal that the loanee-women are conscious of the "double burden of household chores and

income-generating activity, which they have to bear. Viewed from this aspect, their engagement in income-generating activities and financial contribution to the subsistence of the family does not seen to be associated with any major alteration in their status or decision-making power in the family. The existing patriarchal values of the society dictate that women will perform the household chores. It hardly matters if women have to work outside home. They are hardly left with any opportunity to decide how much of the burden of household chores they will share or which household chores they will do and which others would be done their husbands.

Even then, Table 6.23 suggests that the majority of the loanee-women do not perceive the additional work done by them or hours spent by them as an "excessive burden". They do not consider themselves, as it transpires from the opinions expressed by them "over-burdened". Why is it so? The present researcher may at best hazard a guess. It is as follows: "The advantages and convenience gained by the loanee-women through the income-generating activities seem to these women to outweigh disadvantages of double burden" of their household work and work outside home.

The guess is made on the basis of what most of the loanee-women disclosed to the researcher in course of interview. The statement made by them suggest a cue to their perception. Some of them may be noted here. Some loanee-women said, "Earlier the life in the family as a whole appeared a burden. Acute scarcity of almost everything haunted every moment of our existence. How to feed the children ? How to run the household ? Such nagging questions made our existence precarious. Life itself was, therefore, unbearable. We have got a respite with the earning from the work done with the loan from the Grameen Bank. Our financial contribution to the family has lessened the burden of poverty. Hence the work from which we are getting this earning is not an excessive burden." A few others remarked, "Yes, the burden of work has increased. But it has added to our ease and convenience also. Earlier, we had to fetch the drinking water from the tubewell at a distance. Now we have tubewells in the premises of our houses. Earlier, we had to rise before the daybreak as we had to go to the field for toilet. Now we have our own toilets in the premises of our houses. And, all this has become possible with the money earned by ourselves." Some loanee-women said, "New Plot of land has been purchased with the money earned from the work started with the loan from the Grameen Bank. Additional crop from that land has added to the well-being of the family. And, the ownership of the land is mine."

There were a few who said, "Money gives us power. If the work-load has increased, our power too has increased. So the increased work-load is not an excessive burden." A few others remarked as follows, "I'm now earning. When I have money at hand, I am not scared of the burden of work While statements like the above suggest as to why the loanee-women bear the additional responsibility or burden of work, it is also important to note that many loanee-women have expressed the craving for some amount relief from the burden of household chores and for sharing of a portion of this burden by their husbands. They regret the absence of adequate appreciation of their difficulties by their husbands. They regret the absence necessary alteration in the over-all patriarchal value. This point is more sharply emphasised by those nine percent of the loanee-women who cannot but consider the additional work they have to undertake because of engagement with income-generating activities as a burden. A few of them remarked, "Truth to tell, women have a hard luck. They remain ever oppressed in the patriarchal society of Bangladesh. And women's independent earnings from income-generating activities, backed by organisations like the Grameen Bank, can hardly make a dent in the value system of patriarchy".

Table 6.24

Loanee and Non-loanee Women, by Their Opinion Regarding the Role of Husbands and Wives in Running the Household

Perception	Loanee Women %
Work-load has much increased	35
Work-load has increased	44
Work-load has not increased	21
Total	100 (N = 100)

Table 6.24 presents a comparison of the opinions of the loanee-women and non-loanee-women regarding the responsibility of the husband or the husband and the wife in running the household. It, however, does not give any information as to whether any respondent thinks that the wife is solely responsibile for running the household though it does contain information regarding the percentage of women who think that the husbands are solely responsible for running the household. The reason for this is that during the pilot study not a single respondent — loanee woman or non-loanee woman — told the researcher that the woman had the power to bear or that the women should bear the exclusive responsibility of running the household. Some of them even expressed surprise, when they were asked whether women should have the sole responsibility. Their prompt reaction was why should the wife bear the exclusive responsibility for running the household so long as the husband is alive ? Hence this question seeking respondents' opinion regarding women's exclusive responsibility was dropped from the interview schedule for the study.

The invisibility and / or deliberate oversight of women's productive work and contribution to the material well-being of the family is almost universal in societies like Bangladesh that are governed by patriarchal values. And, this fact is closely associated with the deep-seated belief that it is the men who run the families (Johra, 1989, p. 222). This kind of opinion is an indicator of the subordinate status of women in the family. Reporting the status of women in Madhya Pradesh of India, Devi also observes, "The common belief is that man's higher status within the family emanated from his earning the means of livelihood" (1989, p. 281). But if the women have a share in earning the means of livelihood of the family through their income from some visibly income-generating activity, there may be a change in the belief, at least among the earning women themselves, regarding the perception of the responsibility of the husband and wife in running the family. Has there been any change in the attitude of loanee-women as to who has got the responsibility of running the family? The researcher does not have any direct answer to this question since she did not have the opportunity to record the belief of these women prior to their involvement in income-generating activity. She, however, wants to see whether the fact of earning separate income and contribution to the subsistence of the family by the loanee-women is associated with any difference between them and the non-loanee-women in this respect. Table 6.24 shows that there are differences of opinions of the two categories regarding the exclusive responsibility of the husband or the joint responsibility of the husband and wife in running the household. The table shows that the difference between the two categories of women has been statistically significant at .01 level. 24% (about one-fourth) of non-loanee respondents have expressed the opinion that the responsibility of running the family belongs to the husband but the corresponding percentage figure for the loanee-women is only ?

Most of the (93%) loanee-women, who have expressed the opinion that the responsibility of running the family belongs to both the husband and the wife, have told the researcher that the family and the children are created together by the husband and the wife, hence both of them should have a share in the responsibility for running the family. 75% of the respondents said to the researcher at the interview (though this fact is not shown in the table) that the burden of responsibility for running the family falls more heavily on the wives or mothers than on the husbands of fathers. For, in poor families, afflicted with serious paucity of goods and services that are required, it is the wife or the mother who has, on many occasions, to somehow "manage" the household, the husbands/father is found in such situations, to shirk the responsibility. The latter goes out of home and spends a considerable time outside home. At home, the wife or the mother is to face the nagging children and other members of the family.

Many of these women have also told the researcher during the interview that in a poor family which is always haunted by scarcity of different articles required or demanded by the children and other members of the family, it is not possible for the husband to meet all, or even a large portion of, these demands. The husband loses temper as a result and becomes irritated and starts scolding the wife or the children and other members of the family. Under such circumstances, quarrels between the husbands and the wife become a constant feature of the family. The loanee respondents told that before they started earning separately, they had suffered constant bickering with their housbands because of the reasons stated above. But since they started sharing the financial burden of the husehold, the incidence of quarrels between them and their husbands diminished to a great extent. This, of course, improved the status of the former in the family. The loanee-women narrated several other experiences like the one mentioned above, which are not amenable to quantitative treatment, and hence cannot be presented in a tabular form.

As one comes to the responses of the non-loanee-women, it is found that in their cases also, the majority has expressed the opinion that the responsibility for running the household belongs to the husband and the wife together. But they have deplored, in private, their inability to help the family financially, since they have no separate source of income. What should not be ignored that one-fourth of the non-loanee respondents the opinion in favour of the husband's responsibility for running the household.

It is, one may guess, associated with the absence of any opportunity for income-generating activity and the related outlook among these women.

Table – 6.25

Loanee and Non-loanee Women, by Their Opinions Regarding the Desirability of Taking Decisions Conjointly by Husband and Wife

Opinion on desirability	Loanee Women %	Non-loanee Women %
Husband should seek consulation	12	4
Both spouses should seek consulation	70	56
Wife should seek consulation	18	40
Total	100 (n = 100)	100 (n = 50)

X^2 = 9.64; df = 2 ; Significant at .05 level.

Table 6.25 seeks to further highlight the nature of perception of the respondents (as expressed through the respondents' opinions) regarding their status vis-a-vis their husbands'. It gives a comparative picture of the loanee-women and the non-loanee-women in relation to their opinions regarding the desirability of consultation between the wives and the husbands prior to taking decisions on different matters.

The exercise is prompted by the prevailing idea that since women in societies like Bangladesh are culturated in the values of a traditional, patriarchal system, they would accept the male domination as natural in every aspect of life. They would hardly have the self-confidence that they can offer helpful suggestions to their husbands for reaching decisions in different matters. The lack of self-confidence of women and the associated ideas regarding the superior power and / or knowledge or intelligence of the husbands are supposed to be a feature of the subordinate status of women vis-a-vis men. (cf. Kabir and Amin, 1995, p. 2).

The issue, however, becomes problematic in the light of observations made by Ramu (1988, pp. 52-53), Das (1976, p. 133,) Kakar (1981, p. 118). Ramu rightly points out that power-in its dimension of authority — is rooted in tradition, codified by custom and sanctioned by norms. Being an elderly male and / or, one may add a husband, confers a certain degree of power and it is ascriptive in this sense. "By contrast, influence in achieved. It is an ability on the part of the spouse to impose her or his point of view in subtle ways and manoeuvre relations in order to accomplish a desired outcome" (Ramu, *op.cit*, p. 52). Influence is based on the personal attributes, e.g., docile or domineering, submissive or aggressive bearing. It depends on the socio-economic circumstances and knowledge as well. Besides, a successful application of influence is closely related to the nature of interpersonal dynamics between spouses. "When strategically employed it [i.e., influence] has just about the same potency as power to shape the final outcome of decisions" (*idem*). Das remarks that in tradition-bound countries like India it is only men who could exercise power through institutionalised political positions, and in this sense, women have no power. "However, if we try to conceptualise power as an asymmetrical relation, in which one person treats another as an object, then the image of women, as totally powerless, needs serious consideration. Young women might have been treated as objects, but as they grew older, the influence they had on the affairs of men was of no mean importance" (1976, p. 133) Kakar more sharply presents the fact. Although the wife of the family patriarch may indeed pay a formal deference to him, especially, in the presence of outsiders, "she may exercise considerable domestic power, not merely among the other women of the household, but with her husband, and she often makes many of the vital decisions affecting the family's interest" (1981, p. 118).

In the light of the above observations, Ramu very correctly remarks, "Therefore, it is necessary to distinguish between the location of power and the manner in which it is exercised by spouses" (op. cit. p. 53). But this manner of exercising power is associated with the conception of the spouses regarding the feasibility of exercising power. If the wives do not have the initial idea that they should or can exercise influence over their husbands in arriving at a decision, or that there is at all any need on the part of the husbands to consult their wives before taking any decision in any matter, the question of their exercising any influence over their husbands in decision-making hardly arises. The researcher, therefore, wanted to have an idea regarding the respondent's perception of the matter and the differences if any between the loanee and non-loanee-women in this particular sphere.

The table shows that there is a difference in this respect between the loanee-women and the non-loanee-women in the sample studied by the researcher and the difference has been statistically significant at .05 level. The table shows that while 12% of the loanee-women think that husbands should consult their wives before taking any decision in any matter relating to the interest of the family as well as their personal matters or those pertaining to their life in places of their work, the corresponding percentage in case of the non-loanee-women is only 4 (i.e., 4%). Further, 70% loanee-women think that both the spouses should consult each other before taking any decision, but only 40% of the non-loanee-women think that way.

It may be inferred that this difference is associated with the differentia between the two categories, viz., the engagement of the loanee-women in a certain kind of income-generating activity and the absence of any such scope in case of the non-loanee-women.

As the researcher recalls the discussions between her and the loanee respondents, she remembers that the majority of the women expressing their opinion in favour of joint consultation between the husband and wife before taking any decision told the researcher that they were not that conscious of the importance and desirability of the matter, prior to their contact with the Grameen Bank. In course of their interaction with the Grameen Bank, they noticed that many loanee-women talked of the suggestions they received from their husbands regarding the activities in the *kendra* of the Grameen Bank as well as ideas regarding the best way of utilising the loan received by them from the Bank when they consulted their husbands. The loanee respondents too, found it helpful. They too consulted their husbands on these matters, in addition to the matters relating to the well being of the family. And, they had a similar expectation regarding their husbands. They expected that their husbands too, should consult them before taking decisions even in matters relating to their [*i.e,* the husbands'] place of work.

Though the table does not contain the information, 30% of the loanee respondents, expressing the opinion that both spouses should seek consultation with each other, reported to have gained experience of the world outside home and self-confidence because of their contacts with the persons and institutions outside their home in course of their receipt and utilisation of loans. Hence, they were, they felt, in a position to render useful advice to their husbands, should the latter consult them.

By contrast, 40% of the non-loanee-women did not betray this kind of consciousness and expectation. They told the researcher during the interview that they did not have much knowledge of the world outside home and the complex problems or life. They were not at all in a position to appreciate the problems faced by their husbands in their work place and therefore no purpose would be served, should their husbands consult them and seek their opinion. Further, since the husbands or males had an acquaintance with the larger world and experience, they had a better understanding of the problems – domestic or non-domestic. Hence they themselves were competent enough to take decisions and there was hardly any need on their part to consult the wives.

Table – 6.26
Loanee and Non-loanee Women, by Their Perception of Happiness

Perception	Loanee Women %	Non-loanee Women %
Loanee women are happier than the non-loanee-women	81	78
Both the loanee and non-loanee-women are happy	14	10
Non-loanee-women are happier than the loanee women	5	12
Total	100 (n = 100)	100 (n = 50)

$X^2 = 2.58$; df = 2, Not significant at .05 level.

Table 6.26 gives further information regarding the respondents' own comparative assessment of the conditions of loanee-women and non-loanee-women, More precisely, it presents data about the respondents' opinions regarding the relative happiness of the loanee-women and the non-loanee-women. The purpose has been to examine whether there is any difference between the loanee-women who make an earning from income-generating activities and the non-loanee-women who do not have any earning from income-generating activities in their opinions regarding the greater happiness of the loanee-women than the non-loanee-women.

Here, one may legitimately point out that "happiness" is not a term precise enough to convey the same kind of meaning to everyone. Analysing the different statements made by the respondents during the pilot survey in response to the queries as to whether they are happy or they are happier than others and what is meant by happiness when they say they are happy (or not happy) or happier, the researcher has come to infer that the meaning or sense conveyed by the respondents in reply to the relevant queries approximates to the following meanings of the words, "Happiness" and "Happy", as given in *Oxford English Dictionary* (OED, 1979). According to OED (1979), *Happiness* means "The state of pleasurable content of mind, which results from success or the attainment of what is considered good" and *Happy* means "Having a feeling of great pleasure or content of mind, arising from satisfaction with one's circumstances or condition". The preceding statement regarding "Happy" has been taken as "Operational Definition" of the word, "Happy" for the purpose of the present study.

Table 6.26 shows that there is no statistically significant difference between the loanee and the non-loanee-women in terms of their perception as expressed through their opinions regarding the greater happiness of the loanee-women. Rather, a reading of the frequencies in the table shows that 81% of the loanee-women and 78% of the non-loanee-women state that the loanee-women are happier than the non-loanee-women.

Thus in both the categories, an overwhelming majority (more than three-fourths) of respondents have opined that the loanee-women are happier.

A much smaller portion of women in both the categories (14% in case of loanee and 10% in case of non-loanee-women) have opined that both loanee and non-loanee-women are happy.

A still smaller portion (that is, only 5%) of the loanee-women think that the non-loanee-women are happier than the loanee-women. The percentage of non-loanee-women, in the category of respondents holding the above opinion, is higher i.e., (12%) than that of loanee-women. Again, the percentage (12%) of the non-loanee-women talking of greater happiness of non-loanee-women is higher than the percentage (10%) of the non-loanee-women saying that women of both loanee and non-loanee categories are happy. But what is noteworthy is that in the group of non-loanee-women the proportion of respondents having the opinion that the non-loanee-women are happier than the loanee-women is less than one-sixth of the proportion of non-loanee respondents holding the opinion that the loanee-women are happier than non-loanee-women.

One may infer from the above that there is an association between the greater happiness (as indicated in the opinion of about 80% of the respondents in both the categories) of the loanee-women and their independent earning from income-generating activities.

This inference seems to be buttressed by the comments made by the respondents—loanee and non-loanee—regarding different aspects of life during their conversation with the researcher at the time of interview. Some of them may be noted below.

One of the loanee respondents holding the view that the loanee-women are happier than their non-loanee counterparts has said, "Women like me now get the opportunity to exchange information and views with others. As a result, we have more information of what is happening around us. We are now in a position to think how the condition of the family can be improved. We are no longer abjectly dependent on our husbands for everything concerning the family, nor are we just passive onlookers without any power to do the needful.

Another woman has remarked, "If the income of the family increases, it provides a modicum of relief to a poor family tormented by nagging scarcity of the daily necessities of life. The occasions for quarrels between the wife and the husband, who earlier was the only earner in the family, have become more infrequent than earlier. If the husband, on return home, encounters nagging demands for different things, he can hardly keep his cool. Being exasperated, he may start beating his children and wife. This was precisely the picture earlier. But now the wife's earning makes for the deficiency in the husband's income. And, the occasion for quarrel between husband and wife, which was prompted by the husband's inability to meet the familial needs voiced by the wife, has become less recurrent. Most of us who have their independent earning share this kind of experience. And, women like us are happy".

Another respondent reports, "We were earlier taken for granted. Our husbands did not attach any importance to us. They did not consult us any issue. They took us for credulous women. Indeed, we had to accept whatever they told us. We did not have any opportunity to test the veracity of their statements. But we are no longer gullible individuals. Because of our interaction with others, in course of our activities in connection with our economic venture, we have come to understand what is what. And, our husbands do reckon with this fact in their dealings with us. Our husbands earlier went out without informing us, their wives, of where they were going. But at present they do not and cannot take this liberty." One of the loanee-women in the sample interviewed by the researcher observed that, "Earlier the husband did not give me his whereabouts, when he went out of home. If I dared ask him, he used to immediately stop my queries. He would say, Eh, you, the idiot woman, how dare you ask me ? I've some important business to discuss with ..... [He would give some fictitious name] What's the use of talking to you ? Do you understand anything?' But now my husband discusses with me a lot of matters, he wants to learn from me what happens in our Grameen Bank *kendra*. He often proposes to take me to the cinema-show which was earlier unthinkable. Though my husband wants me to accompany him to the cinema hall, I do not go. I like to save the money. But I am happy now for the above reasons."

A fifth woman of the above category has said, "I can now handle a lot of currency notes and coins. Earlier our husbands hardly gave us a note or a coin. I too, was nervous about keeping accounts of money, if the sum was large. But I am now not afraid of carrying with me a sum of *Taka* 4000 or *Taka* 5000, and keeping accounts of how the money is spent. And, it is a cause of great satisfaction for me. Also, I can now spend money for children's education and can buy them sundry articles which they ask for. Don't you feel that it gives a lot of happiness to a mother?"

Many non-loanee-women also have expressed the view that loanee-women are happier than non-loanee-women. One may mention here the comments of one or two respondents of this variety. One such respodent has said, "Those who are engaged in income-generating activities with loan from some agency are happier than we. They can financially contribute to their family. Many such women have contributed to the economic betterment of their family. And, the better economic condition of their respective families is visible enough." Another lady has remarked, "It is quite evident that those women who make independent earning from some income generating activities have bettered the economic condition of their respective families. Quite a few of these women like other members of their respective families could not afford two square meals a day. But now they seem to have solved the problem of food. Not only that, they now wear clothings of good quality. Also, many of them have rebuilt their houses. They are happy. They're happier than we. We cannot afford the comforts they can manage for their families." A third lady confides, "I do think that they [the women earning money from income-generating activities] are happier than we. Believe me, I too want to pursue some income-generating activity with loan from the Grameen Bank. Independent earning gives the women status in the family and society; the women can then contribute something to the material well being of the family. But it's my hard luck that my husband and other members of his family do not give me the permission to do it. I also, because of fear of quarrels in the family, have to refrain from applying for any loan."

While on this theme one or two samples of the remarks of the respondents, who have opined that women of the both the categories, may also be presented here. Thus, one loanee respondent has observed, "I can't say who is happier than who else ? Both the loanee-women and the non-loanee-women are happy in their respective manners. If we were not poor, should we go to the Bank for loan ? Yes, our financial crisis is not now as serious as it was earlier and it has given us a sense of relief. But what bothers the loanee-women like us is how to ensure the payment of instalments of the loan and interest thereon. It is not easy for loanee-women to collect the money of the instalment she is required to pay off but she has to bother about whether the other women of her group have been able to collect the money necessary for paying off the instalments due from them. The non-loanee-women are free from this concern." A non-loanee woman has said, "Those who are earning money from some income-generating activity with loan from some agency are doing not too badly. They seem to be living happily. But we, too, are happy in our own way. We do not have to bother ourselves as to how we shall pay off the amount borrowed from the loan-giving agency. We are free from that anxiety."

Finally, we may submit two more statements—one by a loanee woman and the other by a non-loanee woman—averring the greater happiness of non-loanee-women over loanee-women. A non-loanee woman has remarked, "Those who do not have to engage in any income-generating activity with money from a loan-giving agency are happier than those who have to do so. Women like me who do not have to take loan for income-generating activity do not have to face the humiliation the loanee-women have to suffer when they fail to pay off the instalment of the loan taken by them and the interest thereon. The employees of the Grameen Bank put such defaulters to great shame. Even if a woman pays off the instalment due from her, she has to suffer rebuke because of failure of other members of her group. I cannot withstand all this. I am happy, may be happier than loanee-women, because I won't have to face this." Part of what is said above is admitted by a loanee woman also, who thinks that non-loanee-women are happier than loanee-women. She has observed, "Poverty compels me to face the hazards involved in accepting loan for income-generating activity. I am held responsible and face castigation by the Grameen Bank employees not only when I myself become a defaulter but also when any other member of the group I belong to, fumbles and falters in repaying the instalment of the loan she received and interest thereon. In addition to this, I have to work for longer hours than before. I do not get any respite from the household chores. I have to do work for earning money in addition to performing my household duties. Don't you feel that ours is not an unenviable lot? Non-loanee-women do not have the double burden, nor do they have to bother with timely repayment of instalments of loan. They are happier than we."

Table – 6.27

Non-Loanee Women, by the Primary Reason for Their not Taking Loan from The Gremeen Bank

Sl. No.	*Reason*	*Non-Loanee Women*
1.	Grameen Bank's rules are not liked	12
2.	On grounds of religious consideration (religious injunction against usury, prejudice and criticism of *Mullahs* or *Imam*)	10
3.	Lack of courage because of non-availability of husband's co-operation	9
4.	Disapproval by husband and or elderly family members because of status consideration	6
5.	Failure in post-training test for admission into Grameen Bank membership	5
6.	Lack of willingness of the respondent herself.	4
7.	Excessive household work	3
8.	N.A.	1
	Total	50

(N = 50)

It is found in Table 6.27 that not only the majority of loanee-women but 78% of the non-loanee-women also feel that the loanee-women are happier than non-loanee-women. Then, one may like to know as to why the non-loanee-women (at least, a sizable section of them) have not taken loan and started some income-generating activity. Table 6.27 gives some information regarding that point. It is based on the statements made by the non-loanee respondents or opinions expressed by them.

The table should be read with one important caveat in mind. While one respondent starts narrating the factors associated with her not taking loan from the Grameen Bank, a number of factors are mentioned in a quick succession. The researcher has hardly met a respondent who mentions just one cause for her not taking the loan. Of course, it is not difficult to distinguish the main or chief factor from the rest of the factors mentioned by a respondent to be associated with her non-acceptance of the loan.

In arranging the data for Table 6.27, the researcher has taken into consideration the fact which has given prime importance by a respondent.

Table 6.27 reveals eight such factors associated with non-acceptance of loan by the non-loanee-women.

1. Grameen Bank's rules are not liked

The table shows that 12 i.e., 24% or nearly one-fourth of the non-loanee respondents have expressed the opinion that the rules, regulations, and practices followed by the Grameen Bank are not to their liking or are not liked by their husbands or other members of their families including their sons and this fact has stood in the way of acceptance of loan by them from the Grameen Bank. They have given several instances. The rule requiring the regular attendance of the loanee-women in the weekly meeting in the Grameen Bank *kendra* (local centre) and join the exercises in physical training held there. That is to say, one rule of the Grameen

Bank stipulates that every loanee woman will herself go to the *kendra* to pay off the instalment of the loan due from her. The reason behind insistence on this physical presence is that the staff of the Grameen Bank as well as the loanee-women get an opportunity for discussion or exchange of views or clarification in the weekly meetings attended by the loanee-women. The staff of the Grameen Bank would insist that the meeting should be started by the loanee-women themselves. At the outset of a meeting, the loanee-women would exchange greetings and repeat certain slogans in a chorus and then take physical exercises, say, through the continuous process of sitting and standing. The Grameen Bank authorities follow these practices in order to break the shell of coyness of the village women. But these are not looked upon with favour by the village people in general. The loanee-women face the allegations of improper or shameless behaviour. On hearing this kind of critical remarks of the villagers against the loanee-women, the non-loanee-women do not feel like approaching the Grameen Bank for loan. Sometimes, as a few non-loanee-women have reported, their grown up sons seriously object to the proposal that their mothers i.e., the women reporting, would go to the *kendra*. Acceptance of loan from the Grameen Bank would mean slogan-shouting and undergoing exercises in a public place. These would invite for their mothers jeering or sarcastic reflections from other villagers. "Why invite this unnecessary trouble?" They would ask their mothers. "How can we ignore this unpleasant possibility?" asked several non-loanee respondents.

The Grameen Bank seems, according to some non-loanee respondents, extremely particular, e.g., harsh in exacting the instalments of loan received by and due from the loanee-women and interest thereon. Generally, the loanee-women are organised in groups of five. Now, it is not enough for a loanee woman to pay off the instalment due from her. If the rest of the four members of the group becomes a defaulter, the entire group is held responsible and is heavily criticised by the Grameen Bank personnel. The instalment due from the defaulting member will have to be paid by those who have paid off the amount due from them. It appears to 5 non-loanee respondent as unsolicited botheration and even harassment.

2. On grounds of religious consideration (religious injunction against usury, prejudice and criticism of *Mullahs* or *Imam*) :

(a) The reasons adduced by ten respondents to non-acceptance of loan by them seem associated with religious belief or injunctions against it by local religious leaders like *Mullahs* or *Imam*. Two such respondents have said that in their husbands opinion, if a woman takes loan from the Grameen Bank, she cannot observe the custom of maintaining *purdah*. Also, to take interest on loan or to pay interest on loan is *haram* i.e., prohibited or wrong in Islamic belief. These two respondents belong to the families of two *Imams*.

Another woman belonging to the family of a *Haji* (a person who has performed pilgrimage to Mecca and hence is considered to be a religious person and respectable man) has mentioned the same reasons as stated by the two women of *Imam* families for not accepting the loan.

Four women are neighbours of these women belonging to the families of *Imams* and *Haji*. They have stated that because of their residential proximity to the families of *Imam* and *Haji*, they are specially vulnerable to the neighbours' criticism of their venture for loan from Grameen Bank. They are, therefore, prevented by their husbands from going to the Grameen Bank. The comment of one of these respondents made in this connection is very interesting and deserves to be quoted here. It shows the critical awareness of a village woman. The woman has said to the researcher, "They say that to take or pay interest on loan is unlawful or wrong. But I know it very well that these families of two *Imams* and the *Haji* take agricultural loan from the *Krishi Bank* (Agricultural Bank). Do they get the loan without interest? Do they not have to pay interest on the amount which they receive as loan from the Krishi Bank? When they pay interest, is it not '*haram*' or unlawful or wrong? If that is not *haram*, why should paying interest on loan received by women from the Grameen Bank be considered *haram*? But our husbands will not follow this simple logic and the hollowness of the criticism made by the members of these families of the idea or proposition of accepting loan by us from the Grameen Bank. Rather, they (our husbands) would prevent us from approaching the Grameen Bank for loan because of fear of criticism by the members of these families of *Imams* and *Haji*.

The remaining three respondents belonging to the category not taking loan because of religious considerations have said that to borrow money from the Bank (for which one has to pay interest) is not proper according to *Shariah* (revealed law). One or two of the comments made by them are as follows. "Why go to the Grameen Bank for loan on which you have to pay interest, when usury is not permitted in religion? Have faith in *Allah*. He has created mouths and He will feed these mouths."

"No barkat or prosperity lies in the money received on loan. Loan does not bring luck to all."

3. Lack of courage because of non-availability of husband's co-operation :

Nine women are found in the category of respondents who have reported their lack of courage to make any venture for income-generating activities with loan from the Grameen Bank because of the absence of their husbands' agreement and co-operation.

Four respondents of this category have said that their husbands are absolutely lukewarm to any income-generating activity by them with loan from the Grameen Bank. But they (these women) themselves do not have courage enough start an income-generating activity with loan from the Grameen Bank. How would they pay off the loan, if they fail in their venture? And, they do not have enough knowledge and information, or skill or intelligence. So they have not dared to make the venture.

The remaining five respondents in this category have informed that their husbands are not only indifferent but would be positively nuisance in the way of the prospect for any success in their effort to start some income-generating activity with loan from the Grameen Bank.

Their husbands will, they fear, grab the sum received from the Grameen Bank and spend the same according to their own sweet will but will not take any responsibility for repayment of instalment of the loan and interest thereon. It is a part of their previous experience that whenever they made some small savings enduring great hardship, the same were expropriated by their husbands who spent the amount according to their own liking. And, the same thing would happen with the loan from the Grameen Bank.

Their husbands would appropriate or misappropriate the money received by them from the Grameen Bank. (Two of these five respondents have said that both of them earlier got a small amount as loan from another organisation. But that amount was immediately taken away by their husbands who, however, did not take any responsibility for the repayment of the loan. Ultimately, they could repay the loan by bringing money from their natal families or parents' families. Their natal families were hardly better off than their husbands' families and therefore they had serious difficulties in collecting the money. They do not want a repetition of the same by taking loan from the Grameen Bank. They or their natal families do not have the capacity to meet the contingency arising out of non-repayment of loan owing to their husbands' irresponsible behaviour. Nor do they have any ability to restrain their husbands from taking away from them, the money borrowed by them from the Grameen Bank or any other source.

This fact of helplessness of the women in relation to their husbands in the present male-dominated socio-economic set-up is more nakedly exposed in the fear expressed by another woman in this category. She has told the researcher that it is certain that if she borrows any money from the Grameen Bank, it will be immediately usurped by her husband. And her husband, an irresponsible and unscrupulous man as he is, would alone migrate to the city with that money never to return to her in the village. Men have, in general, this kind of mentality, that they can abandon their wives any time they like without any qualm of conscience. And, women or wives have hardly and remedy against it. "Why, therefore, invite the trouble by accepting loan from the Grameen Bank?" she asked.

4. Disapproval by husband and/or elderly family members because of status consideration :

The third category of women has mentioned the disapproval of the husbands and/or other elderly members of the virilocal family to be important reason for their abstention from accepting the loan from Grameen Bank. Each of the six women in this category has told the researcher that though at present her husband's family faces great financial hardship, her husband and/ or any other elderly member of the family have objected to the proposition that she should approach the Grameen Bank for loan on the ground that this would detract from the social honour or status enjoyed by the family in the local socio-cultural milieu. One such woman has remarked, "It's true that, at present, my husband's family is economically poor. But this family was earlier very well off. My father-in-law was highly venerated by the villagers. Even today our neighbours respectfully mention his name. How can I sit on the same level with those female clients of the Grameen Bank, who come of families of lower social ranks? My husband says that he would rather die of starvation than suffer social dishonour. He, therefore, does not like the idea that I should go to the Grameen Bank and take loan from there." Another woman has told the researcher that her parents-in-law have sharply objected to the idea of her going to the Grameen Bank and beg money from it along with women of lowly families. It would undermine the prestige of the family in the village. A third woman has reported the strong objection of her elderly brother-in-law on grounds of social status or honour to be the factor behind her not approaching the Grameen Bank.

5. Failure in post training test for admission into Grameen Bank membership :

Several non-loanee-women sought the membership of the Grameen Bank. But they have failed to get the membership because of their failure in satisfying certain formal requirements for admission into the membership of the Grameen Bank. One of the prerequisites for admission of the Grameen Bank is the ability to sign one's name. Further, an intending woman has to undergo a certain kind of training where the trainees are informed of a few basic facts and rules. A trainee after completion of the training is required to understand and remember these facts and rules. But the women under consideration have said that they are unable to meet these minimum requirements of the Bank. Three women have said that they have not been taken in by other members of the respective groups with which they were associated. For, they cannot sign their names despite great effort. Also, they cannot keep in memory the facts and rules they are informed of during the training.

Two women have said that they found entry into two different groups. But, ultimately, after the completion of the training, they failed in the test where the eligibility of the groups for admission into membership of the Bank was assessed. These two women could not answer any question asked by the Branch Manager of the Grameen Bank. They could hardly complete a single sentence in presence of the Branch Manager.

6. Lack of Willingness of the respondent herself :

Four women have expressed their unwillingness for taking loan from the Grameen Bank to start any income generating activity. One of them has said that once she purchased a cow with money borrowed from her own brothers. She had the hope of making some profit from selling milk of the cow. But, as ill luck would have it, the cow died within a few months from the date of purchase. And, it was a tremendous blow to her. She could pay off the debt with great hardship. What's the guarantee that a similar misfortune will not befall her if she attempts some income-generating venture with loan from the Grameen Bank ? Further, she could not pay off the entire money borrowed from her brothers. Since they were her own brothers, they spared her. But in case of the loan from the Bank, the Bank authorities would not grant any remission in repayment of the loan. They would exact the entire amount from a loanee, even if she fails in her venture initiated with the amount borrowed by her from the Bank.

Three women have told the researcher that they are not interested in starting any income-generating activity with money borrowed from the Grameen Bank or any other loan-giving agency. They would rather try to do something with small savings made by themselves. To make it possible, these women are sincerely trying to raising poultry, though on a very small scale. All these four women are of the view that loan is not helpful for everybody. True, some people have benefited from utilisation of loan. But many people have failed in their ventures started by them with the amount which they received as loan from agencies like the Grameen Bank. Then their situation became worse and really pitiable.

7. Excessive household work :

Three women have not tried for loan from the Grameen Bank, since it is not, they feel, possible for them to engage in any income-generating activity with loan from the Bank simultaneously with the performance of their household chores. The burden of household work is heavy and no help is available from anybody else for doing it. Since there is nobody else in the family to help them in their household work, it is not at all feasible for them to attend the weekly meetings in the local *kendra* of the Grameen Bank for paying off the instalments of the amount borrowed and interest thereon or to go to the *kendra* as and when they are sent for by the Bank authorities. Their children are very small.

APPEND IX A
Interview Schedule

Women and Grameen Bank : A Sociological study in the District of Narsingdi in Bangladesh.

Note : The answers to the questions presented here would be used strictly for the research and academic purpose and would not be exposed to others. The identification of the respondent would not be disclosed also.

Serial Number : Name of the Village:

Date Union : Panchdona

Respondent : District : Narsingdi

Bangladesh.

1. **Name :**
2. **Age :**
3. **Educational Qualification :**
   (a) Illiterate
   (b) Only can sign the name
   (c) Upto Class II
   (d) Upto Class V
   (e) Upto Class VI
   (f) Upto Class X
   (g) Matric (S.S.C)

4. Occupation

5. Duration of Marriage :

6. Type of Family :

(a) Nuclear

(b) Non-Nuclear

7. Total number of family members : —

S. No.	Relation ship with res- pondent	Age	Educa- tion	Going to school or not	Occupa- tion	Income
1.						
2.						
3.						
4.						
5.						
6.						
7.						

8. What are the main sources of income of the family ? (Specify)

9. Annual Income —

(a) Income from domestic animals

(b) Income from agriculture

(c) Income from house-rent

(d) Income from ponds

(e) Income from kitchen-garden

(f) Income from orchard

(g) Others

10. Approximate average monthly income of the family —

11. Total amount of Land Owned :

Kind of land	Areas of Land	Had before	Now acquired
Vita (space for dwelling-house) Pond Cultivated Mortgaged			

12. Other assets

Description of	Number	Purchased or acquired Owned by
Cot		
Table		
Chair		
China and glass ware		
Wooden Hanger		
Almirah		
Clock/Wrist Watch		
Radio		
Cycle		
Silver		
Gold		
Shop		
Rickshaw		
Handloom		
Sewing machine		
Tublewell		

13. Who takes/take the decision in the following matters ?

Items	Decision taken by
1. Expenses for daily shopping	
2. Expenditure on guest	
3. Expenses on festivals	
4. Daily cuisine	
5. Expenditure on Children's items, such as clothes, gifts, toys, snacks and so on	
6. Expenses on food	
7. Buying things for other family members	
8. Buying sundry articles for the household	
9. Buying clothes for self	
10. Expenses on house repair/ building	

11. Children's school admission
12. Appointing tutors for children
13. Choosing the school where children would be admitted
14. Extent of children's education
15. Negotiating children's marriage
16. Expenses on children's marriage
17. Selecting the health institution where other members of the household would be treated in case they become ill
18. Selecting the health institution where other members of the household would be treated in case they become ill
19. Selecting the health institution where the respondent herself would be treated in case she becomes ill

14. Description of everyday work : —

	H/W	H+W	C	W+C	other
(a) House clearing					
(b) Washing plates and utensils					
(c) Fetching water					
(d) Collecting fuels					
(e) Making rolling a bed					
(f) Preparation for Cooking					
(g) Cooking					
(h) Serving food					
(i) Washing Clothes					
(j) Bathing the children					
(k) Looking after children					
(l) Coaching the children					
(m) Nursing					
(n) Taking them to the doctor					
(o) Buying sundry articles for the family and vegetables, cooking ingredients					
(p) Others					

15.A. Control over Family Income, Expenditure and Savings

	Wife	Both	Husband	Other
1. Who controls Expenditure of husband's Income ?				
2. Who controls expenditure of money earned through the sale of poultry and dairy products ?				
3. Who controls expenditure of other sources of income in the family?				
4. Who is entrusted with safe keeping of husband's income ?				
5. Who is entrusted with safe keeping of family savings?				

15.B. Control over your (Only Loanee respondents) own income : —

(a) Who is entrusted with the safe keeping of your income ?

Self ☐

Both husband and wife ☐

Husband ☐

(b) Who controls expenditure of your income ?

Self ☐

Both husband and wife ☐

Husband ☐

16. Freedom to sell your (respondents') property

(a) Can sell after due intimation to husband

(b) Can sell only after due permission from husband

(c) Cannnot sell anyway

17. Do you talk to male outsiders who do not belong to your family?

(a) Yes, and talk directly always

(b) Yes, and talk directly, but not always

(c) Yes, and talk directly, but only in the presence of my husband.

(d) No, my husband does/yes, but talk through a mediator

18. Do your husband and other family members ap prove your talking directly to a male who does not belong to your family ?

(a) Does not object

(b) Does not approve always

(c) Never approves

19. Do you have to abide by the disapproval of your family in this regard ?

(a) Yes

(b) Yes, only in instances

(c) No

20. Have you got freedom of moving around

(a) Yes, permission as well as and escort is required

(b) Yes, permission is required but an escort is only a matter of choice
and is not compulsory

(c) Yes, intimation is provided but can move alone, without an escort

(d) Do not have to seek permission, or the necessity of doing so does not arise. An escort is only a matter of choice.

21. Who took the decision about the number of children ?

The decision was :

(a) Entirely wife's / Equally that of husband and wife/Husband's sole prerogative

22. Information of the exercise of your right to vote:

(a) Are you a voter :

(b) Do you cast your vote ? Yes / No

(c) Who decides whom you will cast your vote for ? Self/Both (Husband and Wife) Others than the respondent decide.

23. Information regarding your leisure time (if any):

(a) When you get up in the morning ?

(b) When do you go to bed at night ?

(c) When do you get leisure ?

(d) How much the leisure time ?

(e) What do you do at that time ?

24. Information regarding leisure-time of your husband :

(a) When does your husband get up in the morning?

(b) When does he go to bed at night ?

(c) When does he get leisure time ?

(d) What does he do at that time ?

(For the respondents who have taken loan from the Grameen Bank)

25. When did you take loan from the Grameen Bank?

26. Total amount of money borrowed from the bank

27. In what type of income generating activities did you invest your loan money ?

Specify ....

28. Have you bought something from the earnings of your income generating activities ?

Yes / No

If Yes, Specify ....

29. Does anybody assist you in your income generating activities ?

Yes / No

If Yes, whom do you get the assistance from ?

30. What is your approximate monthly income from the income generating activity ?

31. What is your opinion regarding the roles of husband and wife in running the household ?

(a) Husband alone should bear the sole responsibility

(b) Both should share the responsibility

32. What is your opinion regarding the desirability of taking decisions, conjointly by the Husbands and Wives ?

(a) Husband should seek consultation

(b) Both spouses should seek consultation with each other

(c) Wife should seek consultation

33. What is your opinion regarding your income-generating activity ? Has it increased your work-load ?

(a) Hasn't increased

(b) Has increased

(c) Has increased a great deal.

34. Do you think this income generating work is creating an excessive burden or just a perssure of extra work ?

Please specify why you say so.

35. In your opinion which of the three categories of women are happier.

(1) Non-loanee-women are happier than loanee-women.

(2) Both are happy

(3) Loanee women are happier than non-loanee-women.

Why do you say so ?

(For Non-loanee Respondents only)

36. What is the primary reason for your not taking loan from the Grameen Bank ?

Bibliography

Abdullah, T.A. and S.A. Zeidenstein. (1982) : *Village Women in Bangladesh ; Prospects for Change* Oxford : Pergamon Press.

Adnan, S. (1988). "Birds in a Cage" Institutional Change and Women's Position in Bangladesh", Paper persented at the IUSSP Conference on Women's Position and Demographic Change in the Course of Development in Oslo.

Afsar, Rita., (1989). "Credit and women in Development : *The Bangladesh Experience,*" in *Women in Development in South Asia*, Kanesatingam, V. (ed.), New Delhi : Macmillian India Limited.

Aggarwal, R.C., (1992). "Womanpower – The Neglected Factor in Development" in *Women and Development*, Kalbagh, C, (ed.), New Delhi : Discovery Publishing House.

Ahmad, Alia., (1991). *Women and Fertility in Bangladesh.* New Delhi : Sage Publications.

Ahmad, Perveen., (1980). *Income Earning as Related to the Changing Status of Village Women in Bangladesh : A case study*. Dhaka : Women for Women Study and Research Group. (Bangladesh)

Ahmed, Israt & M Kabir., (1994). "Influences of Women's Development Programmes on Women's Status and Fertility in Bangladesh : Evidence from Focus Group Discussions" in *The Eastern Anthropologist* Vol. 47, No.4, Oct-Dec. 1994: pp. 369-377.

Ahmed, Mahbub (Dr.), (1985). *Status, Perception, Awareness and Marital Adjustment of Rural Women : The Role of Grameen Bank.* Dhaka : Published by Grameen Bank (Bangladesh).

Ahmed, Q.K. et. al. (ed.), (1985). : *Situation of Women in Bangladesh.* Dhaka : Ministry of Social Welfare and Women's Affairs Government of Bangladesh.

Arab News, (1989). August 7.

Aziz, K.M.A., (1989). "Gender creation from Birth to Adolescence in Rural Bangladesh" in *Gender and the Household Domain : Social and Cultural Dimensions*, Krishnaraj, M, and Chanana, K., (ed.), New Delhi : Sage Publication.

Babbie, E., (1992). *The Practice of Social Research.* California : Wadswarth Publishing Company.

Banerjee, Nirmala, (1985). *Women Workers in the Unorganized Sector : The Calcutta experience.* Hyderabad : Sangam Books (India) Pvt. Ltd.

Bangladesh Bureau of Statistics (BBS) (1986). Dhaka : Government of Bangladesh.

Bangladesh Bureau of Statistics. (1989). Bangladesh Economic Survey 1988-89. Dhaka : Government of Bangladesh.

Bangladesh Population Census : Narsingdi Zila. (1991). Bangladesh Bureau of Statistics (BBS) 1995, August. Dhaka: Government of Bangladesh.

Bangladesh Population Census Narsingdi Zila Series, (Unpublished). Under Processing data, Date 28.4.93., Bangladesh Bureau of Statistics (BBS) Dhaka.

Bangladesh Population Census., (1991), Volume 1, Analytical Report (National Series) : Bangladesh Bureau of Statistics (BBS)., Dhaka : Government of Bangladesh.

Bangladesh Statistical Pocket Book., (1994). Bangladesh Bureau of Statistics (BBS)., Dhaka : Government of Bangladesh.

Bhasin, Kamla. (1994). *What is Patriarchy ?* New Delhi : Kali for Women.

Bhatty, Z., (1987), "Economic Contribution of Women to the Household Budget : A Case Study of the *Beedi* Industry" in *Invisible Hands : Women in Home Based Producation.* Andrea, M. S. and Vittanen, (ed.). New Delhi : Sage Publication.

Bhatty. Z. (1980). "Economic Role and Status of Women : A case study of women in the *beedi* Industry in Allahabad." Geneva : ILO Working Paper.

Bhattacharyya, G.K. and Johnson, R.A., (1977). *Statistical Concepts and Methods*. New York : John Willy.

Bhuiya, Rabia. (1985). "Legal Status of Women in Bangladesh" in *Situation of Women in Bangladesh,* Ahmed Q.K. et. al. (ed.), 1985. Dhaka : Ministry of Social Welfare and Women's Affairs. Government of Bangladesh.

Bhuiyan, R. (1984). "Legal Status of Women in Bangladesh and Needed Changes for Improvement of the Socio-economic Status" paper presented at the National Seminar on Women in Development, Ministry of Social Welfare and Women's Affairs and Path Finder Funds, Dhaka, 1984.

Blalock, H. M., (1979). *Social Statistics*. McGraw-Hill Series in Sociology, McGraw-Hill International Editions.

Blood, Robert, O. and R.L. Hamblin. 1963. "The Effects of Wife's Employment on the family Power Structure", in *Modern Introduction to the Family,* N.W. Bell and E.F. Vogel, (ed.). New York : Free Press.

Blumberg, Rae Lesser., (1985). "A Walk on the 'WID' Side: Summary of field Research on 'Women in Development' in the Dominican Republic and Guatemala", Draft, Agency for International Development. Paper presented at the International Conference on "Gender and Farming Systems", Gainesville, FL, April, 1986.

Blumberg, Rae Lesser., (1989a). "Toward a Feminist Theory of Development" *in Feminism and Sociological Theory*, Ruth A. Wallace, (ed.) 1989. New Delhi : Sage Publication.

Blumberg, Rae Lesser., (1989b). "Work, Wealth, and a Women in Development 'Natural Experiment' in Guatemala: The ALCOSA Agribusiness Project in 1980 and 1985", in *Women in Development : A.I.D.'s Experience, 1973-1985*, Vol. 11. Ten field Studies, Paula O. Goddard, (ed.), Washington, DC; Agency for International Development.

Blumberg, Rae Lesser., (1991)., "Income under Female Versus Male Control : Hypotheses from a Theory of Gender Stratification and Data from The Third World" in *Gender, Family, and Economy : The Triple Overlap*, Blumberg, R.L., (ed.). New Delhi ; Sage Publications.

Blood, Robert O. and Wolfe, Donald M., (1960)., *Husbands and Wives : The Dynamics of Married Living*., Illinois : The Free Press of Glencoe.

BRAC and Women's Development : An Exploratory Study., (1990). Dhaka : Bangladesh Rural Advancement Committee (BRAC) Research and Evaluation Division.

Cain, M., S. R. Khanam and S. Nahar., (1979). Class, Patriarchy and Women's Work in Bangladesh. *Population and Development Review, Vol. 5, No. 3, pp. 405-38.*

Castillo, Gelia. T., (1977). *The Changing Role of Women in Rural Societies : A Summary of Trends and Issues.*

Casterline, J. and I. Alam. (1984). "Socio-economic Differentials in Recent Fertility" WFS Comparative Studies No. 33.

Chafetz, Janet Saltgman and A, Gary Dworkin., (1986). *Female Revolt : Women's Movements in World and Historical Perspective.* Totowa. NJ : Rowman and Allanheld.

Chafetz, Janet, Saltzman., (1989). "Gender Equality : Toward a Theory of Change" in *Feminism and Socialogical Theory*, Wallace, Ruth, A, (ed.). New Delhi : Sage Publication.

Chakrabortty, Krishna., (1978). *The Conflicting Worlds of Working Mothers.* India : Prograssive publishers, Calcutta.

Chatterjee, Searle Mary., (1981). *Reversible Sex Roles : The Special Case of Benares Sweepers.* New York : Pergamon Press.

Chauvery, Nayak and Kala., (1992). "Relative Male-Female Contributions to Household Earnings" in *Women and Development*, Kalbagh, C. (ed.). New Delhi; Discovery Publishing House.

Chaudhury, R.H. and N.R. Ahmed., (1980). *Female Status in Bangladesh.* Dhaka : Bangladesh Institute of Development Studies.

Chen, Marty., (1986). "Poverty, Gender, and Work in Bangladesh", in *Economic and Political Weekly Vol. XXI, No. 5*, 1986, 1st Feb. Bombay.

Conklin, George H. (1981). "Cultural Determinants of Power for Women within the Family : A Neglected Aspect of Family Research", in *Women in the Family and the Economy : An International Comparative Survey* (ed.), G. Kurion and R.Ghosh. Connecticut : Greenwood Press.

Crandon, Libbet with Bonnie Shepard., (1985). *Women, Enterprise and Development*. Chestnut Hill, MA : Pathfinder Fund.

Dandekar, Kumudini, (1959). *Demographic Survey of Six Rural Communities.* Gokhale Institute of Politics and Economics and Bombay ; Asia Publising House.

Das, Veena. (1976). "Indian Women : Work, Power and Status" in Indian Women From Purdah to Modernity, B.R. Nanda, (ed.). Delhi : Vikas Publisling House.

Desai, Neera & M. Krishnaraj. (1990). *Women and Society in India.* Delhi : Ajanta Publications (India).

Devi, D.R. (1989). "Status of Women in Madhya Pradesh", in *Women and Population Dynamics : Perspective from Asia Countries*, Mahadevan, K, (ed.) New Delhi : Sage Publication.

Devis, K., (1948). *Human Society*. New York : Collier Macmillan

Dixon, Ruth. (1978). *Rural Women at Work Baltimore* : The Johns Hopkins University Press.

Dube, S.C. (1967). *Indian Village*, Bombay : Allied Publishers Private Limited.

Duza, A., (1989). "Bangladesh Women in Transition Dynamic and Issues" in *Women and Population Dynamics: Perspective from Asian Countries*, Mahadevan K., (ed.) New Delhi : Sage Publication.

Establishment Survey., (1982). Bangladesh Manpower, Planning Centre. Dhaka : Government of Bangladesh.

Farouk, A. and M. Ali. (1975). *The Hardworking Poor—A Survey of How People Use their Time in Bangladesh.* Dhaka: Bureau of Economic Research, Dhaka University.

Farouk, A. (1980). *Time Use of Rural Women.* Dhaka : Bureau of Enonomic Research, Dhaka University.

Foldan, Martha., (1988). "Renegotiating the Marita Contract: Intrahousehold Patterns of Money Alloction and Women's Subordination Among Domestic Outworkers in Mexico City" in *A Home Divided : Women and Income in the Third World,* Daisy Dwyer and Judith Bruce, (ed.). Palo Alto, CA : Stanford University Press.

Fuglesang, Andreas and Dale Chandler., (1986). *Participation As Process—What we can learn from Gremeen Bank, Bangladesh.* Norway : Norwegian Ministry of Development Cooperation Norad.

Fuglesang, A and D. Chander, (1993). Participation As a process. Dhaka : Grameen Bank.

Gerth, and Mills, C. Wright., (1953). *Character and Social Structure.*

Grammen Bank Annual Report., (1992). Dhaka : Grameen Bank.

Gulhati, Leela., (1975). "Female Work Participation", in *Economic and Political Weekly*, Vol. 10 Nos. 1-2., Bomaby.

Heer, David. M. (1963). "The Measurement and Bases of Family Power : An Overview". *Journal of Marriage and the Family* 25. pp. 133-139.

Hossain, Mahabub., (1986). *The Impact of Grameen Bank on Women's Involvement in Productive Activites.* Dhaka : Grameen Bank.

Huq, Jahanara, (1979). "Economic Activities of Women in Bangladesh : the Rural Situation" in *Situation of Women in Bangaldesh*, Women for Women (ed.). Dhaka : Women for Women.

Huq, Muzammel (1985). "Case Study : Grameen Bank", in Situation of Women in Bangladesh, Ahmad et.al. (ed.), Dhaka : Grameen Bank.

Islam, Mahmuda., (1979). "*Social Norms and Institutions" in Situation of Women in Bangladesh.* Dhaka : Women for

Women Research and Study Group, (ed.) At the Request of Women's Development.

I. Rahman., (1986). *Impact of Gramen Bank on the Situation of Poor Rural Women,* Working Paper No. 1., Grameen Bank Evaluation Project.

Dhaka : Bangladesh Institute of Development Studies.

Jahan, Rounaq., (1975). "Women in Bangladesh" in *Women For Women : Bangladesh 1975*. Bangladesh : University Press Limited.

Jhora, Fatima., (1989). "Arthanaitik Prekshapate Bangladesher Mahila" (Women of Bangladesh and the Enonomic Background) in *Bangladesh Unnayan Sameeksha*, Vol. 6 (Annual Number 1395) pp. 210-223 BIDS.

Kabir. K. et. al. (1977). "Rural Women in Bangladesh : Exploding Some Myths" in Role of Women in Socio-economic Development in Bangladesh. Dhaka : Bangladesh Economic Association.

Kabir, M. Dr. and Dr. Ruhul Amin., (1995). "The Impact of poor Women's participation in Village Based Development Programmes on Fertility" in *The Jounal of Rural Development* Vol. 25, No.1, January, 1995, BARD, Comilla, Bangladesh.

Kakar, Sudhir. (1981). *The Inner World : A Psycho-analytic Study of Childhood and Society in India.* Delhi : Oxford University Press.

Kalbagh, Chetana. (ed.), (1992). *Women and Development*. New Delhi : Discovery Publishing House.

Kalbagh, Chetana. (ed.), (1992). "Poverty, The Family and Economic Conditions : A Study of Domestic Workers" in *Women and Development* Kalbagh, C. (ed.), New Delhi : Discovery Publishing House.

Karlekar, Malavika., (1982). *Poverty and Women's Work : A Study of Sweeper Women in Delhi.* Delhi : Vikas Publishing House.

Kazi, Shahnaz., (1989). "Some Measures of the Status of Women in the Course of Development in South Asia" in *Women in Development in South Asia*, Kanesalingam, V. (ed.) New Delhi : Macmillan (I) Ltd.,

Kenkel, William F. (1961). "Sex of Observer and Spousal Roles in Decision-Marking." *Marriage and Family Living* 23 (May) 185-186.

Kenkel, William F. (1963). "Observational Studies of Husband-Wife Interaction in Family Decision Making" in *Marriage and the Family*, M.B., Sussman, (ed.). Boston : Honghton Mifflin Company.

Khan, Salma., (1988). *The Fifty Percent Women in Development and Policy in Bangladesh*. Bangladesh : The University Press Limited, Dhaka.

Khandker, S.R. (1988). 'Determinants of Women's Time Allocation in Rural Bangladesh', *Economic Development and Cultural Change*, Vol. 37, No. 1, pp. 111-26.

Khanam, Rashed Akhter U.H., (1990). "Women and National Planning in Bangladesh Perspective Plan : Objectives and Strategies : Women, Employment and Techonology" in *Women and National Planing in Bangladesh*, Begum et.al. (ed.). 1990. Dhaka : Women for Women : A Research and Study Group.

Kolenda Pauline. (1967). : "Regional Differences in Indian Family Structure", in *Regions and Regionalism in South Asian Studies : An Exploratory Study*, Robert Crane, (ed.). Durham, N.C. : Monograph Number Five of the Duke University, Programme on Southern Asia.

Lengermann, P.M. and Brantley, J.N., (1988). "Contemporary Feminist Theory", in *Sociological Theory*, Ritzer, G. (ed.) New York : Alfred A. Knopf.

Linton, Ralph., (1936). *The Study of Man.* New York : Appleton-Country-Crafts.

Roldan, Martha., (1982). "International Patterns of Money Allocation and Women's Subordination : A Case study of Domestic Outworkers in Mexico City, Unpublished Paper circulated to participants in *Women, Income, and Policy Seminar*. Popular Council, New York, March.

Mabud, A. Mohammad. (1985). *Women's Development, Income and Fertility in Bangladesh.* Dhaka : The External Evaluation Unit, Planning Commission, Dhaka Canadian International Development Agency.

Mahadevan, K., Aghajanian, A. Jayasree, R. and Moni, G.S. (1989). "Status of Women and Population Dynamics : A Conceptual Model" in *Women and population Dynamics : Perspective from Asian Countries*, Modhavan, K., (ed). New Delhi Sage Publication.

Mahtab and Ahmad (1979).

Mathew, Sarah., (1989). "*Social Attitudes to Women's Education*", in *Women in Development in South Asia*, Vikanesalingam, (ed.). New Delhi : Macmillian India Limited.

Merton, R.K., (1957). *Social Theory and Social Structure* Glencoe, Ill. : Free Press.

Mizan, A.N., (1992). *Rural Women's Economic Participation and Decision-making Power in the Family : A Study on Grameen* Bank in Bangladesh, Department of Sociology in the Graduate Shool, Southern Illionis University, USA. Unpublished Ph.D Thesis.

Monthly Statement of Grameen Bank., (1993), June., Bangladesh : Published by Grameen Bank, Dhaka.

Noman, Ayesha., (1983). *Status of Women And Fertility in Bangladesh*. Dhaka : the Universisty Press Limited.

Non-formal Education in Bangladesh (1975). The Report of the Committee of Non-formal Education. Dhaka : Planning Commission, Government of the People's Republic of Bangladesh.

Noponen., (1987). *Invisible Hands : Women in Home-based Producation,* A.M. Singh and A. Kelles-Viitanen, (ed.) New Delhi : Sage Publication.

Nur, Najma, Begum., (1988). *Pay or Purdah : Women and Income Earning in Rural Bangladesh*. Dhaka : Human Resources Development Programme, Winrock International Institute for Agricultural Development. In Collaboration with Bangladesh Agricultural Research Council.

OED., (1979). *The Compact Edition of the Oxford English Dictionary* (Complete Text, Reproduced Micrographically). London : Book Club Associates by arragement with Oxford University Press.

Palli-Karma-Sahayak Foundation Annual Report., (1990-91). Dhaka : Palli Karma-Sahayak Foundation.

Papanek, Hanna., (1971). "Purdah in Pakistan : Seclusion and Modern occupations for Women" in *Jounal of Marriage and Family*, August 1971 ; pp. 517-30.

Qadir, S.R. (1981). *Women's Income Earning Activities and Family Welfare in Bangladesh*. Dhaka : Unicef.

Quddus, Solaiman, Karim., (1985). *Rural Women in Households in Bangladesh* : With a Case-study of Three Villages in Comilla.

Comilla : Bangladesh Academy for Rural Development, Kotbari.

Quamruddin, K.A.A. (1977). "A Review of Laws Relating to Marriage and Divorce in Bangladesh", Paper presented at the Seminar, "The status and Legal Rights of Women in Bangladesh", held in Dhaka 10-12 December, 1977.

Rahman, Atiur. (1987) : *Dual Role of Tradition in Social Mobilization : The Grameen Bank and Rural Poor in Bangladesh.* A paper presented at the 21st Bengal Studies Conferece. Unviersity of Wisconsin at Oshkosh, May, 8-10.

Rahman, Atiur (Dr)., (1995). "Rural Development from Below : The Case of Grameen Bank in Bangladesh" in *Poverty Focused Rural Development : A Hand-book of Regional Training Programme,* Md. Abdul Quddus, (ed.).

Comilla : Bangladesh Academy For Rural Development (BARD).

Rahman, S. et. al., (1991). *From Calories to Capacity Building :Proverty Alleviation Programmes and Delivery Systems in Bangladesh.*
Dhaka : Grameen Bank, Head office

Ramu, G.N., (1988). "Wife's Economic Status and Marital Power : A case of Single and Dual-Earner Couples" in *Sociological Bulletin,* 37 (1 and 2), March-September, 1988: 49-69, Bombay.

Ray, Jaynanta Kumar., (1987). *To Chase Miracle : A Study of the Grammen Bank of Bangladesh.* Dhaka : The University Press Limited.

Reddy, G. Narayana., (1985). "Women's Role in Economy and Society" in *Mainstream* November 2, 1985 : 46-48.

Report on Labour Force Survey (1990-91). Bangladesh Bureau of Statistics. Dhaka: Government of Bangladesh.

Ritzer, George. (ed.) (1988). *Sociological Theory.* New York: Alfred A. Knopf.

Ross, D.A. (1973) The Hindu Family in its Urban Setting Delhi, Indian Edition.

Rural Industries Survey Project., (1982). Dhaka : Bangladesh Institute of Development Economics.

Rutstien, S. (1983). "Infant and Child Mortality Levels, Trends and Demograhic Differentials", *World Fertility Survey Comparative' Studies*, No. 24 Netherlands : Voorburg.

Safilios-Rothschild, Constantina (1982) "Femal Power, Autonomy and Demographic change in the Third World" in Anker Richard, et. all. (ed.), Women's Roles and Population Trends in the Third World. London : Croom Helm. pp. 117-130.

Satler, Ellen, (1979). "Demographic Features of Bangladesh with Reference to Women and Children", in *Situation of Women in Bangladesh,* Women for Women (ed.). Dhaka : Women for Women Research and Study Group.

Sethi, Raj Mohini., (1989). "Women and Development : A Profile of Active Agricultural Producers" in *Sociological Bulletin*, 38(2), September, 1989 : 217-233, Bombay.

Sethi, Raj Mohini., (1981). *A Study of Agricultural Labour in Panjab*, Dept. of Sociology, Punjab University, Chandigarh, Unpub.; cited in Desai, Neera and M. Krishnaraj, 1990, *Women and Society in India.* Delhi : Ajanta Publications.

Selltiz. C. et. al, (1965). *Research Methods in Social Relations*. Kent : Methuen and Co. Ltd.

Sen, Rita. (1991). *"Gainful Employment and Status of Muslim Working Women in two Slums of Chittagong and Calcutta.* Unpublised Ph.D Thesis.

Sen, Rita., (1992). *Social Constraints For Working Women: notes from a rural area of Jamalpur*. Dhaka : Research and Evaluation Division, Bangladesh Rural Advancement Comittee.

Schuler, Sidney Ruth et. at., (1992). *The Impact of Women's Participation in Credit Programmes on Family Planning in Rural Bangladesh. DRC Working Paper No. 3.*, Dhaka ; Development Reserarch Centre.

Shahana, D. (1989). "Legislation for the Improvement of the Socio-economic Condition of Women : The Indian Case" in *Women in Development in South Asia (ed.)*, Kanesalingam, V. New Delhi : Macmillian India Limited.

Shams, M.K., (1992). *Designing Effective Credit Delivery System for the Poor : The Grameen Bank Experience.* Bangladesh : Published by Grameen Bank, Dhaka.

Sharma, Ursula., (1980). *Women, Work and Property* in Northwest India. London : Tavistock Publications.

Shehabuddin, R., (1992). *Empowering Rural Women : The Impact of Grameen Bank in Bangladesh.* Dhaka : Grameen Bank.

Statistical year Book of Bangladesh. (1982). Bangladesh Bureau of Statistics. Dhaka : Government of Bangladesh.

Statistical Year Book of Bangladesh, (1994). Dhaka : Government of the People's Republic of Bangladesh

Stoeckel, J. and M. A. Chowdhury. (1973). Fertility, Infant Mortality and Family Planning in Rural Bangladesh. Dhaka: Oxford.

The Bangladesh Census of Agriculture and Livestock : 1983-84 Zila Series : Narsingdi. Bangladesh Bureau of Statistics (BBS) Dhaka : Government of Bangladesh.

The Constitution of the People's Republic of Bangladesh. (1991). Dhaka : Government of Bangladesh.

The Second Five-year Plan., (1980-85). Ministry of Planning. Dhaka : Planning Commission, Government of Bangladesh.

The Social Encyclopendia., (1985). Adam Kuper and Jessica kuper (ed.). London : Routledge and Kengan Paul.

Todd, H. (1989). "The bank that work for the poor".

SPUR : October.

Towards Equality : Report of The Committee on the Status of Women in India. (1974). Department of Social Welfare. New Delhi : Government of India.

United Nations, Department of Economic and Social Affairs, (1975).

Wallace, Ruth A. (ed.). (1989). *Feminism and Sociological Theory*, New Delhi : Sage Publication.

Weber, M., (1978) (1922)., *Economy and Society* I & II. (Original Greman edn. Wirtschaft and Gesellschaft, Tiibingen., Berkeley & Los Angeles : University of California.

Weisblat, A.M., (1975). *Role of Rural women in Development: Seminar Report.* New York : The Agricultural Development Council, Inc.

Westergaard, Kirsten. (1983). *Pauperization and Rural Women in Bangladesh : A Case Study.* Comilla : Bangladesh Academy for Rural Development, (BARD), Kotbari.

Wilkening E. A. And L. K. Bharadwaj. (1967). "Dimensions of Aspirations Work Roles and Decision-Making of Farm Husbands and Wives in Wisconsin" *Jounal of Marriage and the Family* 29 (Nov.), pp. 703-711.

Wolf, Charlotte., (1985). "Status" in Kuper and Kuper 1985 *The Social Science Encyclopedia*, London : R.K.P.

Yunus, Muhammad. (1984) *Jorimon of Beltoil Village and Others : In Search of a Future.* Dhaka : Grameen Bank (Bangladesh).

Yunus, Muhammad., (1987). *Credit for Self-Employment : A Fundamental Human Right.*

Bangladesh : Grameen Bank, Head office, Dhaka.

Yunus, Muhammad., (1989). *Strategy For the Decade of Nineties*. Bangladesh : Grameen Bank, Head Office, Dhaka.

Yunus, Muhammad. (ed.). (1991). *Jouimon and others : Faces of Poverty*. Dhaka : Published by Grameen Bank (Bangladesh).

Index

A

Agricultural
  Labour Women, 31
  Labourers, 37
Alleviation of Poverty, 90
Arbitration Council, 85

B

Bangladesh (BD), 15, 16, 20, 24-26, 32, 33, 35, 41, 46-49, 51, 53, 54, 59-67, 73, 74, 77, 79-81, 85, 86, 88-91, 93, 103, 116, 119, 120, 138, 145, 170, 177, 188, 194, 195, 201, 219, 224, 238, 243, 263, 271, 274
  Constitution of-, 238
  Divorce and Remarriage in-, 66
  Female Population in-, 69
  Hindus and Buddhists in-, 60
  Institute For Dev. Studies, (BIDS), 104
  Islamic Society of-, 227
  Male Dominated Society of-, 60
  Muslim
  Families in-, 84, 208
  Society of-, 56, 174, 228
  Women in-, 83
  In-, 54
  Nuclear Families in-, 251
  Patriarchal Society of-, 269
  Population, 138
  Productive System, 72
  Rural
Bangladesh, 60 see also under rural
  Bangladesh
  Society in, 59
  Women in-, 61, 73, 74
  Status of Women in-, 79
  Women in-, 60, 65
  Women's Education in-, 66
Bangladesh's
  Social Customs, 87
  Villages, 99
Bangladeshi
  Culture, 61
  Muslims, 233
  Women, 23, 53, 56, 59, 87, 100
Beedi Industry Allahabad, 28
Bengali Women, 243
Bhatapara, 15, 116, 119, 128, 146, 153
Bhatpara Mauza, 153-155
Birth Control, 64, 65

C

Calcutta/Chittagaon Slums, 249
Central Bank of Bangladesh, 93
Child Marriage Restraint Act, 81, 82
Children Education, 101, 281
Chittagaon University, 92
Civil Laws, 81
Civilian Labour Force, 24
Class System, 18

Code of Criminal Procedure, 86
Comilla District (BD), 35, 64
Commercial Banks, 92
Contraceptive Prevalence Survey, 64
Craftsmen, 78
Cropping Pattern, 139

D

Data Collection Techniques, 121
Decision Making, 31, 36, 38, 39, 41, 45-48, 50, 54, 55, 70, 108, 119, 129, 154-156, 169, 170, 172, 174, 175, 178, 180, 191,196, 208, 211, 212, 224, 225, 235, 238, 243-245, 247, 249, 251-253, 257-259, 262
  Power, 268
  Process, 25, 26, 31, 33, 35, 39, 40, 107, 109, 115, 116, 128, 164, 165, 169, 211, 238, 248, 249, 253, 256, 258-260
  Western, 26
Developing Countries, 26, 31
Development Projects, 32
Dissolution of Muslim Marriage Act, 81, 83, 84
Divorce, 22, 81, 83, 105
Dowry, 88, 89, 105, 106, 193
Dowry Prohibition Act (1980), 88, 89
Dowry-less Marriages, 101

E

Economic
  Activities, 15, 20, 29, 30, 32, 33, 37, 73, 74
  And Social Development Program, 96
  Contribution by Women, 233, 238, 239
  Contribution to Family, 186, 188, 196-198, 200, 207, 211, 213, 219, 220, 229, 230
  Growth, 94
  Participation, 25, 32, 212
Economy, 16
  National, 94
  Political, 21
  Education, 38, 42, 43, 49, 53, 60, 62, 67-69, 70, 106, 156, 160, 164, 169, 191, 193, 194, 198-200, 247, 248, 260, 262
  and Training Facilities, 77
  Formal, 62
  Loanee/Non-Loanee Women, 157
  Of Rural Women, 243
  Religious, 62
Employment, 70, 71, 77, 79, 105, 173, 187, 193, 215, 256
  Market, 26
  Of Women, 211, 249, 263
  Role of Males, 71
  Status, 72

F

Family
  Decision Making Process, 32, 109, 112, 126, 164, 165, 247
  Funds, 221
  Planning Methods, 64
  Planning, 102, 106, 213
Farm Management, 36
Female
  Education, 67
  Employment, 71
  Labour, 36, 72, 73
  Literacy, 67
  Population, 72
Feminist Theories, 19, 20
Fertility Pattern, 22
Festivals, 174, 175
Folklore and Religious Tradition, 62
Food Preservation, 74
Freedom to Sell Property, 133
Fund Giving Agencies, 165

Fundamental Rights, 80
Fundamentalists, 85, 86

G

Gandhi, Rajiv, 86
Gender
  Bias, 204
  Inequality, 107
  Stratification Patterns, 21
  Stratification Theory, 17, 20
Grameen Bank, (Bangladesh), 15, 16, 25, 26, 90-96, 99-101, 103, 104-107, 109, 111, 112, 116-119, 124, 127, 128, 131, 156, 157, 160, 161, 164, 165, 175, 178, 180, 187, 189, 190, 192-194, 197, 210, 211, 222, 227, 229, 230, 233, 236, 239, 253, 256-259, 263, 268-270, 276, 281-293
  Female Borrowers, 105
  Pachdona Branch, 116, 118, 119, 124, 125, 154, 187
  Programmes, 25
  Project, 19
  Rules, 285
  Types of Facilities Provided, 96
  Children's Welfare Fund, 98
  Emergency Loan, 97
Group Fund Loan, 96
  Individual Savings Deposits, 99
  Shareholding Schemes, 98
  Social Development Programme, 100, 101
  Special Savings Schemes, 98
  Welfare Programmes, 102
  Women Participants, 105
  Workshops, 101, 102
  Objectives, 102

H

Health
  and Sanitation, 102
  Care Services, 204, 210
Himachal Pradesh, 37
Homeopath or Kaviraj, 206
House Building Loans, 96
Household
  Decision Making, 27, 35
  Income Sources, 142, 143
Housekeeping, 265
Husband Dominated Families, 212

I

Illiteracy, 262
Income Generating Activities (IGA), 42, 45, 53, 90, 111, 119, 120, 128, 154, 264, 266-269, 271, 282, 283, 288, 289
Income Generating Opportunities, 77
Indian
  Council of Cultural Affairs, 135
  Muslims, 85
  Women, 191
Indonesia, 65
Inheritance, 81
Inheritance Rights, 87
International Fund for Agricultural Development, 93
Interview Schedule, 125, 126
  Text, 294-301
Iran, 21
IRDP (Integrated Rural Development Project Schemes), 39
Irrigation, 139
Islamic
  Beliefs, 287
  Law, 54

J

Joint Family Structure, 252
Jotira, 92, 93
Jute Products, 78
  Krishi Bank, 288

L

Labour

Force Survey, 70
Market, 24, 33, 79
Lace Makers Women, 31
Land and Property Ownership, 43
Landless Rural Poor, 104
Law of Inheritance, 85, 86
Legal System, 20
Life Expectancy, 43, 59
Life Options, 22
Literacy, 27, 70, 143, 247
Literacy Rate, 67, 68, 153
Loanee
Group of Women, 180, 182, 185, 207, 209
Women Occupations, 162
Loanee/Non-Loanee Groups of Women, 180

M

Madarasas, 154
Madhya Pradesh, 271
Management, 34
Marriage Contract, 82-84
Medical Institutions, 209, 210
Medical Personnel/Institutions, 205
Mehr, 82
Middle East, 33
Migration, 43
Modernization, 119
Mother's Centres, 77
Muhammad Yunus, 91-94
Muslim
Countries, 65
Family Law Ordinance, 81, 82, 84
Law, 82, 83, 85, 88
Personal Law, 86, 87
Personal Laws (Shariah), 88
Society, 65, 88, 186
Patriarchal and Patrilineal, 49
Women, 81, 82, 187, 243, 249
Women (Protection of Rights on Divorce) Bill, 1986, 86
Women of India, 86

N

Nagar Pachdona, 153-155
Narsingdi District (BD), 15, 116, 119, 124, 125, 138, 142, 145-147
Household Income Source, 147
Sex-wise Population, 148
Thana Ranking, 147
Nikahnama, 52
Non-Feminist Theories, 19
Non-Governmental Organization (NGO), 77
Non-Loanee Group of Women, 180, 182, 185, 207, 209, 212, 253

P

Pachdona, 15, 116, 117, 124, 125, 138-140, 153-155
Pakistan, India and Bangladesh, 33
Panchdona
Literacy, 151
Mauza, 153, 154
Sex-wise Population, 151, 152
Union, 145, 151, 153
Social System, 18
Patriarchal
System, 173, 188, 274
Values, 208
Patriarchy, 30, 49, 51, 221
Paul, Narsingha, 138
Personal Laws, 81
Philippines, 34
Planning Commission (Bangladesh), 71
Political Parties, 230
Polygamy, 84, 85
Poverty Alleviation Programme, 93
Psychoanalytic Theories, 18
Punjab, 37

Purdah, 55, 56, 61-63, 69, 89, 92, 106, 119, 120, 187, 227, 232, 240, 287

R

Rangpur/Dinajpur Area, 74
Revenue Villages, 146
Right to Vote, 238
Rights
  And Privileges, 239
  Of Women, 65
Rituals and Social Ceremonies, 38, 191
River
  Arialkhan, 139
  Brahmputra, 139
  Haridoa, 139
  Meghna, 139
  Paharia, 139
  Sitalakhya, 139
  System, 139
  Titas, 139
Role of
  Rural Women in Development, 34
  Women, 16
Rural
  Bangladesh, 26, 50, 55, 73, 252
  Development Activities, 39
  Sector, 25
  Women Economic Dependency, 92
  Women, 25, 26, 50, 61, 63-65, 69, 78, 100
  Women's Economic Role, 25

S

Sex-wise Literacy, 144
Shah Banu Case, 85
Social
  Control, 237
  Intercourse, 237
  Justice, 101
  Sanctions, 215
Stratification, 40
Structures, 41, 42
Socialism, 16
Society (ies), 16, 17, 29, 21, 23, 25, 33, 42, 43, 61, 62, 69, 81, 93, 215, 225, 239, 263, 282
  Bangladeshi, 243
  Gender Stratification, 20
  Male Dominated, 21, 201, 201, 203, 224
  Patriarchal, 174, 219, 232
Stratified, 21
  Traditional, 42, 46
Status of Women in-, 23
  Western, 251
  Socio-Economic
  Status (SES), 29, 64, 104, 259, 260
  Features, 156
Socio-Cultural System, 238
South Asia, 30, 33, 90
South Asian Countries, 33
Status of
  Rural Women, 27
  Women, 15, 23, 25, 31, 40, 41, 42, 70, 89, 224
  Women in India, 52
Sunni Law of Inheritance, 86
Sylhet, 154

T

Teacher—Student Ratio, 194
Tenancy, 142
Third World Countries, 20
Tradition Bound Societies, 135, 174, 201, 262
Training and
  Education, 100
  Occupations, 43
Tribal States, 143

U

UN Children's Fund, 93
Unorganized Sector in India, 221
Unskilled Labour, 78
USA, 211

V

Value System of Patriarchy, 270
Vocational Training, 35
  Programme, 77
Voting Rights, 239

W

Wage Rates, 37
Women
  Decision Making Role, 33
  Educational Attainment, 249
  Emancipation of-, 17
  Himachal Pradesh and Punjabi, 36
  In Societies in Bangladesh, 274
  Legal Rights, 79
  Legal Status, 79
  Status, 26
  Traditional Skills, 77
  Voters, 56
  Workers, 28
Women's
  Casting of Votes, 56
  Contribution, 40, 66
  Contribution to Agricultural Work, 37
  Cooperatives, 77
  Decision Making Power, 24, 32, 35, 252
  Economic
  Activity, 29
  and Social Status, 60
  Contribution, 25-27, 31, 109, 111, 135, 155, 174, 176, 180, 221
  Participation, 169
  Social, Psychological Independence, 45
  Status, 25, 108
  Education, 249
  Employment, 24, 104
  Freedom of Movement, 131
  Freedom to Talk to Male Outsiders, 56, 131, 228, 232
  Participation, 24, 120, 129, 185
  Personal Education, 216
  Position, 52
  Problems, 21, 23
  Relative Economic Power, 21, 22
  Rights, 215
  Status, 24, 28, 30, 43, 44, 45, 47, 48, 64, 108, 109, 112, 115, 119, 128, 135, 136, 216
  Subordinate Position, 17
  Subordination, 66
Working Women (WW), 23, 28, 266
World Capitalist Economy, 20
World Health Organization, 50

Z

Zila,
  Brahmanbari, 138
  Gazipur, 138
  Keshoriganj, 138
  Narayanganj, 138
Zoya Hassan, 85